Choosing Reality

Choosing Reality

A BUDDHIST VIEW
OF PHYSICS AND THE MIND

B. Alan Wallace

Snow Lion Publications
Ithaca, New York
Boulder, Colorado

Snow Lion Publications
P.O. Box 6483
Ithaca, New York 14851 USA
607-273-8519
www.snowlionpub.com

Printed in USA on acid-free recycled paper.

ISBN- 1-55939-199-5

The Library of Congress catalogued the previous edition of this book as
follows:

Wallace, B. Alan.
    Choosing reality : a Buddhist view of physics and the mind / B. Alan
Wallace.
        p. cm.
    Includes bibliographical references.
    ISBN 1-55939-063-8
    1. Reality. 2. Physics--Philosophy. 3. Physics--Religious aspects
--Buddhism. 4. Science--Philosophy. 5. Religion and science. I. Title.
QC6.4.R42W35   1996
110--dc20   96-6934
                                                                  CIP

Table of Contents

Acknowledgments

I would like first of all to express my deep gratitude to His Holiness the Dalai Lama, who, during his visit to Amherst College in the autumn of 1984, encouraged me in the studies that made this work possible. I would also like to thank Amherst College, including its faculty, administration, and student body, for enabling me to pursue these studies.

More specifically, my thanks go especially to Arthur Zajonc, Associate Professor of Physics at Amherst College, for his encouragement and invaluable guidance. Likewise, my sincere thanks go to Robert Thurman, Professor of Religion at Amherst College, for his many helpful comments on chapters 14-17.

I would also like to thank John Servos, Assistant Professor of History at Amherst College, for his reading and comments on chapter 3, and Joseph Epstein, Professor of Philosophy at Amherst College, for his comments on chapter 3. My thanks go also to physicist Victor Mansfield of Colgate University for his careful reading and many constructive comments on chapters 1-17. My gratitude also goes to physicist Melvin Steinberg of Smith College for his comments on chapters 1-17. In addition I would like to thank my friend Brenda Loew for reading the entire manuscript and for pointing out areas that needed clarification. My deep gratitude also goes to Dr. Jeremy Hayward for his extremely helpful editorial comments. Finally, I would like to thank my editor at Snow Lion, Kate Bloodgood, for her careful polishing of the final manuscript.

To the best of my knowledge, this is the first attempt to apply the mode of philosophical inquiry of the Buddhist Madhyamaka view to the foundations of physics. Initial works of this nature are bound to be flawed, and I only hope that the shortcomings of my efforts stimulate others to elucidate this rich subject with greater mastery and insight.

Chapter One
Worlds Apart

Over the past few centuries, Western civilization has produced a jewel to adorn human culture as a whole. It has challenged religious and metaphysical assumptions that were in need of critical reassessment, delved with penetrating inquiry into aspects of nature that had escaped our notice, and provided us with tremendous advances in diverse areas, including communication, transportation, and health. While originating chiefly in Europe, it has been adopted and furthered by societies around the world—its influence on our lives and thinking is pervasive. This jewel is, of course, our natural science.

Among the sciences, physics is still widely regarded as the exemplar for scientific research and theorizing, not only for the physical sciences, but for the life sciences, psychology, and sociology. The combined approach of empirical research and mathematical analysis that is so appropriate for physics has provided us with an enormous accumulation of information, while shedding little if any light on the meaning of human existence. We err, however, if we expect natural science to solve issues of a metaphysical or religious nature, for it was never designed to probe such questions. Many of the great formulators of science as we understand it—men such as Kepler, Descartes, and Newton—were deeply religious men who looked to scripture for their spiritual needs. Their insights into the physical world might heighten their faith in God's wondrous powers of creation, and through such insights they might feel they more clearly understand the nature of the Creator; but scientific research was not intended as a substitute for revelation.

As science continues to develop, however, it appears to enter increasing conflict with the doctrines of Judaism and Christianity, which in fact profoundly influenced the origins and development of science. Contemporary views of geology, evolution, and cosmology repudiate biblical accounts of the origins of the earth, life, and the cosmos. Physics provides no coherent way of viewing the miracles reported in the Bible, and neuroscience finds no place for the Christian concept of a human soul. What science does leave us with is a vast, impersonal universe consisting of matter and energy, in which life and consciousness occurred by accident. In this context human existence is insignificant except possibly insofar as it allows for scientific insights into its own irrelevance.

In the face of the conflict between science and religion, some people choose to reject the latter on the grounds that it has been disproved by science. Others dismiss many scientific tenets due to their incompatibility with revelation, and still others bifurcate their minds by adopting both scientific and religious doctrines, without allowing themselves to dwell on points of incompatibility between the two. In recent years attempts have been made to transcend the split between science and religion by seeking parallels between insights in modern physics and those in mysticism. Books on this theme, such as Fritjof Capra's *The Tao of Physics*, have gained wide popularity and stimulated much worthwhile thought. Clearly they have responded to a need for wholeness and the yearning to combine the deepest scientific truths and spiritual insights into an integrated understanding of reality.

Drawing parallels between mystical experience and contemporary views in physics may be enticing, but it also has its perils. If we endorse the value of mysticism on the basis of certain theories in today's physics, how shall we respond if in the future those theories are regarded as yesterday's misconceptions? In 1939, Alfred North Whitehead commented:

> Fifty-seven years ago it was when I was a young man in the University of Cambridge. I was taught science and mathematics by brilliant men and I did well in them; since the turn of the century I have lived to see every one of the basic assumptions of both set

aside....And yet, in the face of that, the discoverers of the new hypotheses in science are declaring, *"Now at last, we have certitude"*—when some of the assumptions which we have seen upset had endured for more than twenty centuries.[1]

Several years later he picked up on this theme with the remarks:

> I have been fooled once, and I'll be damned if I'll be fooled again! Einstein is supposed to have made an epochal discovery. I am respectful and interested, but also skeptical. There is no reason to suppose that Einstein's relativity is anything final, [no more] than Newton's *Principia*. The danger is dogmatic thought; it plays the devil with religion, and science is not immune from it.[2]

There may indeed be lasting truths discovered by modern physicists—theories that are similar to the insights of great mystics—as suggested by Capra. However, as we shall see later in this book, these truths have not been arrived at or demonstrated by strictly scientific procedures. All scientific theorizing is a human activity saturated by nonscientific influences. The hope that subjective mystical insights may be confirmed by pure objective science is a chimera.

Scientific dogma refutes biblical dogma, biblical dogma refutes the dogmas of Eastern religions, and today's science refutes even the most cherished, fundamental assumptions of yesterday's science. This state of affairs has led to a new movement that might be called the Cult of Uncertainty. Its dogma is to place credence in no theory or belief, and in standing for nothing, it regards itself as unassailable. Skepticism may be irrefutable, for it presents nothing to refute; but on its own it is also sterile.

Any pursuit of understanding and meaning requires faith, the acceptance of certain underlying assumptions that are necessary if one is to use a given mode of inquiry. Faith also implies a degree of humility in one's quest for truth. It is this that enables the seeker to employ certain theories and practices before having fully understood them or verified them by means of personal experience. Proponents of religions emphasize the crucial role of faith, though it is unfortunately often presented in the form of uncritical belief. Indeed, some regard faith alone (in the latter sense) as sufficient for salvation.

Faith is also a prerequisite for philosophical inquiry: the philosopher needs the confidence that such inquiry actually pertains to truth, that reality can be thought about. In addition to faith, philosophizing also requires reason. If a theory is internally inconsistent, illogical, or inconsistent with experience, it is unlikely to be accepted as sound philosophy.

Science also requires a type of faith, although it rarely goes under that label. Whereas religions normally make a clear statement of their articles of faith, science introduces its underlying assumptions more surreptitiously. The universe as it exists apart from human perceptions and conceptions can be known by means of scientific methods; although the world exists independently of our concepts, its components and laws can be grasped by concepts; although science repeatedly abandons its earlier theories, it is progressing steadily toward a correct representation of the universe as it is. These are just a few of the articles of faith that are held by most scientists and their followers today. In science lectures these assumptions are rarely mentioned and even more rarely questioned. Yet most science students emerge from their education having imbibed them, often without any conscious or critical appraisal. Such issues are not strictly scientific—though they pervade most scientific education and research—so their discussion does not find a place in the study of science.

Like philosophy, science also requires logic, and this plays a central role both in mathematical analysis and in the formulation of theories in spoken language. But unlike metaphysics, science further requires empirical methods for testing its theories. If a hypothesis, be it ever so elegant and appealing, cannot be put to the test of empirical refutation, it is likely to be dismissed by scientists as mere philosophizing.

With its threefold approach of faith, logic, and increasingly refined empirical investigation, science arose from the intellectual tyranny of the Middle Ages. Since then it has provided us with a wealth of knowledge about the physical world, and in the process it has formulated a new article of faith: all of reality essentially boils down to matter and energy subject to the mindless, immutable laws of nature. Life is reduced to an epiphenomenal by-product of complex configurations of chemicals; and mind is a coemergent property of the organization of the neural system. Such physicalist reductionism is not simply a conclusion based upon scientific research. Rather, it provides the metaphysical context in which such research and theorizing are pursued; and as such, much evidence is interpreted as being supportive of this view.

The use of mechanical instruments and mathematical analysis has been enormously productive in the physical sciences. But such methods have yielded scanty insight into the nature of the mind. More importantly perhaps, the physicalist view denies that mind as a subjective phenomenon is deserving of scientific research: since it is nothing more than an epiphenomenon of matter, a thorough understanding of the nervous system will provide all pertinent information about the mind. Does this attitude not have a familiar ring? How easy it is to imagine a medieval churchman admonishing his contemporaries: since the physical world is nothing more than an epiphenomenon of God, a thorough understanding of the scriptures (and possibly Aristotle's writings) will provide all pertinent information about nature.

Modern science established its identity by insisting upon directly probing into the natural world as opposed to submitting to authority as the means for understanding. Its original instruments were relatively crude by today's standards, but by using them to their fullest, scientists have developed finer, more sophisticated tools. These instruments are wonderfully suited to objective physical research, but their use in directly probing the mind is extremely limited. Nature in its wholeness includes both objective physical events and subjective mental events. A science that ignores or fails to produce means for investigating the latter must be an unnatural kind of science. Its theories must be incomplete and may be profoundly misleading.

For generations the notion that scientific theories represent objective, independent physical reality has been seriously challenged by philosophers of science. Indeed, there are few today who adhere to such straightforward scientific realism. Among the many problems with the realist position is the fact that multiple, mutually incompatible theories can often be presented that equally account for a given body of experimental evidence. A philosophically unreflective approach to science gives the impression that objective reality screens out false hypotheses, leaving only one true theory. In fact multiple hypotheses are often put forth, and the choice among them is based on various human factors.

Does science give us knowledge of the objective world? At the very least we have grounds for seriously calling this into question. If we conclude that it provides us with no ultimately reliable, objective knowledge, we may ask: what, then, is the purpose of creating scientific theories? One response is that such theories do make natural events intelligible in their relation to our human existence. A second purpose is that they are extremely useful in learning to deal with natural events that have a strong bearing on our well-being. One facet of that purpose is the development of technology.

Let us now return to the question of scientific research into the nature of the mind. If theories are unable to represent objective physical reality, can they any more reliably represent subjective cognitive reality? Might even direct investigation into the nature of mental events yield multiple, mutually incompatible theories to account for the same body of empirical evidence? This may very well be so, in which case, of what use are such cognitive theories? The situation is similar to that for physical theories: cognitive theories can make the mind intelligible in terms of our present worldview; they can enable us to deal more effectively with the mental causes of both joy and sorrow, contentment and discontent; and they may provide means for transforming and refining the mind in ways previously not imagined.

At present, Western civilization has no cognitive science comparable to its physical science. On the basis of this discussion thus far, one might assume that they are two autonomous disciplines. As we employ more revealing techniques for exploring the nature of consciousness, however, we may find ourselves delving into some of the deepest facets of the physical world. As insights into the nature of consciousness are related to physical science, physicists may find themselves confronting the profound role of the mind in their own field of inquiry. Indeed, if the universe is not composed of two autonomous substances of mind and matter (or matter alone), such integration of physical and cognitive science is bound to take place.

How shall we develop a cognitive science that penetrates so deeply into the nature of awareness? Cognitive science in its present Western form investigates mental states objectively in the sense that the researcher performs tests on other people's mental functions. Since the scientist has no direct access to anyone else's mind, this approach treats the mind as a "black box." The information that is analyzed concerns input and output from the mind and senses, but cognition itself is not directly examined. This would entail a subjective perspective, which is still regarded as unprofessional in today's scientific arena. This "black box approach" to the mind provides one means of questioning that can provide a certain body of knowledge about cognitive functions. But it leaves us in the dark as to other important aspects of the nature and potential of consciousness.

A central theme of this book will be that a particularly useful method for exploring the mind entails refined introspection: let the mind directly probe the mind, for no other instrument has that ability! As soon as we try to do so, however, we run into problems: the mind in its present state is a very unreliable instrument for the observation of mental states. It is exceedingly unstable, strongly subject to compulsive conceptualization, and lacking in clarity. These are some of the reasons why the school of introspectionism died just a few decades after its birth about a century ago.

Perhaps it is time to give the mind another chance. Are there ways to transform the mind into a stable, reliable, clear instrument of observation? In seeking methods toward this end, we may simply rely upon our own resources—that is, start from scratch—or we may look around for techniques that have already been developed by others. If we follow the latter, time-saving course, we may have to break down some conceptual barriers that we have set up among science, philosophy, and religion. Why? Because the most effective means for transforming human consciousness in this way have been developed by the great contemplative traditions of the world. Those of the East in particular do not distinguish science, philosophy, and religion as autonomous disciplines, as we are prone to do in the West. In our culture meditation and contemplation are widely regarded as means for relaxation and, in the religious context, for deepening one's experience of the divine. Are there contemplative techniques that can provide us with knowledge that can be integrated into our scientific understanding of the world? This we must judge for ourselves, and it is one aim of this book to introduce some of these techniques for appraisal. Of course, like the methods of physical science, they can be thoroughly appraised only if they are implemented.

The contemplative practices discussed in these pages are drawn from Buddhism. In addition to the techniques themselves, some of the resultant psychophysical theories will be briefly introduced. In many respects these differ, in some ways profoundly, from contemporary Western ideas. How shall we respond to such differences? If the methods by which they are formulated are unreliable, they can simply be dismissed. If those methods earn our respect, however, a profound insight of Werner Heisenberg, one of the great architects of quantum theory, may help us in reconciling incompatible theories: "What we observe is not nature in itself but nature exposed to our method of questioning."[3]

When we first encounter a theory that either contradicts or transcends our own, we may insist that it be verifiable by means of our present methods of questioning. As Heisenberg's statement suggests, this may not be possible; indeed, it may be impossible to rephrase one theory in terms of another that is derived from a radically different mode of inquiry. Yet there is a strong human urge to formulate grand unified theories, while rejecting evidence that does not fit. The assumption underlying this motive is that reality itself is one grand unified system that can be represented by our theories. If this assumption is unfounded, the quest for an ultimate, comprehensive supertheory is futile. In that case, we must be satisfied with the more modest pursuit of developing complementary theories, each one seen as relative to the mode of questioning that produced it.

Must the goal then be abandoned of knowing reality as it is apart from human sense perceptions and language? As we shall see, there are compelling reasons to believe that theories can never represent any reality existing independently of them. The conceptual mind, then, can never grasp a reality independent of thought; and the five senses clearly cannot penetrate beyond the veil of sensory appearances. The only possible access we may have to phenomena that transcend human concept and sensory perception is by cultivating states of awareness that themselves transcend language, concepts, and sensory experience.

How are we to know that such experience is authentic and not mere fantasy? From our present vantage point, we can scrutinize the contemplative methods that are employed in this quest. Clearly we have no ultimate criterion for what does and what does not constitute sound practice in this regard. Nevertheless, there is no reason to place credence in methods that appear unreliable. In Buddhist practice, claims to the authenticity of such transcendent experience are made on the basis of the soundness of the mental discipline that results in such experience, the subjective appraisal of the experience itself, and the useful, lasting effects of such insight.

The above discussion might suggest that by developing contemplative states of nonconceptual awareness, one can finally realize what is really out there, the true nature of the objective world. But this is not so. In such nonconceptual experience there no longer persists any sense of "out there" as opposed to "in here." The distinctions between subject and object, mind and matter, absolute and relative are all transcended. Words and concepts are incapable of describing such experience, and this, of course, is as it should be.

In the Buddhist context, how shall we regard the use of disciplined contemplation as a means for investigating the phenomenal world and the nature of ultimate reality? Is it a religious pursuit, a form of philosophical inquiry, or scientific research? It is not easy to classify, for it includes aspects of all three while resisting inclusion in any one of those categories to the exclusion of the other two. Contemplative inquiry may help to integrate diverse fields of knowledge as well as to deepen them individually. In this book we shall begin to explore its potential applications and relevance to contemporary life.

Chapter Two

Exploring the Nature of Empty Space

Since the time of Thales, dwelling on the eastern shores of the Mediterranean some twenty-five hundred years ago, Western thinkers have pondered the nature of the physical universe, posing the question: what is the fundamental substance of which the world is made? A great variety of responses have been made. Thales speculated that the basic stuff of the universe is water, whereas modern physicists, probing the structure of atomic nuclei, hypothesize that quarks may be the fundamental building blocks of the material world. Research continues as scientists develop yet more powerful tools for exploring more minute elements of matter; and present hypotheses are in no way considered to be final or incontrovertible.

As we begin our investigation into the relation between scientific theory and physical reality, let us inquire into a complementary subject that concerns not the nature of matter but the arena in which physical objects arise, move about, interact, and pass from existence. This is the subject of space, more specifically the vacuum. After placing this subject in a historical context, we shall survey a specific mode of recent empirical research into the nature of the vacuum. We shall then observe how experimental data are interpreted in light of a physical theory. As we explore the subject more thoroughly, we shall note other, competing theories that also account for the same data; and this will lead us into a more philosophical line of inquiry concerning the relation of theory to reality.

The early atomists Leucippus and Democritus originated the idea of a void existing in its own right, absolute and independent of contained things. Aristotle sharply refuted this view, declaring that the concept of the vacuum is nonsense. What is empty, he argued, is nothing, and what is nothing has no existence. Moreover, if a vacuum were to exist, it would provide no resistance, and consequently all forces would produce infinite speeds. Thus, from the era of Greek antiquity, the concept of the vacuum has implied to some thinkers the problem of infinite divergences.

Aristotle's views concerning space and the vacuum strongly influenced medieval thought, as well as later theories set forth by such men as Descartes and Leibniz. Descartes claimed that space exists only by virtue of a continuous distribution of matter; Leibniz, denying that space exists where there is no matter, maintained that it has no independent reality. Newton's views on this subject as articulated in his *Mathematical Principles of Natural Philosophy* differ sharply from the above. For him, absolute space is a logical and ontological necessity; it exists in its own nature, without relation to anything external. He thus adopted a view tracing back to the pre-Aristotelian atomists, and as his system of mechanics spread, so did his concept of absolute space.

Einstein's special theory of relativity, presented in 1905, was the first major, scientific challenge to Newton's assumption of absolute space. In proposing that the speed of light signals traversing space is invariant with respect to different inertial reference frames, Einstein refuted the classical notion of space as the absolute medium in reference to which absolute motion occurs. The invariance of this maximum speed—which turns out to be the speed of light—led to the realization that space, while not possessing an absolute frame of reference, is more than mere nothingness. It would seem to possess physical structure.

During the opening decades of this century, another physical theory was developed that challenged a number of classical concepts, including that of the vacuum. This was, of course, the quantum theory. Quantum theory asserts that although a region of space can in principle be emptied of ordinary matter, this vacuum is neither empty nor featureless. Rather, it has a complex structure that can in no way be eliminated. Moreover, it is now thought that the vacuum contains a residual energy that persists even when all matter and thermal radiation have been experimentally eliminated from a volume of space. The existence of such energy was predicted in 1911 by Max Planck, the originator of the notion of quanta, in a modification of his original theory. This came to be known as the *zero-point energy* of the vacuum. Although Planck himself, as well as his colleagues, swiftly discarded the specific conceptual grounds for this revised theory, his mathematical prediction of a residual energy in the vacuum remains.[1]

If such a zero-point energy does exist, it would seem to be an inherent property of space. Since there is no known means of removing it, once matter and radiant energy have been eliminated, it would indeed be the energy of the vacuum. There is even serious speculation that the entire universe may have originated from the vacuum. The energy-time uncertainty relation asserts that the standard deviation in time multiplied by the standard deviation in energy is greater than or equal to a numerical constant. We need not be overly concerned at this point with the precise meaning of the term *standard deviation*. What is of importance is that this uncertainty relation allows an arbitrarily small fluctuation in energy to occur for an arbitrarily long period of time. Thus, even if the net energy of the entire universe were approximately zero, an arbitrarily long-lived universe might fluctuate into existence out of the vacuum. Such a zero net energy is not absurd, for the positive matter-energy might be cancelled by the negative gravitational potential energy existing in the cosmos. In fact, rough order-of-magnitude estimates of the observed mass density of the universe suggest that the two quantities are remarkably close. For the time being, however, this theory remains highly speculative.

To sum up, according to modern physics, the classical vacuum state, free of all matter and fluctuating fields, is not physically realizable. Neither matter nor energy can be relied upon to be absolutely nonexistent in any region of space. Consequently, both relativity theory and quantum theory, for different reasons and in different ways, unequivocally declare that empty space, or the vacuum, has structure. Its precise nature is still being explored and many problems remain, but all of modern physics asserts that it is not a featureless, quiescent, propertyless void. Empty space is clearly, yet in some sense mysteriously, more than nothing.

This discussion suggests that the average energy of the vacuum is zero. However, this is not necessarily so. Let us focus for the time being on the electromagnetic vacuum, the ground state of an electromagnetic field system that contains no photons. A literal reading of well-known calculations performed in quantum electrodynamics suggests that the density of this vacuum energy is infinite.

Take any volume of space, empty it of matter, and remove all the photons, or elementary quanta of energy of the electromagnetic fields within it. What is left inside that vacuum? The unmodified calculations indicate that the residual energy is infinite, and this conclusion is not flatly contradicted by empirical evidence. More graphically stated: the energy inherent in one cubic centimeter of empty space is greater than the energy of all the matter in the known universe. This energy density is present throughout all of space, including regions where matter and other forms of energy are present. It is not confined to regions of pure vacuum. Seen in this light, the zero-point energy of the vacuum appears as a vast omnipresent ocean of infinite energy, and all other forms of energy—thermal, gravitational, and so on—appear as the thinnest of films upon the surface of this fathomless sea. Couched in such language, one may even begin to wonder whether this may have religious implications: is this infinite energy a facet of God's omnipresence? And it stimulates a number of philosophical questions, such as: might this ground-state energy of space be the fundamental, unified source of all physical and cognitive phenomena? Most physicists tend to avoid such speculations concerning this infinite divergence. In fact, the majority of advanced texts on quantum electrodynamics skirt the issue.

Thus, we are faced with the question: is the infinite vacuum energy physically real, or is it simply a mathematical anomaly devoid of physical relevance, a mere artifact of an abstract theory? Physics is generally understood to distinguish itself from metaphysics by being concerned only with theories that lend themselves to empirical verification or refutation. If no experimental evidence can be found to test a theory, practicing physicists are bound to lose interest. Thus, they might disregard the infinite energy of the vacuum on the grounds that it is unobservable, since no instrument has been invented that is able to measure infinite energy. But before we abandon the subject altogether, we may ask: is there any indirect evidence in support of this zero-point energy? In their textbook *Quantum Field Theory*, Claude Itzykson and Jean-Bernard Zuber declare that variations in that energy can be measured, specifically in the experimental confirmation of a theoretical prediction known as the Casimir effect.[2]

In the spring of 1948, the theoretical physicist H. B. G. Casimir presented a paper in which he proposed a way of calculating a finite difference between the vacuum energies of two cavities of different volumes. Ideally, both cavities would contain infinite vacuum energy. But, as Casimir pointed out, when the experiment is conducted in a laboratory, the nonideal walls that enclose the two cavities do not act as perfect reflectors for all frequencies of electromagnetic fields. This fact allows one to introduce a cut-off point for the relevant frequencies within the cavities. Now imagine a single cavity with a wall that can slide back and forth, increasing and decreasing the enclosed volume. Since the vacuum energy of the larger cavity is greater than that of the smaller cavity, the difference in energies between the cavities creates a force that acts on the opposing walls. This force is not due to gravity or electric charges on the walls; rather, it is a zero-point force derived from the electromagnetic energy inherent in the vacuum. Casimir theoretically calculated the direction and magnitude of this force and suggested that it could be experimentally put to the test. This has been done repeatedly, and his predictions have proven correct. On the face of it, the experimental confirmation of a force that is produced from differences in vacuum energy indirectly establishes the physical reality of that energy. Instead of being satisfied with that straightforward conclusion, however, let us look more closely at the interpretations of these experimental results.

We have noted that there is some question as to whether the energy of the vacuum is infinite or zero. Recall that, according to Itzykson and Zuber, an experimental confirmation of the Casimir effect implies a measurement of a variation of the infinite energy of the electromagnetic vacuum. Physicist I. J. R. Aitchison points out that the zero-point energy of the vacuum is far too securely founded simply to ignore it, and he states that no completely satisfactory resolution for the difficulty of its own infinite divergence exists.[3] Thus, an empirical demonstration of the force predicted by Casimir must be of great interest in terms of testing the physical reality of the infinite energy of the vacuum.

E. A. Power points out that despite the infinite divergence of the zero-point energy of the vacuum, it can still be regarded as a constant; and since physics is generally concerned with only the energy differences, the energy of the vacuum can simply be set at zero.[4] Mathematically this adjustment from infinity to zero is brought about by techniques of regularization or renormalization. On the other hand, Power seems uncertain about this procedure when he goes on to point out that there is one compelling branch of modern physics that is concerned not merely with the differences in energy states but with their absolute values.[5] This branch is the general theory of relativity, which prohibits physically unjustifiable, ad hoc methods of redefining energy values. Gravitational energy in particular is an absolute quantity in nature, and its value must not be arbitrarily altered.

Now we have a problem: the empirical confirmation of the Casimir effect has been cited equally as grounds for believing in the physical reality of infinite zero-point energy of the vacuum and of an average zero energy of the vacuum. Over the past four centuries physics has advanced tremendously by making frequent use of the following combined approach of theoretical and empirical research: (1) A physical theory is formulated with the use of mathematical calculations, (2) a specific quantitative prediction is made on the basis of that more general theory, and (3) experiments or observations are performed that confirm the specific prediction, thereby empirically demonstrating the validity of the initial theory. Now in the present case we are presented with a problem, for the experimental confirmation of the Casimir effect has been presented as evidence for two mutually incompatible conclusions: an energy of the vacuum that is said to be both infinite and zero. Both of these conclusions are made in the context of a single theory, quantum electrodynamics, but the Casimir effect itself sheds no light on the actual value of this energy.

The problem of interpretation does not stop there. In the opening lines of his aforementioned paper, Casimir remarks that calculations for a similar problem were previously derived by taking the London-van der Waals force as a starting point and altering it to account for the effects of special relativity.[6] The London-van der Waals force has a completely different source than the vacuum energy: it is produced by the behavior of the atoms that form the walls of the cavity in the Casimir experiment. The calculations for the effects of London-van der Waals force and for the effects of the zero-point force, however, yield exactly the same prediction. Thus, an experimental verification of that prediction equally confirms both theories, though they are conceptually quite different. Oddly enough, this ambiguity concerning the Casimir effect is generally ignored in references to it and its experimental confirmation.

Let us continue our investigation into the mystery of the real significance of the Casimir effect. Quantum electrodynamics allows us to conclude on the basis of the confirmed experiment either that the energy of the vacuum is zero or that it is infinite. In either case the vacuum is assumed to have a structure. Can we at least conclude that the objective physical reality of the structure of the vacuum is an unambiguous conclusion of the experimental demonstration of the Casimir effect? Unfortunately not, for in 1975, J. Schwinger[7] showed a way of accounting for the Casimir effect within the context of his "source theory,"[8] which assumes the vacuum to be without structure. The mathematical results that he obtains with that theory are identical with those predicted by Casimir.

May we at least conclude that the approach of contemporary quantum mechanics is the most promising line of inquiry into the objective reality of the energy of the vacuum? Physicist Timothy Boyer has developed a theory of stochastic electrodynamics that brings even that conclusion into question.

At the beginning of this century, Max Planck laid the foundation for modern quantum theory in response to a problem involving thermal radiation in a cavity.[9] The relevant entropy-energy formulas of Wein and of Rayleigh and Jeans, which were derived in the context of classical thermodynamics, were contradictory and presented no solution to the so-called ultraviolet catastrophe. Planck's formula expressing his famous radiation law arose as a natural modification of the connection between the entropy and energy of thermal radiation, which formed an interpolation of the above two formulas. As Boyer points out: "Only after noting the success of this modification did Planck return to try to find a theoretical justification for the modification. He found an explanation in the notion of discrete units of energy, the notion of quanta."[10]

Planck's radiation formula conformed with experimental evidence, and he saw that it could be justified by modifying the classical calculation of thermodynamic probability by the use of quanta. Since 1969, Boyer has written a series of technical papers demonstrating that the introduction of the notion of quanta is quite unnecessary. Planck initially introduced the concept of quanta into physical theory to account for certain experimental results involving thermal radiation. In the ensuing decades, as quantum mechanics has developed into an extremely successful theory, the physical reality of quanta has widely come to be taken for granted. Boyer challenges this assumption by resolving the initial problem in thermal radiation without introducing quanta.

The main new concept in Boyer's work is the existence, at absolute zero of temperature, of a classical, fluctuating, electromagnetic background radiation that produces the same effects as the ground state of the radiation field in quantum electrodynamics. Thus, he speaks of classical, rather than quantum, electromagnetic zero-point energy. In short, he arrives at the conclusion that "the idea of quanta forms a subterfuge for what is a natural part of a theory of classical thermodynamics including electromagnetism."[11] Boyer, using his classical theory of a vacuum energy, also looks into the experiment suggested by Casimir, and his calculations yield exactly the same prediction for the force between the walls of the vacuum.

Early in this century, Einstein proposed a number of situations that he thought could be most naturally explained in terms of quanta. Boyer reviews those examples and shows how they can be reinterpreted, without quanta, in terms of classical electromagnetic zero-point radiation.[12] In fact, it is no secret among those well versed in the foundations of quantum mechanics that the original justifications for the necessary physical reality of quanta are now seen as quite tenuous.

———————◆———————

As we have inquired into the nature of the vacuum and its zero-point energy, we have come across a diversity of mutually incompatible theories that all account for the Casimir effect. There are yet other theories relating to the vacuum that have not been mentioned, such as supersymmetry, which states that the energy of the vacuum is zero, and another cosmological theory that suggests that it is finite. At this point the straightforward approach of producing a general quantitative theory, a specific prediction, and empirical confirmation clearly makes no unequivocal statement about objective reality. Upon initially investigating a subject such as the vacuum, we may be fascinated and eagerly anticipate the experiment that will verify the physically true theory. We may feel like travelers setting out on a clear-cut path through a dense forest. Eagerly we look forward to coming upon a promontory that will give us a broad, clear view far out over the surrounding countryside. But as we tread deeper into this forest, we encounter more and more forks in the path, and each one is marked with a sign declaring, "Promontory, this way." Are all the signs correct, or was a malicious prankster at work? Does only one path lead to the promontory that we long to reach, or might there be multiple promontories offering a diversity of views? Or are all the paths dead ends leading to no promontories, merely giving us the opportunity to exercise as we wander in the dark?

Upon confronting a diversity of theories that equally account for the same body of experimental evidence and that yield identical predictions, we may become disheartened and lose interest. Or we may assume that only one of those theories (or an unformulated one) represents physical reality. This latter attitude encourages us patiently to identify the one true path by a gradual process of elimination; but it also entails the assumption that the choice will be narrowed down; that is, that new competing options will not crop up as quickly as we eliminate old ones. The belief that there is an objective physical reality that can finally be represented by one and only one theory is a metaphysical assumption held by many scientists today.

A third response to this problem of diversity is to step back from the methods of physics and to reflect on the nature of scientific modes of inquiry. Thus, acknowledging this problem may lead us more to philosophical inquiry rather than to proper scientific research.

Not long ago a friend and I attended a lecture by a fine theoretical physicist speaking on the nature of the vacuum. The lecturer began by informing his audience that he would now convince them that the vacuum has structure and an inherent energy, as asserted in quantum field theory. He then presented a lucid, compelling account of this theory of the vacuum and its various empirical confirmations, including the Casimir effect. At the conclusion of this talk, my companion, with whom I had been researching the vacuum, raised his hand and asked: "Doesn't Schwinger's source theory equally account for all the experimental evidence you have cited, while standing in direct opposition to quantum field theory?" In response the speaker smiled and said that this was indeed the case. He went on to remark that such a situation of multiple incompatible theories accounting for the same phenomena is common throughout physics. The choice among such theories, he added, is a matter of metaphysical predilection.

What a remarkable about-face! First we were told that we would be convinced, on experimental grounds, of the structure of the vacuum as asserted in quantum field theory. Then we are informed that the same experiments equally confirm a theory that denies any structure of the vacuum, and that the choice between them is a metaphysical one. If the presence of multiple incompatible theories accounting for the same phenomena is, as we were told, common in physics, what does this science have to tell us about the nature of the objective universe? It would seem at this point that physics as such presents us with a number of options, among which we can try to choose the realistic one on the basis of our own metaphysical predilections!

We have encountered several competing theories that attempt to explain the Casimir effect, each of which accounts for the experimental evidence. But we have not exhausted all the present theories, let alone all the conceivable theories that might be equally explanatory of the relevant phenomena. Can we place a limit on the number of possible theories to account for a single body of evidence? Who can put a limit on the creativity of the human imagination, or on theories that lie beyond our imagination? Might there be in principle an infinite number of reasonable theories to account for the same phenomena? If so, in what sense does physics bring us closer to a true understanding of physical reality? Moreover, if our choice of an account of the universe is ultimately a metaphysical one, why should we limit the possible choices to those presented by science? These are some of the questions that we shall explore in the following chapters.

Chapter Three

The Conception and Preservation of Energy

In the preceding chapter, we were introduced to the notion of an energy inherent in empty space. We briefly investigated one of the major bodies of empirical evidence in support of this idea, namely, the experimental confirmation of the Casimir effect. In trying to make sense of the implications of this discovery, however, we found that it has been cited as evidence both for an infinite energy density of the vacuum and for an average zero energy density. What is the nature of this mysterious entity that can be reduced from infinity to zero simply by means of mathematical manipulations? Are such normalization techniques used because the idea of infinite energy density is physically absurd or incomprehensible?

Quantum theory, along with most of the rest of physics, is concerned only with the differences in energies, not their absolute values. Yet general relativity does ascribe absolute quantity to energy—it cannot be changed from one value to another simply out of convenience. Which of these two incompatible attitudes with regard to energy is true of nature? Furthermore, quantum theory regards energy as being quantized, whereas Timothy Boyer's theory of classical stochastic electromagnetic fields denies the need for such quantization. Here again, what is the true nature of energy in its own right?

Science does not yet have answers to these fundamental questions, so we must be patient. In the meantime it may serve us well to look more closely at the birth and development of our concept of energy in the context of modern science. If energy had simply been objectively discovered using purely scientific techniques, it would be hard to imagine how such fundamentally incompatible ideas could persist concerning its nature. So let us look back to the modern origins of this concept and see what other influences might have a bearing on it.

We may begin this brief historical review by going back to the theories of Newton and Leibniz in the seventeenth century. At this point there was no agreement even on basic terminology. Newton used the term *force* to refer to something imposed on essentially inert matter, and this something is not conserved. Leibniz, in contrast, defined the living force (*vis viva*) of a body as a dynamical quantity that is conserved in all interactions. This concept is more closely akin to, and in fact helped to produce, our modern concept of kinetic energy.

In his *Specimen Dynamicum* Leibniz sets forth his notion of living force. He first draws a distinction between primitive and derivative forces. Primitive forces cannot suffice to explain phenomena, for they relate only to general causes and characterize the nature of substances. Derivative forces are those by which bodies act on one another. It is these forces that produce motion, and they arise through a limitation of primitive forces. The living force and the dead force (*vis mortua*) are derivative active forces, while the impenetrability of bodies and their resistance to motion are derivative passive forces. Derivative active and passive forces are both regarded as phenomenal manifestations of primitive forces.

Leibniz defined the living force of a body as the product of its mass and the square of its speed. He adopted this quantity from Huygens, who thought it had no profound significance for the science of mechanics. Leibniz, though, regarded the conservation of this quantity as a fundamental law expressing the inherent activity of nature and the order and self-sufficiency of natural processes. He writes in reference to this principle: "We ought to establish...[a] law of nature which I hold as being most universal and most inviolable...there is always a perfect equivalence between the full cause and the total effect...each entire effect is equivalent to the cause."[1]

While living force arises in the actual motion of a body, dead force is the tendency of a body to achieve a state of motion. Thus, the former arises from an infinite number of infinitesimal impulses of the latter. In Leibniz's view, matter is elastic, and change never occurs instantaneously but must pass through all intermediate degrees. This notion is an expression of his metaphysical principle of the *law of continuity*. Although living force seems to disappear when a moving body comes to a stop as a result of friction, Leibniz assumed that it is simply absorbed into the internal structure of the bodies in question. While dead force is transient, living force remains in existence, conserved and never diminished.

In Leibniz's theology, God created a universe operating according to the perfect and self-sufficient laws established at creation. Due to the conservation of living force, natural processes are maintained without intervention by an external agent. Newton, however, maintained that every action in nature reflects the exertion of a new force on the thing acted upon. In nature there is a continual dissipation of motion that must be counteracted by active principles; hence, the world cannot be reduced to absolute mechanism. He condemned Leibniz's notion of a world machine that can continue to run forever without divine intervention. In his *Opticks* he dismisses Leibniz's view of the conservation of living force as being sufficient to account for all natural phenomena, declaring this "a notion of materialism and fate,...[that] tends (under pretence of making God a *supramundane* intelligence) to exclude providence and God's government in reality out of the world."[2] Indeed, as mechanics developed over the following decades, nature's need for divine intervention or guidance (in maintaining the planets in their orbits, for instance) did seem to disappear.

Thus, at the birth of classical physics there was a fundamental divergence of views by the two greatest natural philosophers of the time concerning the nature of force, energy, and matter. Newton's and Lebinz's mathematical expressions for force differed, as did their conceptions of the matter that is acted upon by forces. Newton regarded matter as inert, and he challenged Leibniz's theory of the conservation of living force on theological grounds.

The principle of conservation can be traced at least as far back as the fifth century BC in the speculations of the Greek philosopher Parmenides. Leibniz found it compatible with his theological views, and he criticized Newton's system of mechanics as being supernatural. In the contest between these two intellectual giants in the history of science, neither adversary seemed concerned with pure science, divorced from metaphysics and theology. Nor, in their lifetimes, did nature settle their disputes.

The formulation of the law of conservation of energy in the nineteenth century is one of the most striking instances of simultaneous discovery in the history of science. One factor contributing to this discovery was the belief, widespread in the eighteenth century, in the interconversion of natural powers and the unity of nature. Speculations on the relationships among the phenomena of heat, light, electricity, and chemistry were frequently based on a unified ether theory, which emphasized the balance of forces, the unity and interconversion of natural phenomena, and the self-sufficiency of nature. More specifically, the *Naturphilosophie* of Leibniz, the author of the metaphysical conservation theorem, could have provided an appropriate philosophical background for the discovery of the principle of energy conservation. Reaching its height of popularity during the first two decades of the nineteenth century, this view posited a universal science with the organism as its fundamental metaphor, and its adherents constantly sought a single unifying principle for all natural phenomena.

In terms of scientific research, the conversion processes and mathematical analyses of heat and electricity in the nineteenth century were prerequisites for the formulation of the principle of energy conservation. Part of the foundation for this principle was the refutation of perpetual motion. Early in the nineteenth century, as new conversion processes were developed, some scientists, ignoring irreversible energy transformations, reasoned that any power can produce any other and be produced by it. Therefore, there must be a uniform, quantitative equivalence between each pair of powers; otherwise, a properly chosen series of conversions would result in the creation of power. On this basis, a law of conservation was formulated as early as 1829. In 1840, Michael Faraday proposed such a principle, and in 1842, Julius Mayer declared that forces are indestructible, convertible entities. Mayer's thesis, however, was philosophical in nature; and, lacking a solid experimental basis and mathematical formulation, it was ignored for at least a decade.

Mayer's theory and the work of James Prescott Joule are often contrasted, the former exemplifying a nonscientific, speculative approach to nature and the latter typifying the sober, empirical, and mathematical approach of a physicist. The point is well taken. Nevertheless, it is worth noting that Joule did not present a quantitative formulation of a general principle of conservation of energy. Rather, he maintained that he had scientifically established the mutual convertibility of heat and work. He did in fact believe in the indestructibility and self-sufficiency of natural powers, but on the grounds that only God can destroy agents of nature. It is "manifestly absurd," he declared, "to suppose that the powers with which God has endowed matter can be destroyed."[3] Both he and Faraday argued that the indestructibility of such powers is an indication of the wisdom and foresight of God.

For Mayer the notion of an underlying, imperishable metaphysical force seems prior to research and almost unrelated to it. The same has been said of Hermann von Helmholtz,[4] who in 1847 provided the first systematic and mathematical formulation of the principle of the conservation of energy. In an essay presented in that year, he treated mechanical phenomena, heat, light, electricity, and magnetism as different manifestations of energy. On this basis he devised a conservation law in the form of a mathematical and mechanical theorem. This formulation was closely linked to his assumption of the universal validity of the mechanical view of nature. This, he assumed, was the criterion for "the complete comprehensibility of nature,"[5] and he emphasized the unifying role of the energy concept in relation to an ontology of matter and the program of mechanical explanation. In taking this view, he assumed that natural laws are Newtonian, they are objectively real, and they cause phenomena.

From the foregoing discussion it is apparent that during the first half of the nineteenth century there was some confusion in terminology relating to the conservation of energy. The word *energy* used roughly in the modern sense, dates from 1807, but for decades thereafter different scientists variously spoke of "natural powers" and "forces" that are conserved. *Energy* was first used as a general and fundamental physical concept by William Thomson in 1849. He identified two types of energy, which he called *statical* and *dynamical* and maintained that all forms of energy are of a mechanical nature. Thus, energy became for him the unifying principle in physics. In his view, it is an objectively real, quantitatively immutable entity that is convertible and links all of nature in a web of energy transformations. Like so many other scientists, he too expressed a theological position in support of his theory: energy is an immutable natural agent that cannot be created or destroyed except by God. His metaphysical assumption was that the energy concept would provide a foundation for a comprehensive, mechanical explanation of natural events.

Thomson's use of the word *energy* resolved terminological and conceptual confusions, and his emphasis on diverse energies being manifestations of mechanical energy brought out the unifying role of this concept. By the 1850s, this term was in common usage, though it was not until 1867 that the dual classification of potential and kinetic energy was introduced.

The principle of energy conservation was a broadly unifying factor in nineteenth-century physics. As we have seen, the motivation for its adoption into scientific theory arose largely from a metaphysical assumption of the unity of nature. Leibniz, the author of the metaphysical conservation theorem, formulated this concept long before conclusive empirical evidence was available to substantiate it. He simply intuited, for example, that live force (akin to the modern concept of kinetic energy) must be conserved, even though experience suggested otherwise. Mayer and Helmholtz first adopted the conservation principle on metaphysical grounds, while Joule, Faraday, and Thomson formulated scientific theories of this principle in conformity with their theological views. It seems they never held the view that science could be conducted properly only when it is divorced from metaphysics and religion, yet the conservation theory that they pioneered remains a dominant principle of twentieth-century physics.

Physicists have always, although often not explicitly, come to conclusions about physics out of metaphysical assumptions (some derived from their religious beliefs), as we see from the history of the idea of energy. They still do so; in fact they cannot avoid doing so, as we saw in the discussion of the vacuum energy. So there is a need to recognize this more explicitly, and to examine just what are these metaphysical assumptions, particularly in regard to the relation between theory and reality.

Chapter Four

Views of Science and Reality through History

The history of physical theories in modern science reveals a great diversity of beliefs concerning the nature of space, time, energy, and matter. Although there is widespread agreement among physicists concerning the use of mathematical techniques, the validity of empirical data, and the value of certain models of physical processes as heuristic devices, there is still a fundamental diversity of opinion concerning the nature of physical reality. The most basic problem is the relation between physical theory and physical reality.

Many scientists and their followers in the nineteenth century adhered to a view of physics now described as *scientific realism:* true physical theory represents an independent objective reality. Theoretical entities—such as gravity, fields, energy, and the ether—operate behind the veil of appearances; their existence is discovered by unbiased research. The laws of nature are revealed by the scientific method, entailing mathematical analysis and empirical verification; they describe physical events that occur independently of the human mind.

During the latter part of the nineteenth century, this metaphysical assumption was challenged by such physicists as James Clerk Maxwell, Ernst Mach and Jules-Henri Poincaré. Their views are closely aligned with a philosophy of science now known as *instrumentalism,* which holds that the function of a physical theory is to offer an intelligible, systematic conceptual pattern for observed data, thereby uniting phenomena that are otherwise surprising, anomalous, or wholly unnoticed.[1] Theoretical concepts such as fields, energy, electrons, and so on do not correspond to independent, objective entities; they are simply conceptual constructs, or instruments, that physicists find useful in making predictions about measurements. Consequently, according to this view, physical theories are not true or false; they are simply more or less useful in accounting for observed phenomena.

The fundamental opposition of realist versus instrumentalist views did not emerge for the first time in the nineteenth century. The beginnings of this controversy can be traced back to Greek antiquity.[2] One of the challenges that Plato set for his students was to devise a mathematical stratagem that would account for the motions of heavenly bodies.[3] The first reasonably complete astronomical theory known to history was formulated in this spirit by Eudoxus. His motive was to "save the appearances," and his theory entailed a mathematical description rather than a physical explanation. A theory that "saves the appearances" accounts for observed phenomena so that their present occurrence is seen as a matter of course and future occurrences are accurately predicted. Such a theory makes phenomena intelligible by predicting their behavior, without explaining why they behave as they do. Aristotle, on the other hand, was concerned with an astronomical theory that explained *why* celestial bodies move as they do. The hypotheses of such a theory must be justified by the nature of those bodies, and not simply account in an ad hoc manner for their movements.

Given the challenge of saving the appearances, Greek astronomers were quick to discover that more than one theory could account for the same observed phenomena. Hipparchus (second century BC) proved, for example, that the course of the sun can be represented either by supposing that it describes a circle eccentric to our world or by letting it be carried by an epicycle. In the latter case, the revolution of this epicycle must be achieved in exactly the same time in which its center has completed a circle concentric with the earth.

Ptolemy (second century AD), whose astronomical system was extensively elaborated during the Middle Ages, was another thinker who adopted an instrumentalist view concerning physical theory. In his system, the spheres and orbits of the celestial bodies, by which appearances were to be saved, were regarded as hypotheses in the strict sense of the word: assumptions made for the purpose of a particular argument and by the same token not posited as true.[4] The Greek and medieval astronomers who adhered to Ptolemy's instrumentalist view were not at all disturbed by the fact that the same appearances could be saved by two or more quite different hypotheses, such as an eccentric or an epicycle. They were concerned simply with finding the simplest and most complete theory for practical purposes.

While Aristotle claimed to have found the fundamental principles of both the sublunary and celestial realms, the fifth-century Greek philosopher Proclus declared that there is a fundamental distinction between the kinds of human knowledge of those two realms. While humans can understand sublunary things, he maintained, our hypotheses concerning heavenly things are at best approximations, for the same conclusions can be drawn from different hypotheses concerning the same phenomena. Only the divine mind (logos) knows what the heavens are really like. A realist at heart, Proclus was thus obliged to introduce an element of uncertainty into human understanding of celestial objects.

As Ptolemaic astronomy was adopted and further developed first by Arabic thinkers and later by medieval Christian scholars, Ptolemy's original intent was forgotten. The Arab philosopher Averroës (twelfth century), for example, required more of astronomy than that it simply account for appearances. Its hypotheses must be justified in accordance with principles of physics set down by Aristotle. Bernard of Verdun, a medieval Scholastic doctor, further retreated from the wisdom of the Greeks by maintaining that a false hypothesis—that is, one that does not describe physical reality—cannot possibly yield exact, correct predictions. Thomas Aquinas, on the other hand, recognized along with Averroës that a hypothesis may yield predictions that agree with observation, without that hypothesis thereby being established as a demonstrated truth. Medieval Christian astronomers placed two basic demands upon the hypotheses of astronomy: (1) they should be as simple as possible, and (2) they should save the appearances as exactly as possible.

The task that Copernicus set himself was to save the appearances by means of hypotheses conformable to the principles of physics. Like Averroës, he regarded an astronomical theory as satisfactory only if it is constructed on the basis of hypotheses that are true. Taking the philosophical position of his medieval predecessors, he, too, deviated from Ptolemy by taking a realist view of the hypotheses of astronomy.

Kepler adopted both Copernicus's heliocentrism and his attitude regarding hypotheses. He recognized that mathematics alone cannot decide among diverse hypotheses—that is, mathematical formulas are not self-interpreting. Rather, the choice must be made on the basis of justifiable physical principles. Moreover, he was convinced that if a hypothesis is not true, its falsehood will be revealed when it is applied with sufficient precision to ever more varied cases.

Galileo, too, demanded that the hypotheses of astronomy be established on the ground of physics. As the father of modern science, he is revered for his insistence that experience, not the authority of tradition, decide which among competing hypotheses conforms to reality. With his dedication to realism, he seems to have ignored that contradictory hypotheses may equally account for the same observed facts. Moreover, in his contest with the Inquisition, he exhibited an even more simplistic attitude concerning the proof of a hypothesis. In imitation of the *reductio ad absurdum* proofs that are used in geometry, he suggested that experience, by convicting one system of error, confers certainty upon its opposite.[5]

The first religious opposition to the heliocentric theory came not from the Roman Catholic Church but from Martin Luther. Recognizing that its chief proponents regarded it as being a true hypothesis and not merely a useful instrument for making predictions, Luther condemned it as contrary to Scripture. His disciple Philip Melanchthon advised young people to rely upon religious authority and not to be misled by the hypotheses of "clever scientists." In his words: "They will then understand that God has revealed the truth; they should accept it with respect and acquiesce in it."[6]

Until the culmination of the conflict between the Inquisition and Galileo in 1616, the Church of Rome not only permitted but encouraged discussion of the Copernican system, as long as it was confined to the language of science and did not impinge on theological matters.[7] The dignitaries in the Vatican apparently believed that Copernicus presented his theory as a hypothesis in the traditional sense of the word: a useful means to save the appearances and make accurate predictions, without any claim to truth. Galileo's chief opponent in the controversy with the Church was Cardinal Robert Bellarmine. A general of the Jesuit Order, he found nothing to be prohibited in the Copernican theory as long as it was introduced simply in order to save appearances. Indeed, he maintained that "to say that the assumption that the Earth moves and the Sun stands still saves all the celestial appearances better than do eccentrics and epicycles is to speak with excellent good sense and to run no risk whatever. Such a manner of speaking suffices for a mathematician."[8] However, he went on to insist that one should not think that the sun is in truth at the center of the universe.

Thus, the Church naturally held a realist view regarding its own scriptures and tolerated contrary scientific theories only if they were presented from the instrumentalist point of view. Galileo found such intolerance unacceptable. The Church's inability to accept a realist interpretation of heliocentrism resulted in its condemnation of the Copernican system in 1616. Shortly thereafter, Cardinal Maffeo Barberini, soon to become Pope Urban VIII, met with Galileo to discuss scientific theory and reality. The Cardinal pointed out that to prove one's own hypothesis, one must demonstrate that its predictions could not be obtained by a different system and that such a system would involve contradiction. The fact that a hypothesis, such as the heliocentric theory, satisfactorily explains certain phenomena does not necessarily prove that it is true, for those phenomena could have been produced by some entirely different means which are not understood by the human mind.

Seen in this light, the conflict between Galileo and the Church appears to focus on the ontological assumptions concerning physical theory. Galileo was unpersuaded by the Cardinal's critique of his realist view of scientific theory, and he must have recognized that the Church was unwilling to apply that same critique to its own interpretations of theories presented in the scriptures. Since Galileo was impenitent in his realism, in 1633 Urban VIII allowed the Peripatetics of the Holy Office to express their intransigent realism by issuing a further condemnation of the Copernican system. Galileo was forbidden to teach that system in any manner whatsoever. From now on astronomy was to be subject to theology and philosophy, and the Copernican hypotheses were not to be used even to make predictions.

Although Copernicus, Kepler, and Galileo were all confirmed realists, the contest among scientists between instrumentalism and realism was far from settled. Newton himself was of two minds on the matter. In his *Principles*, he restricted himself to setting forth the mathematical principles of mechanics as a means of understanding apparently diverse physical phenomena, notably both terrestrial and celestial dynamics. With this system he was able to vanquish the mistaken assumption—tracing back to Aristotle—that sublunary and celestial bodies are subject to fundamentally different natural laws. His theory also challenged Proclus's view that only sublunary events can be humanly known with certainty. In this treatise he made a point of not speculating on the ontological nature of such theoretical entities as gravitational force. For Leibniz, Newton's chief opponent, *Principles* seemed merely a mathematical predicting device, akin to Ptolemy's system of astronomy: they both merely saved the appearances, while providing minimal elucidation of the actual nature of physical reality.[9]

For Leibniz and other like-minded Continental thinkers, a complete science must explain the data, as well as account for them. Thus, following the trend of Aristotle, Leibniz adopted a realist view, while criticizing Newton for his instrumentalist leanings. This charge is only partially justified. Newton did indeed seek to abstain from forming ontological hypotheses by confining himself to observable phenomena; and even in his later years he discouraged his students from speculating on the physical nature of gravity. Nevertheless, as evidenced in his *Opticks*, he was not immune to hypothesizing various types of ether that could act as media for gravity, light, and heat. His metaphysical and theological convictions concerning the nature of space, time, force, and matter are also incompatible with an instrumentalist view.

Throughout the eighteenth century, as Newtonian mechanics was extended and refined, it was widely regarded as a mathematical theory designed to predict, but not to explain, physical phenomena. But during the nineteenth century, a process of reification dominated scientific thinking, and mechanics came to be regarded as a true explanation of the hidden processes of physical reality, behind the veil of appearances. This mechanical philosophy can be traced back at least to the seventeenth century, and though it originated from no single thinker, its most influential proponent was Descartes.[10] He held that nature contains no unfathomable mysteries and that it is wholly transparent to reason. While rigidly excluding all cognitive elements from the material world, he asserted that all phenomena of nature are produced by inert matter in motion. A central assumption of his philosophy is that physical reality is not in any way similar to the appearances of sensation. Although he acknowledged the existence of a nonmaterial soul (for humans only), this was not the seat of life; and he described all organic functions in purely mechanistic terms.

Like Descartes, Galileo was committed to the belief that the physical world is composed of certain primary properties and can be known only in mathematical terms. Human minds and individuals are not included in that realm, and in Galileo's view they are relegated to little more than bundles of secondary qualities. Philosopher of science Edwin Burtt says of Galileo's writings: "Man begins to appear for the first time in the history of thought as an irrelevant spectator, an insignificant effect of the great mathematical system which is the substance of reality."[11]

During Newton's time there was a popular view, believed by practically all educated people, that the mind is a unique but small substance in the brain. There was nothing in Newton's writings to upset this view, and everything to support it. Thus, a naive, utterly speculative view of the nature of the mind came to be backed by Newton's great authority. This notion regarded human beings as irrelevant spectators of the world of nature, and it gradually took on the false status of being a scientific fact, rather than a metaphysical speculation.

Over the next two centuries, while theology and philosophy apparently made no progress comparable to that of natural science, the spiritual and cognitive elements of nature seemed to wane in significance. Especially during the period 1850-90, German science in particular was dominated by mechanistic materialism. This expression of scientific realism was promoted, for example, by the German physician Ludwig Büchner.[12] According to him, phenomena are inherently mechanical, and everything in the real, independent, objective world—including all animate and inanimate things—reduces to matter. The scientific method is the one true means of discovering the objective laws of nature, and its implementation requires no philosophical speculation. Experience is the crucial test of a scientific theory, and this is purely a matter of observation unmediated by concepts.

———————◆———————

During the 1870s, the notion of unmediated, conceptually free observation was challenged by Hermann von Helmholtz. While maintaining a firm realist stance, he proposed that there is an unconscious processing that occurs in perception. A final perception is in fact a conclusion that has been created in part by deductive logic. Thus, conceptually unmediated observation plays no role in science or everyday life.[13] Ernst Mach is especially known for his abandonment of the metaphysical baggage that weighed so heavily in mechanistic materialism. According to him, science is a conceptual reflection of facts, which are contents of consciousness given to us by the senses. Only verifiable statements have a place in science, and these must be reducible to statements about sensations. Eventually Mach acknowledged that such a criterion for verifiability was too narrow, since mathematics, for example, cannot be verified in that way. In his later thinking, he included elements that are not reducible to sensations, but he regarded these as conventions, not a priori truths.

Maxwell also challenged the assumption of mechanistic materialism that the facts speak for themselves, in the sense that empirical evidence verifies the one true hypothesis that accounts for an event. Purely on mathematical grounds, he posited the existence of electromagnetic waves, and on the basis of his work physical reality came to be conceived as a domain of continuous fields that are not mechanically explicable. This was at the time the most profound and fruitful change in physicists' conception of reality since Newton; and it was a major scientific blow to the tenets of mechanistic materialism.

In his treatise *The Value of Science*, Poincaré further repudiated one of the fundamental tenets of mechanistic materialism by declaring: "A reality completely independent of the spirit that conceives it, sees it or feels it, is an impossibility. A world so external as that, even if it existed, would be forever inaccessible to us."[14]

———————————◆———————————

In reviewing the history of physics, Einstein recognized that the natural philosophers of the eighteenth and nineteenth centuries believed on the whole that the fundamental concepts and postulates of physics were induced from experience by logical means. In his view the fallacy of that belief became clear only with the general theory of relativity, which used a foundation quite different from Newtonian theory. Moreover, since multiple hypotheses can account for experience to a large extent, logical deduction alone is insufficient for choosing among them.[15]

There are times when Einstein seems to lean toward an instrumentalist view, when, for example, he acknowledges that scientific theories are "free creations of the human mind" in his statement: "The justification of the system [of physics] rests in the proof of usefulness of the resulting theorems on the basis of sense experience. . . ."[16] But that impression is misleading. Einstein declared that the greatest achievement of Newtonian mechanics lies in the fact that it led beyond the phenomenological representation of Mach. Throughout his life he believed in the possibility of a model of reality in the sense of a theory that represents things themselves. He was clearly a confirmed realist.

In view of the struggle between Galileo's scientific realism and the Church's scientific instrumentalism, it is interesting to take brief note of Einstein's views on science and religion. As a youth, Einstein experienced something tantamount to a conversion from Judaism to science,[17] but the relation between religion and science was a lifelong concern. According to him the ongoing conflict between the two, tracing back to Galileo's time, stems from a misunderstanding of their proper roles. The function of science is to ascertain what is, not what should be; and representatives of science have mistakenly sought to arrive at fundamental value judgments on the basis of the scientific method. In so doing, they unnecessarily set science in opposition to religion. The chief function of religion is to make clear the fundamental ends and value standards of human endeavors. In Einstein's view, advocates of religion err in their belief that scripture can justifiably speak of facts and relationships between facts.[18] By according absolute truthfulness to all the statements recorded in the Bible, for instance, religion intervenes into the sphere of science, thus engendering conflict between the two.

Cardinal Bellarmine insisted that science should avoid intervention into the sphere of theology by abstaining from making statements about reality. If scientists would only keep to the proper function of their discipline—to save the appearances in a manner sufficient for a mathematician—science and religion could peacefully coexist. In other words, scientists must be instrumentalists, leaving the realist stance to theologians. Einstein turned this judgment on its head: theologians must be instrumentalists by viewing scriptural statements as means for establishing human values, without attributing to them any factual content concerning the nature of reality. Leave realism to the scientists, and conflict between the two would vanish.

Einstein went on to claim that "in this materialistic age of ours the serious scientific workers are the only profoundly religious people."[19]

Indeed, "You will hardly find one among the profounder sort of scientific minds without a religious feeling of his own."[20] Thus, in his view science totally supplants theology as a means of understanding reality. The encroachment of science into the domain of religion was now complete in terms of factual content. Religion must confine itself to providing value standards, but it must claim no grounds in reality for proposing those standards. In response to Cardinal Bellarmine's statement, "Such a manner of speaking suffices for the mathematician," Einstein might have said, "Such a manner of speaking suffices for the moralist."

The positivist views of Ernst Mach exerted an influence on many scientists, including Einstein, and they made an especially strong impact upon interpretations of quantum mechanics. Mechanistic materialism was one attempt to remove metaphysics from science, but it succeeded only in introducing a particularly naive, unreflective realism into physics. Mach sought to rid science of metaphysics by demanding that each individual statement in a physical theory be empirically verifiable. Logical positivism, developed during the 1920s, went a step further in its intent to banish metaphysics altogether.

According to logical positivism, only three types of statements are allowable: (1) the logically meaningful (for example, mathematics), (2) the empirically meaningful (for example, scientific statements), and (3) proposal statements or commands. Every theoretical statement in physics, for example, must therefore be empirically verifiable, and this implies that every theoretical entity (such as energy, an electron, or a field) must be definable in terms of observational entities (such as measurements or other directly observable physical objects). This insistence is based on the premise that there is a reliable distinction between theoretical and observational terms.

Although Niels Bohr was not a proponent of logical positivism, he too sought a theory of knowledge independent of metaphysics. In his view quantum theory makes no claim to describe or explain any objective quantum world existing independently of systems of measurement.[21] Rather, it is a mathematical formalism that accounts for a wide variety of physical measurements. In his *Dialectica*, Bohr assessed quantum mechanics as follows:

> The entire formalism is to be considered as a tool for deriving pre-
> dictions, of definite or statistical character, as regards information
> obtainable under experimental conditions described in classical
> terms and specified by means of parameters entering into alge-
> braic or differential equations. . . . These symbols themselves are
> not susceptible to pictorial interpretation.[22]

Once again we are presented with an ontological view akin to that of Ptolemy: a physical theory is presented as correct not because it explains an independent physical reality, but because it is effective in saving appearances. The school of interpretation of quantum mechanics that arose chiefly from Bohr's perspective may be deemed "ontologically agnostic," and it flourished initially during the heyday of logical positivism.

In this historical overview we have seen the debate between scientific realism and instrumentalism arise between the followers of Ptolemy and Aristotle, Cardinal Bellarmine and Copernicus, Leibniz and Newton, and Bohr and Einstein. These two philosophical perspectives regard physical theories in fundamentally different ways, and no amount of scientific research has been able to settle the controversy.

Chapter Five

Scientific Realism Today

The debate between instrumentalism and realism, tracing back to Plato and Aristotle, remains unresolved in contemporary physics, but few physicists today express much concern about this controversy. This should hardly come as a surprise, for neither the education nor the daily occupation of many physicists normally entails much philosophical reflection. However, it is just such individuals who teach science in grade schools, secondary schools, colleges, and universities and who provide information about advances in science to the general public through the popular media.

In the course of our education we learn much about science, and this plays a major role in forming our view of the world and our place in it. We keep this scientifically based worldview abreast of the times by attending to the popular media throughout adulthood. As our scientific knowledge accretes, we may scarcely be introduced to questions concerning the relationship between science and reality. These questions belong to the domain of philosophers of science, and their reflections are rarely discussed in science classrooms or the media. The popular media go to great lengths to keep us informed of contemporary scientific knowledge, but they tend to pass over the underlying question as to what such knowledge has to tell us about reality.

In fact, a general consensus among philosophers of science today rejects the realist notion that scientific theories are simple representations of the universe as it exists independent of our experience. But no alternative view has gained widespread acceptance. Given this state of affairs among the philosophers, perhaps it is no wonder that their ruminations are not regarded as hot news items. Nevertheless, the issues they are grappling with must surely be relevant to everyone whose worldview has been influenced by science.

From a materialist perspective, such concerns may be deemed unproductive, for mathematical theories can be formulated, experiments conducted, and technology advanced without reference to the real meaning of physical theory. Such an indifference usually veils a naive, unreflective realism. A disinterest in metaphysics may result not in abstention from such concerns but in unconscious, unintelligent adoption of a particular form of metaphysics.

Physical science today clearly exerts a profound and extensive influence not only on our physical environment but upon our way of viewing the world as a whole. There is a prevailing effort to reduce chemistry, biology, and psychology to the methods and laws of physics, and this reductionist approach has deeply affected our way of viewing human existence and the universe. Does physical theory describe and explain the real world independent of human experience, or is it simply a conceptual construction created by humans to correlate and predict scientific measurements? Are there other meaningful ways of understanding the relationship between physics and the natural world? Given the tremendous impact of physics on our daily lives, it seems crucial to give such questions prolonged and careful consideration.

What relevance does the term scientific realism have for those of us who are not professional philosophers of science? Check for yourself what sort of perspective you have on scientific assertions, regardless of your philosophy. As you look at this page, you see a sheet of white paper with black markings on it. Touch the page with a finger and feel its smooth texture and its relative coolness or warmth. Now sit back and ask yourself: do I think of the whiteness, texture, and coolness of the paper as qualities of this material existing in it independent of my senses? Do those qualities exist "out there," in or on the paper, unrelated to my awareness of them?

They certainly seem to be attributes inherent to the paper, and if we believe that they exist in that way, then we are adherents of everyday realism. There are problems, however, in this viewpoint. If we assert that such qualities exist out there as they appear to, we are implicitly assuming that our visual and tactile sense faculties play an utterly passive role in the perception of them. That is, these faculties would act simply as clear windows through which color, texture, and coolness flow from the object to the perceiving subject. Much research has gone into studying the functioning of our sense faculties, but none of it has led to the assertion that they function passively as simple receptors of objective color, texture, sound, and so on. Moreover, if we reflect on the wide range of visual faculties of fish, insects, birds, and mammals, for instance, it seems exceedingly hard to believe that they all see the world in the same way. What they see is created in part by the specific types of visual organs that they have.

Thus, after only a little reflection we may conclude that colors, sounds, smells, tastes, and textures as we experience them are not attributes of the objective world existing independent of our sense faculties. Rather they are events that occur in dependence not only upon the attributes of the external world but also the specific nature of our senses. In that sense, although they appear to be utterly "out there" in the objects that we perceive, they do not so exist. If we assert the above statement, we leave behind the view of everyday realism.

Now a new question is raised: if the above sensory impressions exist only in relation to the subjective senses, what is really out there that causes our senses to be stimulated so that we perceive colors and so forth? In other words, what is the nature of the real world as it exists independent of human perceptions? What is truly out there? This question has been asked by thinkers of Greek antiquity, and since then a myriad of theories have been devised to describe and explain the nature of such reality. These range from thoroughgoing idealism to materialism, and insofar as we adopt any such theory, we become adherents of *transcendent realism:* we believe in a theory about the real, intrinsic nature of the world as it exists behind the veil of the senses. It is a metaphysical perspective that purportedly transcends sensory appearances and reaches the inherent nature of reality that lies beyond.

Do we believe that the real, objective nature of color pertains to a certain range of frequencies of electromagnetic waves? Objectively speaking, is sound another form of wave pattern that moves through various media such as the atmosphere and water? Are warmth and coolness really a matter of the kinetic energy of random movements of the molecules that make up the physical world? If we answer in the affirmative to such questions, then we adhere to the view of *scientific realism*. Here science is seen as providing answers to what is really happening out there in the real world. It transcends the misleading, subjective impressions of the senses and penetrates to the objective reality that exists independent of perception.

Although scientific realism as defined above is no longer considered tenable by most philosophers of science, it is still the metaphysical view that saturates most instruction in science today. Yet this metaphysical stance is rarely mentioned in classrooms or the popular media when discussing scientific theories. It is simply taken for granted: a metaphysical viewpoint that is regarded by philosophers as highly problematic is absorbed unconsciously and uncritically. It nevertheless exerts a powerful influence on the thoughts and attitudes of those who hold it.

———————◆———————

The origins of the realist view of physical theory can be traced back to such early thinkers of Greek antiquity as Democritus and Aristotle.[1] Copernicus, Kepler, and Galileo, three pillars of modern science, likewise took a realist stance as the foundation of physical inquiry, and under their influence, physics has adopted the goal of formulating a single, true theory that will account for all the phenomena of the inanimate universe together. This theory must explain, not merely describe or predict, and in so doing it will place all physical anomalies within an intelligible framework of ideas. In the words of the philosopher of science Norwood Russell Hanson: "Intelligibility is the goal of physics, the fulfillment of natural philosophy; for natural philosophy is philosophy of matter, a continual conceptual struggle to fit each new observation of phenomena into a pattern of explanation."[2]

Realists demand of a physical theory that it be factual. Their underlying assumptions are that, independent of human percepts and concepts, there exists an objective world of space, time, and configurations of mass and energy, and that this world is humanly intelligible. As science progresses, its theories gradually approximate the one, true, all-embracing theory that will be a perfect fit with reality. Some realists are confident that science will eventually reach that culmination, while others believe that we will approach that perfect theory only asymptotically, by increasingly accurate approximations.

Einstein, perhaps the foremost realist among modern physicists, held that a belief in a natural world independent of the human mind, yet intelligible to it, lies at the foundation of all natural science. On what grounds can we believe that physical theory corresponds to such an independent physical reality? In what sense can a concept correspond to, or be associated with, a reality that is unrelated to it, in the sense of being independent of it?

Recognizing the naiveté of nineteenth-century scientific realism, Einstein offered no facile response to this problem. In his view "the whole of science is nothing more than a refinement of everyday thinking,"[3] and the same can be said of the realist view of science. In everyday thinking we may have, for example, the thought of a tree falling in a forest. From the past we recall typical complexes of sense experiences of falling trees, and on such bases we form primary concepts that are directly connected to those experiences. The corresponding terms are commonly denoted as *observational terms*. Although our sense experiences do not occur independently of our human senses, we naturally presume that the primary concept of a falling tree does refer to something in the independent, objective world. Were this not the case, argues everyday realism, how could orderly, causal, physical events occur in the absence of consciousness of them, and how could different people experience reality in common? The only plausible reason, according to the realist, is that the natural world exists independently of human percepts and concepts; and the necessary assumption for human understanding and activity is that that world is intelligible to us.

What is the relationship between the primary concepts of everyday thinking and complexes of sense experiences? Such a question lies outside the domain of physical science, and Einstein maintained that it can be comprehended only intuitively. By means of the intuitive connections between concepts and experiences, however, we can fashion scientific theories about complexes of sense experiences. The first stage of science, then, contains only primary concepts and theories relating them.

The second stage contains secondary concepts, associated with *theo-retical terms*, which have only indirect connections with such sensory complexes. Until the close of the nineteenth century, many physicists considered the theoretical term atom to be outside the sphere of phys-ics. But in 1905 Einstein presented a paper on Brownian motion which was regarded by the scientific community as a proof of the physical reality of the atom. Similarly, until the experimental work of Rutherford during the early years of this century, the internal struc-ture of the atom seemed purely a matter of metaphysical speculation. But his results unequivocally suggested the existence of an atomic nucleus that is minute in comparison to the dimensions of the atom as a whole.

These secondary concepts and their relations are fewer than the primary concepts, and the primary are derived logically from the sec-ondary. According to Einstein, physics evolves as it formulates ever fewer concepts and relations from which earlier layers of concepts can be derived. In this way science approaches a single unified theory, with the fewest concepts from which all others can be derived.

Nature is thus regarded as a well-formulated puzzle whose solu-tion is found by scientific inquiry. Just as an intricate crossword puzzle finally allows a single, unique array of words, so does the conceptual solution of nature ultimately allow one unique, unified theory. In the word puzzle wrong words may temporarily seem to fit, but as the game evolves, their insertion is seen to be erroneous, and with intelli-gent persistence they are replaced with the correct terms. Similarly, physics may formulate theoretical terms and relations that are tem-porarily useful and explanatory, without being able to integrate them into a unified theory. But as it progresses, the fallacies of earlier par-tial theories are recognized, and new or revised theories are conceived that more closely fit the pattern of the one true theory.

In the face of the diversity of conceptually incompatible views that we have encountered concerning the energy of the vacuum, a realist would insist that only one of those theories (or a future theory) will eventually prove to be the one accurate account of this physical real-ity. For the time being, competing theories within and outside of the context of quantum mechanics all account for the experimental evi-dence; but with persistent effort the inadequacies of the false theories will become evident. Only one theory will remain that is entirely in-ternally consistent and precisely accurate in its predictions. And that one will be the true representation of the vacuum as it exists indepen-dently in nature.

Chapter Six

Assumptions of Scientific Realism

The foregoing discussion mentions a few of the assumptions underlying Western science, and they are so fundamental that physics as we understand it would be inconceivable without them. The initial assumption of the existence of an objective world independent of consciousness and conceptual constructs is a metaphysical belief. Most scientists are unwilling even to consider that it may not be correct, for it is regarded, often implicitly, as an a priori truth. However, given the history of successive collapses of the a priori status of scientific assumptions—for example, Euclidean geometry and absolute space and time—we have little ground for holding this assumption sacred. Indeed, our everyday experience of the world does lead us to believe in such an independent reality, but if advances in mathematics and physics have taught us anything, it is that common sense assumptions based on sensory experience may be misleading. The curved space-time of general relativity and equally unimaginable quantum mechanical description of the behavior of atomic entities provide obvious examples.

Is the ontological theory of an independent, objective physical world the only conceivable theory that can save the appearances of everyday and scientific experience? Certainly not. Philosophers in diverse cultures over the past few millennia have devised alternative ontologies that also, with varying degrees of success, account for the facts of experience. Until very recently, Western scientists have shown little inclination to question this metaphysical assumption, though recent insights in quantum mechanics suggest that such inquiry is long overdue.[1]

A second assumption holds that this world, independent of human percepts and concepts, is nevertheless comprehensible in terms of our concepts. If the universe exists by its own nature, independent of our concepts, on what grounds can we believe that our theories can accurately describe and explain it? Assuming that physical theories can be true in this sense, in what manner do they represent or correspond to the world itself? Since the birth of modern science, this question has never been answered persuasively.

A third metaphysical assumption is that the universe is like an intricate word puzzle that can ultimately be solved in one way only. Over the course of history, various theories have laid claim to explaining nature comprehensively. Aristotle's physics is a prime example, and its claim of exclusivity and comprehensive accuracy collapsed under the experimental and theoretical scrutiny at the birth of modern science. The world machine theory of reality was touted in the nineteenth century as the one true view and was regarded as essentially complete, barring a few minor clouds on the horizon, such as a peculiarity of radiation that came to be known as the ultraviolet catastrophe. Closer scrutiny of those apparently minor anomalies initiated bold new ways of viewing reality, and these raised a vast number of questions that never occurred to earlier physicists. Now as we draw to the close of the twentieth century, highly respected physicists are encouraging the public once again to believe that the one true unified theory that accounts for all natural phenomena is at hand. Only a few pieces in the puzzle, such as a quantum theory of gravity, are needed to bring physics to its culmination.

Given the history of diversity in physics, we must consider the possibility that multiple theories could equally account for all possible experience. Let us first set aside the problem of identifying any set of facts about the physical world as complete. Now consider a time, possibly in the near future, when scientists will devise a grand unified theory that accounts for all known forces in the universe. Such a theory will be based not only on the experimental facts but on the metaphysical assumptions of its creators. This being the case, it seems perfectly reasonable to expect that a competing grand unified theory could be devised that equally accounts for all the facts, while being based on different metaphysical assumptions. In principle, there is no limit to the variety of such theories that might be formulated, all of them conceptually incompatible. Each would vary depending on the diversity of metaphysical assumptions that precede scientific inquiry.

Now let us address the question of identifying any body of facts as complete. It is true that some noted scientists believe that a unified theory accounting for all of reality is close at hand, but to believe this requires an extraordinary leap of faith. How can we believe that fundamentally new modes of experimentation will not shed light on a new range of anomalous phenomena? A unified theory may explain all the facts available at the time it is formulated, but who is to say that human ingenuity cannot discover a new range of facts? The scientists who promote the prospect of an imminent grand unified theory today are not more intelligent or respected by their peers than the physicists of the previous century who regarded physics as essentially complete. It seems that overoptimism, based on metaphysical naiveté, may once again be leading scientists and their followers into an illusion of inflated knowledge.

———————◆———————

Another common assumption among physical scientists is that everything is made of atoms. Nobel prize-winning physicist Richard Feynman insists that *"there is nothing that living things do that cannot be understood from the point of view that they are made of atoms acting according to the laws of physics."*[2] A closely related principle is the conservation of energy. Feynman asserts that the conservation of energy is a mathematical principle, not a description of a mechanism or anything concrete. He goes on to state: "It is important to realize that in physics today, we have no knowledge of what energy *is*."[3] If, as Feynman seems to suggest, energy is an abstraction, we may wonder whether it is purely a conceptual construct, rather than an independent physical reality. In the former case, what shall we make of the principle of the conservation of energy? The renowned astrophysicist Sir Arthur Eddington comments:

> There is no law of government in the external world tending to
> preserve unchanged special created entities which occupy it; but
> the mind has by diligent search picked out the possible constructs
> which have this permanence in virtue of this mode of construc-
> tion, and by giving value to these and by neglecting the rest has
> imposed a law of conservation of things of value.[4]

If both energy and its conservation are simply conceptual constructs
with no independent referents in the physical world, what are the
implications for the nature of matter? Albert Einstein and Leopold
Infeld summarize one of the foremost discoveries of modern physics:
"According to the theory of relativity, there is no essential distinction
between mass and energy. Energy has mass and mass represents energy."[5] Thus, if energy is simply an abstract concept, a mathematical
principle and not an objective physical reality, must not the same be
true of mass? And if atoms are composed of mass and energy, what
does this imply about their ontological status? Are they, too, simply
conceptual constructs?

In 1957, the philosopher of science Hans Reichenbach expressed
the view of many physicists when he declared: "The atomic character
of matter belongs to the most certain facts of our present knowledge
. . . [and] we can speak of the existence of atoms with the same certainty as the existence of stars."[6] What is the nature of this certain
knowledge of atoms? French physicist Bernard d'Espagnat maintains
that atoms, as well as all other knowable entities, are mere properties
of nothing other than space or space-time.[7] Physicist John Gribbin
points out, however, that while quantum mechanics tells us a lot about
material particles, it tells us scarcely anything at all about empty space.[8]
And astronomer Edward Harrison indicates a further complexity of
the situation when he writes: "There are countless possible spaces
with their own geometries, and all are equally valid and self-consis-
tent."[9] If each of these countless possible spaces equally accounts for
phenomena, how are we to choose among them?

Gribbin proposes another view of the ontological status of atoms
and subatomic particles when he says: "If we cannot say what a particle does when we are not looking at it, neither can we say if it exists
when we are not looking at it, and it is reasonable to claim that nuclei
and positrons did not exist prior to the twentieth century, because
nobody before 1900 ever saw one."[10] American physicist Henry Stapp

posits yet another view concerning particles of matter: "An elementary particle is not an independently existing unanalysable entity. It is, in essence, a set of relationships that reach outward to other things."[11] Werner Heisenberg informs us that "atoms are not things,"[12] and Niels Bohr makes the even broader statement that "there is no quantum world, there is only an abstract quantum description."[13] Before we take comfort in the thought that the reality of atoms is as certain as that of stars, we must reflect that much of our knowledge of the heavens is based on quantum mechanics. Insofar as astronomy and cosmology speak of the nature and dynamics of matter and energy in the universe, they must resort to chemistry and atomic physics, both of which are closely connected with quantum theory. One of the principal architects of that theory denies that it describes an independent physical reality, while another remains ontologically agnostic. In short, while physicists are generally agreed that energy is conserved and that matter is composed of atoms, no one seems to know what energy is, and there is fundamental diversity of opinion as to the ontological status of atoms.

There are a number of secondary assumptions that underlie branches of science and that are indispensable to them. A central belief is that the laws of nature write themselves in the language of mathematics. This view will be examined in some detail in chapter 12. Modern science is also based on the medieval insistence on simplicity and beauty in the formulation of physical theories. Once again, this predilection precedes scientific inquiry. Theories that fail to conform to those principles are therefore unlikely to be formulated, or in the case of their appearance, they are unlikely to be promoted. Some scientists may even adhere to those assumptions despite physical evidence to the contrary. Paul Dirac, for instance, commented: "It is more important to have beauty in one's equations than to have them fit experiment."[14] This is indeed a practical guide for advancing theories that can be integrated with previous physical concepts. Physics could make no progress if it abandoned its theories as soon as observations were made that were incompatible with present ideas. The insistence on beauty is a practical means of developing an integrated theory, but on what grounds shall we assume that the universe obeys our present concepts of beauty? Insofar as we make this assumption, we virtually challenge experimental physicists to confirm that beauty lies not in the eye of the beholder, but "out there" in the impersonal, mindless universe. When pushed to this extreme, the appearances must "save the theory."

Quantum theory takes as its starting point the concepts of packets of energy and wave pulses, and general relativity rests on the notion of gravitational fields. Prior to these two theories, classical mechanics took the notion of a material point as a fundamental assumption. Our sensory experience of physical phenomena, however, does not allow such points to be treated as material points, so mechanics is presented with the theoretical challenge: how can we imagine an object to be built up out of material points, and what forces must we assume are acting among them?[15] Thus, given this assumption, which precedes the formulation of classical mechanics, it is apparent that this branch of physics must inevitably lead us to an atomistic construction of matter.

In contrast to mechanics, electromagnetic theory was founded on such notions as waves, fields, and the ether. Classical physics could not fully unify mechanics and electromagnetism, just as contemporary physics has had little success in unifying quantum mechanics and general relativity. Moreover, quantum mechanics remains plagued by the dilemma that its experiments are described in terms of classical physics, while its tenets proclaim that those concepts do not fit nature accurately. As Norwood Russell Hanson points out: "There is no ultimate logical connexion between the languages of classical physics and quantum physics, any more than between a sense-datum language and a material object language."[16] Indeed, the languages formulated from such diverse initial premises turn out to yield logical differences throughout. It then becomes untenable to regard classical theories as "limiting cases" of contemporary physics.

Twentieth-century physics has certainly retained many of the theoretical terms from the classical era. The concept of elementary particles, for example, has persisted over the centuries, but it is crucial to recognize the profound changes it has undergone. Even within this century the same terms have been used for starkly different objects. The electron, for example, was first regarded as an independent particle of matter bearing negative electric charge. Soon a model was created in which it was seen orbiting about the atomic nucleus, like a planet around the sun. Then it was recognized as bearing attributes both of a particle and of a wave. But particles and waves had always been regarded as mutually exclusive types of entities. The planetary model of the electron could now be seen as a partial, heuristic device at best. (Even though it is misleading, elementary physics textbooks still usually leave students with such a concept of the atom.) Following the advent of Heisenberg's uncertainty principle, the electron has been regarded variously as a mathematical abstraction and as a physical probability distribution. In quantum field theory, it, like other particles, is conceived as an elementary quantum of excitation of a field.

Earlier and later concepts of the electron obviously have very little in common. Yet at no point have physicists been inclined to discard the electron altogether. The notion has been a survivor, undergoing major mutations as it has been subject to the changing climates of physical inquiry. Indeed, but for the continuous use of the word *electron*, we would be hard pressed to guess that physicists were modifying one concept rather than abandoning the old and replacing it with the new. Will the concept of particles survive in future developments of physics? Einstein speculated that in the foundations of any consistent field theory that may eventually appear, there will be no concept concerning particles in addition to the concept of the field.[17]

The concept of the atom was prevalent in nineteenth-century physics, and, with great modification, it has survived into contemporary physics. Reichenbach asserted that the atomic character of matter is among "the most certain facts of our present knowledge," and Feynman promoted the common belief that all living things can be understood in terms of their constituent atoms. Yet we have noted the widely divergent views of the nature of atoms and elementary particles. Which of these deals with "the most certain facts of our present knowledge"?

At this point it may be pertinent to recall one of the most certain facts of nineteenth-century physics. Toward the latter part of that century, Lord Kelvin expressed the general attitude of physicists when he said, "One thing we are sure of, and that is the reality and substantiality of the luminiferous ether."[18] Sir J. J. Thomson, the recipient of the 1906 Nobel prize in physics, declared that all mass and kinetic energy is composed of the ether.[19] Yet only a few decades later, Einstein and Infeld asserted, "All assumptions concerning ether led nowhere!"[20]

Physics textbooks now inform students that the ether never had physical reality. The concept is relegated to the status of a naive, mistaken assumption concerning the nature of electric and magnetic fields, and Einstein is thought to have demonstrated this fallacy. In fact,

Einstein insisted that the concept of the ether be modified, not discarded.[21] But the momentum of physical thought swept away the ether, as if physicists were relieved to dispense with a problem that had been a constant source of frustration. The ether has now been replaced in general relativity with space-time that has structure and is subject to curvature. In quantum field theory the ether is replaced with a vacuum that contains at least virtual energy, bears a structure, is subject to polarization, and exerts observable influences on particles that are introduced into it.

Did not elementary particles such as the electron undergo modifications at least as profound as those of empty space? Why did the electron survive, while the ether did not? The simple answer is that physicists simply decided that the meaning of the term *ether* would be frozen in its classical context, whereas *electron* was allowed to adapt to a sequence of changing theories. This decision was not made on the basis of experimental evidence, nor was it due to strictly scientific, theoretical argument. Rather, it was a matter of terminological preference stemming from nonphysical considerations and biases. In light of this fact, we may well wonder if other scientific dinosaurs such as caloric and phlogiston might not have survived if they had been allowed to adapt to new evidence and theories. Were they any more intrinsically doomed to extinction than the electron? And what concepts will physics discard in the future? Will atoms and elementary particles survive, or will they be replaced with pure fields or some as yet unimagined entity? Once again we are faced with a matter of preference, the origins of which lie outside the strict domains of science.

Chapter Seven

Theory and Discovery in Physical Science

The history of physics shows that certain concepts have taken on the status of indispensable principles, the foremost of these being the conservation of energy. As we have seen, this principle arose initially from a metaphysical assumption that predated hard scientific evidence to support it. But as it was gradually adopted by physicists, empirical support was found, and it attained the status of a scientific law. As research continued, the evidence necessitated the recognition of new types of energy that would balance the ledger in certain conversion processes. In the present century, energy has come to be regarded as interchangeable with mass, and to preserve the conservation principle on the subatomic level, physicists have posited the existence of a whole menagerie of particles. The conservation of energy is a prime example of a scientific truth that was established by experiment early on, and then became so indispensable to physics that violations of it are considered unthinkable.

An examination of the process of scientific inquiry makes it evident that physical theories are not simply derived inductively from experience, as was believed by naive realists of the last century. As Einstein commented to Heisenberg: "But on principle, it is quite wrong to try founding a theory on observable magnitudes alone. In reality the very opposite happens. It is the theory which decides what we can observe."[1] Niels Bohr expressed a similar insight when he wrote:

As our knowledge becomes wider, we must always be prepared, therefore, to expect alterations in the points of view best suited for the ordering of our experience. In this connection we must remember, above all, that, as a matter of course, all new experience makes its appearance within the frame of our customary points of view and forms of perception.[2]

Newton's claim of forming no hypotheses that are not direct results of experience turns out to be no more realizable than his notions of absolute space and time.

Whether in everyday experience or while engaged in scientific research, we are presented with far more experimental data than we are able to assimilate and organize. We are thus compelled to sift through the contents of experience, distinguishing the relevant and meaningful from mere noise. By what criteria do we make this distinction? It cannot possibly be made from the side of the experiential data; rather, it is made on the basis of our preconceived, and often unconscious, ideas and theories. In this way the theory allows us to observe certain data as meaningful, while screening out whatever is left over.

In the words of Peter Medawar, a Nobel laureate in medicine: "The teacher has forgotten, and the student himself will soon forget, that what he sees conveys no information until he knows beforehand the kind of things he is expected to see."[3] This insight is not a new one, but as Medawar points out, it is easily ignored. Nietzsche generalizes on this same theme when he writes that "everything of which we become conscious is arranged, simplified, schematized, interpreted through and through."[4]

History presents a number of flagrant examples of an accepted theory preventing the observation or ascertainment of a natural event that is later retrieved by a new theory. One of the most renowned cases concerns a supernova explosion in the year 1054. For twenty-three days this star shone as brightly as Venus at night and was visible even by daylight. It faded from view altogether after eighty nights short of two years.

During that era, astronomers around the world took a keen interest in observing the night skies, but they did so with different preconceived ideas. The astronomers of Europe were committed to the ancient Greek theory that heavenly bodies are immutable, and none of them left surviving accounts of having witnessed this unallowed phenomenon. Here is another case of the phenomena having to "save the theory," which they could do only by being ignored altogether. Chinese astronomers, on the other hand, were not subject to that Greek assumption, and they left numerous accounts of this startling event. By the sixteenth century, the European commitment to the writings of Greek antiquity had begun to be challenged. Thus, when another supernova appeared in 1572, Tycho Brahe studied it and concluded that stars are subject to generation and decay.

A more recent example entails the discovery of the positron.[5] Until the early 1930s, physicists were committed to the belief that the fundamental unit of positive charge, or electricity, could only be associated with the proton. Prior to 1930, several microphysicists "saw" but did not "observe" tracks of the positron, an elementary particle similar to an electron but having a positive charge. Those tracks were seen as spurious and dismissed as "dirt effects." In 1931 Paul Dirac conducted theoretical research that suggested that empirical evidence should be attainable. In the following year the experimental physicist Carl D. Anderson challenged prevailing opinion by identifying the positron tracks, apparently without knowing of Dirac's theoretical justification. Finally in 1933 two other physicists discovered that the Anderson particle and the Dirac particle were identical.

It seems, then, that innovators in science are frequently those with sufficient courage to challenge widespread assumptions, enabling them to observe phenomena that were concealed from their peers by the veils of preconceived ideas. Norwood Russell Hanson comments: "The paradigm observer is not the man who sees and reports what all normal observers see and report, but the man who sees in familiar objects what no one else has seen before."[6]

If theory largely predetermines which phenomena can make an imprint on human intelligence, it follows that scientific observation must also be influenced by the language in which a theory is expressed. We may then expect that people using such different languages as English, Hopi,[7] and Tibetan might have difficulty in apprehending the same facts. Since we can hardly believe that the world has a bias for expressing itself in European languages, we must conclude that our view of reality is inescapably a European view. While our languages and theories have unveiled certain facets of reality, it can hardly be denied that they have concealed others. Moreover, it seems highly probable that non-European inquiries into truth have shed light on phenomena that remain hidden to us.

Many physicists shy away from seeking to describe or explain physical reality in any words at all. Prose accounts are subject to the vagaries of human language, grammar, and logic, and such thinkers are concerned with grasping reality as it exists independently of human thought and experience. On these grounds they confine themselves to quantitative data and mathematical analysis. The goal of physics is still a grand unified theory, but it is sufficient that it remain a purely mathematical theory, devoid of verbal interpretation. The assumption here is that, as Einstein claimed, nature is the realization of mathematical ideas, and that these ideas, while accessible to the human mind, find their source in objective reality.

The claim that the ultimately real speaks in one unique language is not found in physics alone. Traditional Hebrew belief holds that the Creator and Ruler of the universe expresses Himself in the sacred language of Hebrew. Hindu faith maintains that God speaks in Sanskrit and that this divine language pervades the whole of nature. While all three languages—mathematics, Hebrew, and Sanskrit—purportedly originate from a transcendent source of reality, they are all accessible to the human mind, and in this way human intelligence taps into independent, objective reality. Scientists may assert that unlike the grammar of spoken languages, the rules of mathematics are infallible and independent of the human mind. Investigation into the foundations of mathematics, however, seriously questions that assumption.[8]

The belief that mathematical laws are intrinsic to an independent physical reality tends to overlook the fact that the quantitative data on which those laws are based invariably arise from interactions between measuring devices and measured quantities. Recall the words of Werner Heisenberg: "What we observe is not nature in itself but nature exposed to our method of questioning."[9] When we question nature with quantitative instruments, we obtain quantitative results which, upon being sifted through the screen of prevailing theory, often conform to mathematical laws.

Do either the quantitative data or the mathematical laws inform us of nature independent of our experimental and theoretical modes of inquiry? Einstein would have replied in the affirmative, and he formulated a criterion of independent physical reality as follows: "If, without in any way disturbing a system, we can predict with certainty the value of a physical quantity, then there exists an element of physical reality corresponding to this physical quantity."[10] In reference to quantum mechanics, Bohr countered that "the procedure of measurements has an essential influence on the conditions on which the very definition of the physical quantities in question rests."[11] More broadly speaking, to know what we are measuring, we must know the function of our measuring device.[12] Is it, for example, a voltmeter or an ammeter? The quantity obtained takes on a physical status only upon its being interpreted within a specific theoretical context. A meter reading may indicate a certain quantity, but that number is not self-interpreting. To what physical reality does it correspond? This can be answered only in the context of a theory, and diverse theories may well offer different explanations of the nature of the measured event, as we have seen in the case of the energy of the vacuum.

In short, what Einstein calls a physical quantity is simply a number, and if it does correspond to a physical reality, that quantity alone yields no suggestion of what that reality might be. It is up to us to make sense of it, and we do so on the basis of our human experience and concepts. Secondly, any such quantity that is measured either by disturbing or not disturbing a system is the result of an interaction of the measuring device and the measured event. Recalling Heisenberg's similar comment, it is a measure not of nature itself, but nature exposed to our method of detection.

To draw a parallel: according to the materialist view of nature, the colors that we perceive with our visual faculties do not exist in independent physical reality. Objectively, there are only particles of mass-energy in motion, and when certain of these particles, called photons, interact in very large numbers with our visual organs, colors are subjectively experienced. Our visual faculties are of such a design that when they interact with a sufficient number of photons, visual sensations of color occur; but those colors do not exist in the photons themselves. If those photons interact with our skin, a sensation of warmth may be produced, but that warmth is no more intrinsic to the photons than are the colors that we perceive.

Now physicists bring to bear on photons nonorganic apparatuses of detection, and when these interact with photons, quantities are produced. When we direct our visual gaze at photons, it is a foregone conclusion that if we detect anything, it will be colors. When we direct a quantitative measuring device at photons, it is a foregone conclusion that if it detects anything, it will be quantities. Neither mode of observation gives us information about photons existing independently of all methods of detection. Thus, the realist view that quantities are intrinsic to physical reality, whereas colors are not, appears unfounded.

Thus, the assumption of the independent physical reality of a measured quantity is as questionable as the independent status that we attribute to a physical entity (such as a photon) associated with that quantity. The belief in mathematics as an intrinsic attribute of reality in itself is akin to the belief that the contents of a physical theory are independent elements of nature. Both assertions ignore the participatory nature of scientific research. Just as "everyday realism" naively ignores the active role of our senses in the appearance of colors, scientific realism ignores the active role of our instruments of observation and of our language and conceptual conditioning in scientific research and theorizing.

The participatory nature of such research is well illustrated in the case of the Casimir effect. Recall that within the context of quantum electrodynamics, H. B. G. Casimir calculated that a minute attractive force should be exerted between two walls of a cavity. Is this a zero-point force originating from the vacuum as conceived in quantum field theory? Or do fields play no role in this force, as suggested by Julian Schwinger? Is the experimental effect due to the semiclassical, retarded London-van der Waal's force, or to classical, randomly oscillating electromagnetic radiation, as conceived by Timothy Boyer? Experimental evidence has thus far proven incapable of deciding such questions about the physical reality of the situation, and it is questionable whether it ever will.

Casimir predicted a force of a definite magnitude, and this force varies inversely with the fourth power of the separation of the walls of the cavity. But neither the force constant nor the fact that it is an inverse fourth-power force exists independently in the nature of the vacuum itself. Such properties appear in the context of a given system of measurement, but we have no empirical grounds for believing that they have any existence independent of such a context.

Chapter Eight

The Hypothetical Realities of Physics

In our investigations of the physical world we employ instruments, most of which were designed with a specific physical theory, such as electromagnetism, in mind. Our basic experimental data are produced by interactions between such devices and physical events. Had we used radically different modes of observation—including nonquantitative means—our experimental results would have been different. With the empirical data in hand, we are faced with the challenge of interpreting them. The standard procedure in atomic physics, as well as various other branches of science, is known as *retroduction*.[1] In this process we regard a body of empirical evidence with a specific theory in mind. Much of the evidence is accounted for in a familiar way by the theory, but now let us imagine that some surprising phenomenon is observed. Wishing to explain that phenomenon in terms of our theory, we propose that it would be explicable if a physical entity—a new particle with attributes determined by the evidence—existed. We then conclude that the proposed particle exists.

A prime example of this process occurred in Max Planck's formulation of the idea of quanta of energy. Planck devised the formula expressing his famous radiation law by interpolating the formulas of Wilhelm Wein and of Lord Rayleigh and Sir James Jeans. His modification worked—that is, it accounted for experimental results—and he then sought out a theoretical justification for its success. This was found in the notion of quanta. Norwood Russell Hanson insists that we should accept such a physical concept devised in this way, even if it is nothing more than an "ingenious mathematical combination of physically distinct parameters," for if we do, "a comprehensive and systematic explanation of those diverse and apparently incompatible microphysical phenomena will follow as a matter of course."[2] It seems, however, that Timothy Boyer has been able to save the same phenomena without introducing the idea of quanta. So which account explains the ultraviolet catastrophe in accord with objective reality?

Retroduction is without question a useful procedure for explaining and predicting observed phenomena, but is it a means of discovering preexisting entities existing independently of our mode of inquiry, or does it simply allow us to create hypothetical concepts that are useful for explaining observed phenomena? If we adopt the former view, we assume that microentities forever hidden from perception can be discovered by means of inference, identifying them on the basis of the observable evidence they produce, such as traces in a cloud chamber.

Such a process of identification entails the ostensible discovery of the defining characteristics of the subatomic entity in question. To examine this claim, let us imagine a hypothetical entity called a *dreamon*. Now, one possibility is to define a dreamon in terms of the macroscopic effects that it produces when it interacts with a certain measuring device. When we declare that a dreamon exists, we are then simply stating that something that helps cause those effects exists. That may be a useful shorthand device for organizing data, but the tautological nature of the claim divorces it from any statement about an independent physical reality. This can hardly be called a discovery.

The other option is to define a dreamon in terms of its own intrinsic characteristics, such as charge, mass, and spin. As before, the interaction of some physical entity with our system of measurement produces certain observable effects. Following the retroductive procedure, we hypothesize that if there were a particle with the defining characteristics of a dreamon, it would produce the observed effects. In order to establish that a dreamon actually has a physical reality independent of our system of measurement and theoretical constructs, we would have to demonstrate that only that entity could have interacted with the system to produce those results.

In the macroworld it is frequently possible to infer the presence of a cause (combustion, for example), from its effect (smoke). But we have never been able to make such a direct observation of subatomic entities. Microphysics may thus be likened to a detective story in which we obtain only clues, never an eyewitness of the crime or a confession from the criminal himself.[3] We obtain only circumstantial evidence that gives microobjects nothing more than an "as if" reality, for physics has never been able to demonstrate that its theoretical concepts uniquely account for the experimental facts.

Recognizing the uncertainty of scientific explanations, C. S. Pierce commented that "the conclusions of science make no pretence to being more than probable."[4] Particularly in light of earlier revisions of physical theory, some physicists teach their students that the contemporary notions of electromagnetic waves, fields, subatomic particles, and so on are only probably true. Even after having admitted this at the outset, however, such concepts are then used as if they do correspond to physical reality. It is as if a judge pronounces the evidence to be merely circumstantial, and then proceeds to sentence the suspect to prison.

Another reason for attributing only "probable" status to scientific explanations is that incompatible theories are sometimes employed for the same subject matter. Light, for example (as well as electrons and other subatomic particles), is described in one context as a wave and in another as a particle. There can be no intrinsically real physical entity that is both a wave and a particle, however, for the defining characteristics of those two phenomena are mutually incompatible. A "probable realist" justifies this by claiming that such theories are a temporary makeshift: they are to be abandoned when an internally consistent theory, more comprehensive than either of the previous ones, is developed. Indeed, such a realist may acknowledge that all theories are corrigible and that future theories will only better approximate the one true explanation of nature, without actually reaching that idea.

The philosopher of science Karl Popper expresses a similar theme in his assertion that scientific theories are subject only to empirical refutation, but never unequivocal verification. This statement, however, is only partially true. Twentieth-century experiments have refuted the existence of the ether, but only as it is conceived in the context of earlier physical theories. One may discard one physical concept altogether in favor of another, and when fundamental concepts are changed we tend to speak of "revolutions" in physics. In making such shifts we may fail to recognize that the supposedly antiquated theories could have been modified in an ad hoc way to account for recent discoveries. Empirical facts by themselves do not discard older theories. This comes about only with the addition of metaphysical principles such as the demand for simplicity and beauty.

Probable realism assumes the existence of an independent physical reality and proposes at any point in history that contemporary physical theories are probably accurate. Consistent adherence to this view would imply that in Aristotle's time, his terrestrial and celestial physics was probably accurate; in the seventeenth century absolute space and time probably existed; two centuries later the ether was probably real; and in the first decade of this century, electrons were probably simple particles with definite, simultaneous velocity and position. But from the perspective of the late twentieth century, none of those statements is probable; they are all false.

Probable realism also seems to assume that physical theory progresses through history on a unified front; it is like a line that asymptotically approaches the axis of truth. As we have seen, however, throughout the history of physics, prominent scientists have always differed in their interpretations of empirical data and mathematical formalisms. Newton and Leibniz differed fundamentally in their views of the nature of force, matter, and space, and such dissension continues today in competing interpretations of quantum mechanics. At any point in history, which one among conceptually incompatible theories is to be regarded as probable? In the future, a mathematical formalism may be devised that provides the structure for a grand unified theory. We may expect that this formalism and its associated empirical evidence will also be subject to diverse, incompatible interpretations or physical theories, whose diversity will be confined only by the limitations of their creators' imaginations. Which among them should be deemed probable?

At any point in history, to declare that a certain physical theory is a final, true representation of physical reality would suggest a profound lack of intelligent reflection on the philosophical foundations and history of physics. A more cautious stance is to maintain that a theory is at best probable, but the content and justification for this statement seem to dissolve under scrutiny. A third realist position is to assume that the physical world does exist in its own right, but that science has no means for ascertaining whether its theories are correct or even probable. This is tantamount to the belief that the world is real but unknowable, and it hardly provides any incentive for scientific research, apart from the satisfaction of the game and the usefulness of the ensuing technology.

Chapter Nine

Quantum Reality

This century's insights into quantum mechanics have called into question some of the metaphysical assumptions of scientific realism. Is the world governed by strict causality on the atomic level, as classical physics assumes? Do elementary particles exist in their own right, independent of the system of measurement? Do they have definite, simultaneous velocity and position? Can the physicist explore the fundamental components of physical reality as they exist on their own, or must they always take into account the role of the experimenter and experimental apparatus?

Experimental results in quantum mechanics have helped to raise such questions, but they have not been able to provide answers that are universally accepted by the physics community. The wave/particle nature of microentities is a major source of wonderment. When the concept of an electron was first devised, empirical evidence plainly indicated that it was a particle. But this conclusion was soon followed by theoretical and experimental grounds for concluding that it had wave properties. A particle has a definite size and location and either penetrates other objects or bounces off them like a bullet. A wave in three dimensions, on the other hand, spreads out in space. Any initial size quickly expands so that there are no clear-cut dimensions. Such a wave therefore has no simple, pointlike location, and one wave may pass through another with no sustained effect. In certain situations waves can interact in such a way that they set up interference patterns.

In short, particles and waves seem to be fundamentally different types of entities. No one object can be both a particle and a wave, any more than a single object can be both a bullet and a ripple. Yet electrons, like other subatomic entities, display both particle and wave characteristics, and this is one of the central enigmas of quantum mechanics.

The enigmatic quality of this discovery may be attributed to an apparently innate tendency of the human mind known as *reification*. The initial system of detection in which electrons were discovered yielded results that we attribute to pointlike objects. On the basis of everyday experience, physicists assumed that the electron is a particle, regardless of any system of measurement to which it is subject. This form of scientific realism, like everyday realism, ignores the crucial role of the subjective instrument of observation. Thus, the evidence for its particle nature was reified; that is, it was regarded as a real object existing independently of experiment and theory. It was assumed to be the intrinsic nature of the electron. But when the electron is subject to a different type of measurement system, the interaction between the two suggests the presence of a wave. When we proceed to reify the wave nature of the electron, we encounter a paradox, for it must now be intrinsically both a particle and a wave, and that is impossible.

Democritus partially recognized the problem of reification over two millennia ago. He declared that such properties as color, heat, and taste do not exist in the physical objects themselves, but only in their interactions with the senses. What is the intrinsic nature of the physical world? In his view it is composed of space in which atoms with intrinsic size and shape move about with intrinsic velocities. Here is the metaphysical basis of mechanistic materialism, and it was adopted with only minor variations by Galileo and classical mechanics.

This residual reification was challenged by relativity theory and more so by quantum theory. Until then the role of the observer and the system of measurement was largely ignored. The scientists' instruments of observation were regarded as clear, passive windows into which the intrinsic quantities of nature pass; and the scientists' minds received nature's laws inductively from experience. Such a naive view is no longer tenable. Quantum mechanics presents us with objects that are seen as both waves and particles, but is this any more remarkable than detecting the sun's radiation as both color and heat? Certainly the two cases are not exactly parallel, for the frequencies of visual light and heat are different. But even the same frequency of electromagnetic radiation could be perceptually processed by radically different sense organs, resulting in the observation of radically different phenomena. An insistence on reifying intrinsic elements of the microworld leads to a myriad of logical inconsistencies, and these have been touted as being suggestive of the mystical nature of the world of quantum mechanics. But parallels in everyday experience indicate that if electrons are to be reified as being intrinsically particles and waves, we may as well reify solar radiation as both color and heat. Paradox does not necessarily imply mystical insight; it may simply be an expression of confusion.

Quantum mechanics has enjoyed tremendous success in mathematically accounting for the wave/particle nature of the electron, but this in no way solves the conceptual problem of the physical nature of the electron. The theory is inconsistent, for it describes manifestly nonclassical objects, but nevertheless is based on measurements in which electrons are regarded as classical entities. The problem may be dismissed on the grounds that classical physics is merely an approximation of reality in which quantum effects are too small to be seen. This argument is circular, however, for the subtle concepts of quantum mechanics are formulated with gross classical concepts. The necessity of classical ideas in quantum theory cannot be reconciled with the fact that those ideas are not applicable in representing the quantum world.

Another inconsistency of quantum mechanics occurs in the concept of subatomic entities such as the electron. Due to Heisenberg's uncertainty principle, many physicists now believe that the electron, for example, does not simultaneously bear definite location and velocity. Experimentally, insofar as precise measurement is taken of its velocity, knowledge of its location is precluded and vice versa. This fact seems to be inherent in the very process of measurement of microobjects, and it is due to the unavoidable interference of the system of measurement on the measured entity. But apart from such experimental limitations, the theoretical statement of the uncertainty principle indicates that the degree of uncertainty of the electron's position is inversely proportional to the uncertainty of its velocity, or momentum. Thus, precise knowledge of those two properties at one time is even theoretically unfeasible.

In his book *Quantum Reality*, Nick Herbert labels these two attributes as secondary qualities of the electron.[1] That is, the electron's position and velocity are not innate characteristics of this wave/particle but exist in relation to a specific system of measurement. Note the similarity to Democritus's claim that heat and color are only secondary properties of atoms in that they exist only in relation to conscious visual and tactile systems of measurement. In contrast to the atoms of mechanistic materialism, elementary particles are no longer regarded as bearing the intrinsic qualities of position and velocity.

The inconsistency of this interpretation of quantum mechanics lies in the fact that it persists in imputing other primary qualities to the electron, such as rest mass, charge, and spin. These are its chief innate properties, according to this interpretation, and they are intrinsic to it regardless of the system of measurement. The problem can be stated as follows: how can an electron, whose wave and/or particle status is nebulous, have intrinsic mass, charge, and spin, when it does not have intrinsic location or velocity? Moreover, in relativity theory, even the intrinsic mass of the electron becomes problematic, for the mass of a moving body is different when measured from two different frames of reference.

The mathematical descriptions of the quantum world are reasonably straightforward, and there is widespread agreement as to their accuracy. But what does this tell us, for instance, of the physical reality of the electron? It is at this point that inconsistencies, vagueness, and disparity of opinion arise, and these problems are in no way elucidated by equating such incoherence with religious mysticism. Eastern contemplatives were never subject to the quandary of describing quantum reality with the concepts of European classical physics. Indeed, both modern physics and mysticism question the fundamental nature of reality, but in both areas we must avoid confusing mystification with mysticism.

One of the most common remarks concerning the quantum world is that it is unimaginable, and this suggests to some minds a mystical quality to the science that has made this discovery. Since the time of Democritus, Western thinkers have sought to conceive of the nature of reality as it exists in its own right, apart from our experience of it. Everyday realism assumes that all the qualities that we sense—such as color, heat, and taste—are intrinsic to physical objects. Classical mechanics, following the lead of Democritus, imagines that reality is composed of colorless, tasteless, odorless particles moving silently through space. Quantum mechanics has found that independent physical reality can no longer be conceived as simple discrete particles (due to the wave/particle duality), and their absolute motion is also called into question, for that concept falsely assumes absolute location and velocity.

Those who continue to adopt a realist interpretation of quantum theory continue in the age-old attempt to conceive of physical reality as it exists independently of our systems of measurements. Some go so far as to claim that the ontological status of the microworld is fundamentally different from that of the macroworld. Heisenberg, for example, declares that "atoms and the elementary particles themselves are not as real [as experimental facts about atomic events]; they form a world of potentialities or possibilities rather than one of things or facts.[2] Thus, electrons and their orbits are to be considered as potentia, rather than real things or events.[3]

This is a common attitude in quantum mechanics: the macroworld of everyday experience retains the ontological status attributed to it in classical mechanics, whereas the microworld demands a different status in accordance with quantum mechanics. Thus, experimental instruments, such as a cathode ray tube, are regarded as classical objects, whereas the entities they are designed to measure are nonclassical. Niels Bohr, moreover, recognized the logical necessity of describing the observational means in terms of classical physics.

The strangeness of this logical necessity should be obvious. If an unmeasured subatomic entity exists only potentially, how could two such entities be any more actual or real? Or a hundred, or a trillion? If the basic components of physical reality are mere potentia, large quantities of them do not make them any more real; and a macroscopic object such as an apple is presumably composed of nothing more than a large quantity of electrons, protons, and so on. What is a cathode ray tube composed of apart from unmeasured subatomic particles?

Perhaps the chief ontological mystery of quantum mechanics is the manner in which probability waves, or potentia, interact with a system of measurement. Until the measurement occurs and observational results are produced, the Schrödinger equation describes the electron as a probability wave; but when the measurement occurs, that probability wave collapses, and the electron yields actual, not probable, results. The physicist John von Neumann recognized that if the unmeasured electrons that the Schrödinger function describes are mere potentia, the same must be true of the unmeasured elementary particles of which the measuring device is composed. That device must in that case exist as an unimaginably complex system of probability waves and thus as a mere potential. But in this case, how could interaction with such a potential reality collapse the wave function? Following this line of inquiry with his renowned clarity and brilliance of logic, he found nothing in the physical world capable of collapsing the wave function.[4] This led him to the conclusion that this collapse occurs due to *consciousness of the event,* but this interpretation has its own difficulties. The problem of quantum measurement remains unsolved in contemporary physics,[5] and the source of this problem seems to lie once again in the process of reification.

Early twentieth-century physics conceived of the atom as a positively charged nucleus with electrons imbedded in it. This was replaced with the planetary model of electrons orbiting the nucleus, and Bohr modified this picture by allowing the electrons to disappear instantaneously from one orbit and reappear in another. He offered no physical explanation as to how this mysterious feat was accomplished. With the advent of the wave/particle duality and the uncertainty principle, physicists were forced to renounce any imagery that supposedly represented the physical reality of the atom as it exists independently of measurement. Heisenberg, Max Born, and other prominent physicists made a great point of declaring: let us not attribute existence to that which cannot be known even in principle. Let us call this the *principle of unknowability.*

Such physicists were compelled to restrain their impulse of reification by rejecting all models of what atoms really look like when we are not looking at them or measuring them. But the above principle is difficult to adopt in a thoroughgoing way. The foregoing discussion suggests that all our knowledge of the physical world is inevitably related to our means of observation, but we nevertheless yearn to know what is really out there, apart from our subjective input. In his later writings Heisenberg turned away from the principle of unknowability by declaring unmeasured subatomic entities to be potentia. But is not even this potential status in principle unknowable? How can we know anything of probability waves in the independent, objective world apart from our measurements? This would seem to be one more case of reifying a concept based on mathematical formalisms. No imagery is induced by such an ontological claim, but it does set up a paradoxical dualism between the potential status of subatomic entities and the actual, real status of the macroworld, which is composed of nothing other than those potentia.

Experiment does not inform us of the ontological status, or intrinsic nature, of microobjects as they exist apart from measurement. Given one system of measurement, results are produced that suggest the presence of a wave phenomenon; given another system, the "same" measured object seems to be a particle. In the absence of any system of measurement, we have no evidence of waves, particles, potentia, or anything else. We may conclude, according to the above principle, that an electron existing as an independent entity is in principle unknowable; therefore this independent entity does not exist as a potentiality, for it does not exist at all.

Chapter Ten

Uncertainty in the Quantum World

Over the past few centuries, scientists have explored the nature of smaller and smaller components of the physical world. An underlying motive has been, as the experimental physicist Ernest Rutherford declared, that "if we knew the constitution of atoms we ought to be able to predict everything that is happening in the universe."[1] As physicists probed more deeply into the minute components of matter, they repeatedly encountered anomalous behavior, which they gradually accounted for in orderly ways. In the process, increasingly fundamental causes were recognized to account for otherwise inexplicable behavior, and in this way the orderly universe was maintained. Where could such a search for causes end? Science might conceivably come up with a first, or primordial, cause that lies at the source of all motion. But such an Aristotelian idea would more properly belong in the domain of philosophy or theology.

The more likely outcome of this search is that physicists would encounter natural events for which no definite causes could be identified. They would then be faced with two options: (1) to admit that at least for the time being, the causes of those events remain hidden from our understanding; or (2) to claim that those events occur at random, without cause. In the second case, no causes are identified for the simple reason that they do not exist. Max Born, who was instrumental in introducing the probabilistic interpretation of quantum theory, declared that deterministic causes of such quantum processes as radioactive decay are in principle unknowable, and as such they do not exist.

Physics has historically been concerned with finding simplicity and order in nature, but when it comes to the quantum level it finds apparently random events for which no direct causes can be identified. This situation could be interpreted as a further level of subatomic order of possibly unfathomable complexity; or one could insist upon fathomable simplicity by interpreting it as subatomic chaos. By renouncing causality one retains simplicity at the cost of order. The choice is a metaphysical one, and the prevailing interpretation of quantum mechanics has projected our human uncertainty upon the physical world by claiming that it is inherent in nature. Uncertainty is thereby reified, and the principle of unknowability is transgressed.

There is no reason in principle why Western thought could not have arrived at the same conclusion upon inquiring into the nature of the macroworld. Faced with the vast complexity of natural events that we witness, we could have come to the swift conclusion that such things as illness, weather, and natural calamities occur at random. But if we had adopted that view early on, it would have precluded the growth of Western science.

A similar theme has been adopted in modern cosmology. Astronomer Edward Harrison claims that the universe began in a chaotic state in which everything was irrational and indeterministic.[2] The original emergence of life and consciousness in the universe is also attributed to chance in modern cosmology. When scholastic theology encountered inexplicable elements of reality, it frequently deemed them mysteries. When science encounters such elements, it now tends to regard them as random, chance events.

The advocates of this view of acausality in the quantum world express only a partial adherence to the principle of unknowability. Without the classical assumption of physical causality, quantum mechanics could never have been formulated, for it rests upon the very classical concepts that it refutes. Without the concept of causality we would not today recognize four basic forces in nature, for they are regarded as being responsible for all natural processes.

A strict, consistent adoption of the principle of unknowability must acknowledge that the entire physical world, existing independently of all systems of measurement, is in principle unknowable; and thus it does not exist. But few physicists are willing to go that far. While recognizing that some of the properties of atoms do not exist apart from measurement, physicists still tend to believe in a real quantum world existing in its own right. Since strict causality is not knowable in this atomic realm, however, they conclude that it does not exist. There is an inconsistency here: if strict causality is to be discarded on the grounds of unknowability, then the entire realm of the unmeasured quantum world should be abandoned on the same grounds.

Physicists who seek to maintain strict causality in quantum mechanics insist upon hidden variables, mechanisms in the quantum world that are not prone to measurement. These are introduced in order to save the principle of strict causality, and this procedure is often rejected on the grounds that it is ad hoc and artificial. To many scientists the introduction of hidden variables seems to be the only alternative to denying strict causality in quantum mechanics. A third option, however, is to assert that we simply do not know whether atomic processes are subject to strict determinism. We do not even know whether the only possible causes are necessarily of a physical nature. The enormous success of quantum mechanics in accounting for a wide range of phenomena does not rest on the metaphysical denial of strict causality. It would work just as well if physicists acknowledged certain limits to their domain of knowledge; and this might be more responsible than informing society that the fundamental nature of physical reality is irrational and chaotic.

———◆———

Do at least some of the properties of subatomic entities not have an objective reality independent of the act of observation? In a famous paper, "Can Quantum-Mechanical Description of Reality Be Considered Complete?" Einstein attacked this view.[3] As a confirmed realist, he was convinced that any such theory that denies the real, independent properties of such entities must be incomplete. It is a temporary, partial, makeshift theory that will eventually be replaced by one that directly represents physical reality in space and time, and that does not assert natural events as analogous to a game of chance.[4]

In the same paper Einstein presented a thought experiment which he felt demonstrated the incompatibility of the lack of real properties of subatomic objects and the limitation of the absolute speed of light (believed to be the highest, invariant speed in nature). Known as the EPR paradox, it remained a subject of controversy for decades.

Almost thirty years after the appearance of that article, John Bell suggested a means to test this paradox empirically.[5] In his work, now known as Bell's Theorem, he distinguishes between local hidden variable theories and quantum mechanics.[6] The former are theories that posit objectively real parts of a system that can be isolated from one another. Those theories and quantum theory give different predictions for the experiment that Bell suggested. In 1981, Alain Aspect and his collaborators at the University of Paris's Institute of Theoretical and Applied Optics presented a paper describing their experimental test of the EPR paradox under conditions in which Bell's type of analysis applied.[7] Experimental results showed that the quantum-theoretical predictions were indeed obeyed.

A common interpretation of this experiment states that it compels us to renounce either thoroughgoing realism or the theory that nothing can travel faster than the speed of light.[8] In the minds of some physicists, this clearly refutes realism: experiment is seen as deciding a question of ontology. Other physicists, however, interpret the above results in quite another way. For example, N. C. Petroni and J. P. Vigier suggest the possibility of "exchanges of information" occurring faster than the speed of light, and they reaffirm their belief in real particles subject to absolute causality.[9] Such a fundamental diversity of opinion concerning the physical meaning of this experiment supports the age-old truth that any empirical evidence can be subject to multiple, incompatible interpretations.

During the fall of 1985, at a conference on quantum reality held in Urbino, Italy, to commemorate the fiftieth anniversary of the EPR paper, physicists hotly debated interpretations of the series of experiments on this subject performed by Alain Aspect and his team. However, "only one thing was clear from the discussions that took place: It is difficult to find agreement even on minor issues."[10] W. Duch and D. Aerts conducted a poll of fifty-six physicists and other scholars at the conference, who gave answers that seemed representative of physicists working on the foundations of quantum mechanics. Among them, 30 percent believed that recent experiments had falsified Einstein's assumption of objective particles having definite location and moving at speeds slower than that of light, while 57 percent did not; 21 percent asserted, while 52 percent refuted, that there is an influence faster than light; and 86 percent considered themselves to be realists.

Experiments, even if devised as carefully as those of Aspect, once again fail to compel physicists to adopt anything like a unanimous view of physical reality. As in the case of the EPR paradox, we should not expect the problem of quantum measurement to be solved by some as yet undevised experimental test. Empirical evidence will continue to be interpreted in diverse ways in accordance with such nonscientific influences as metaphysical predilection.

Chapter Eleven

Scientific Realism in Review

While noting that physicists who are concerned with the foundations of quantum mechanics have difficulty in agreeing even on minor issues, we must also recognize that such physicists are but a small
minority of the physics community as a whole. The training that most
physicists receive neither encourages such a concern nor educates
them in addressing their minds to subjects that may border on the
philosophical. One rough-and-ready retort to problems of interpreting the formalisms of quantum mechanics is simply that they work;
and this presumably suffices to ensure the validity of this branch of
physics.

However, the fact that those formalisms on their own make no statement about physical reality, apart from quantitative measurements,
should be apparent. If we are to develop a view of physical reality
based upon quantum theory, those formalisms must be interpreted.
In *Quantum Reality*, Nick Herbert presents no fewer than eight major
contemporary interpretations of quantum mechanics. Most of them
are conceptually mutually incompatible, and all account for appearances equally well. Thus, if quantum mechanics is true because it
works so well, we must ask: Which interpretation is true, for they all
work equally well? Moreover, if quantum mechanics is presented as
somehow penetrating to the same truths as mysticism, which of these
mutually exclusive interpretations of quantum mechanics is the mys-

tical one? And among the myriad mystical experiences and theories that have arisen in human history, which ones are corroborated by modern physics?

Since the time of Greek antiquity, Western thinkers sought to understand the nature of physical reality in its own right, apart from human experience and concepts. Not only have we adopted this goal from the Greeks, we have also assimilated many of their metaphysical assumptions in the pursuit of that goal. Beliefs in autonomous atoms moving through the void and in the presence of mathematics immanent in physical reality, as well as the insistence on beauty and simplicity, are all legacies from our Greek heritage. Newton's assumptions—that mind is separate from nature and that the physical world can be understood while ignoring the existence of human consciousness—also trace back to such Greek thinkers as Democritus. So, too, does Leibniz's principle of conservation find its origin in prescientific thought.

The point is that Western science has not followed a course of inquiry into physical reality demanded by nature itself, nor have we followed the one reasonable approach. Rather, we have followed a course that is based on and continues to be influenced by the Greek and Hebrew roots of our culture. In pursuing this mode of inquiry, we have developed a view of physical reality that differs starkly from those of other civilizations, such as classical China and India. A common tendency among scientists and their followers is to judge alien views of reality as false insofar as they differ from modern science. This dogmatic conviction implicitly assumes that the prescientific, metaphysical assumptions upon which Western science is based are the only true ones. It is misleading to suggest that such a claim is a scientific conclusion.

Modern physicists' descriptions of reality show obvious influences of logical positivism, materialism, phenomenology, existentialism, and pragmatism, as well as other influences from the social environment. Only the most naive appraisal of the history of ideas could lead to the conclusion that the hard facts of physics lie at the source of these philosophies.

With the development of the science of mechanics during the eighteenth century, physicists found less and less need to resort to the hypothesis of a God who arbitrates in the operation of the physical universe. During the following century, with the adoption of the principle of energy conservation and the materialistic model of the universe as a mechanism, God seemed still more superfluous. Indeed, as scientific advances appeared gradually to undermine the credibility of religious doctrine altogether, an increasing number of scientists and their followers discarded religion as a whole. This tendency has continued into the present century.

During the opening decades of this century, one occasionally heard a physicist use a theological argument in support of a physical theory. Einstein, for example, challenged certain probabilistic assumptions in quantum theory on the grounds that "God does not play dice." Most contemporary physicists, however, would side more with Bohr's response that we should not tell God what He can do. The prevailing attitude is that scientific theory must be kept strictly free of religious prejudices. Thus, even if some physicists believe in God, they must not let that bias taint their scientific thinking.

Let us, for the moment, define religious doctrine as a system of belief concerning such issues as the nature of the Ultimate Being, the essential meaning of human life, the origin of the universe, the destiny of the individual following death, and the means to salvation. Viewed in such terms, it becomes immediately apparent that contemporary science is thoroughly suffused with religious doctrine. That doctrine may vary anywhere from agnosticism to unequivocal atheism. In this sense, twentieth-century physics is as profoundly influenced by metaphysics and religion as it was during the time of Newton. This fact may be overlooked by today's practicing physicists, for their training does not encourage them to reflect on the philosophical and religious foundations of their discipline. Scientists cannot really choose whether they will be free of such influences, for scientific thinking does not occur independently from the rest of our thinking. Those who are affected by science can choose only whether they will consciously, intelligently reflect upon its historical development and metaphysical foundations.

Since the time of Newton, there has been virtually universal agreement that physical science has made tremendous progress. Over the years there has been widespread agreement among physicists as to the progress in mathematical and experimental techniques. There has also been a general consensus concerning the heuristic value of popular physical models. The picture of electrons circling about an atomic nucleus, like planets about a sun, for example, is still very much in use, even though it is no longer believed to correspond to any physical reality. What is an electron, really? Is it a wave or a particle? Does it have definite location and velocity? Is it an independent physical reality or purely an abstract concept or a set of physical relations? How many electrons could perform a chaotic random walk on the head of a pin? Physicists' responses to these ontological questions appear to vary as much as the speculations of medieval theologians concerning the ontological status of angels.

Science has long prided itself on its unique progress, in contrast to the idle speculations of philosophy and the unverifiable tenets of religion. Kant expressed this attitude when he reflected that metaphysics is always "keeping the human mind in suspense with hopes that never fade, and yet are never fulfilled . . . while every other science is continually advancing."[1] Let us recall for a moment the diversity of conceptually incompatible views that account for the Casimir effect. This situation of multiple theories equally accounting for the same phenomena is actually quite common in physics, though it is not commonly brought to the attention of students or the public at large. The realists' creed is that such diversity will disappear when a broader range of more precise experiments has been conducted. By a process of steadily more exacting elimination, false theories will be found inadequate, and the culmination of this evolution will be a single grand unified theory that will consistently and accurately account for all phenomena in the one correct way.

According to this view, as scientific research continues there should be ever increasing agreement on first the major aspects and then the subtle points of physical theory. The present diversity of views on the Casimir effect, the implications of the Aspect experiment, and more generally the nature of quantum reality should encourage us to question this realist assumption. There has always been fundamental diversity of interpretations of mathematical theories and experimental evidence, and there is no evidence that this tendency is on the decline. If this is the case, the prospects seem remote for the scientific community ever to agree universally on a single grand unified theory. To paraphrase Kant, the realists keep the human mind in suspense with hopes of such a unified theory which never fade and yet are never fulfilled.

Alfred North Whitehead made an observation similar to Kant's when he noted: "European thought is represented as littered with metaphysical systems, abandoned and unreconciled."[2] He goes on to add, however, that if that means ill-success, the same can be said of science. Over the entire course of its history, physics has moved from one diversity of views to another, and always it has developed hand-in-hand with prevailing metaphysical and religious beliefs. It has indeed progressed, but not in the manner assumed by the prevailing view of scientific realism.

In the historical and philosophical inquiry into the foundations of physics presented here, we have encountered diversity, inconsistency, and at times naiveté in physicists' views of their discipline. Does physics indeed shed light on an independent, intrinsic physical reality? Are the foundations of physics secure? Einstein, who had a lifelong commitment to a realist interpretation of physics, plainly acknowledged: "For the time being, we have to admit that we do not possess any general theoretical basis for physics which can be regarded as its logical foundation."[3]

Chapter Twelve

Mathematical Realism

The preceding chapters bring to light a number of serious problems in scientific realism: multiple incompatible theories explaining the same body of observed phenomena have long been prevalent in physics; this science, too, is known for abandoning even its most cherished tenets from one age to the next; and the formulation, adoption, and rejection of its theories have always been deeply influenced by nonscientific social influences. None of these facts bode well for the belief that our physical theories represent the world as it exists independently of our means of observation and conceptualization, that is, that they reflect objective reality.

Especially in the present century it has become increasingly difficult to imagine the type of world that physics presents to us. We may recall Niels Bohr's comment that the entire formalism of quantum mechanics is simply a tool for deriving predictions and that its symbols are not susceptible to pictorial interpretation. David Bohm remarks of contemporary physicists: "They do use the idea of fields and particles and so on but when you press them they must agree that they have no image whatsoever what these things are, and they have no content other than the results of what they can calculate with their equations."[1] If quantum mechanics fails to provide us with an image or pictorial representation of the actual nature of physical reality, the same may be true of present speculations concerning eleven dimensions in the "superstring" theory or even the more modest four dimensions of general relativity.

If we adopt physics as a means of exploring the objective physical world, we may well ask: why should the world that is independent of our human senses and concepts be amenable to images or representations that are formed on the basis of those faculties? If we reject the notion that objective reality can be represented by such images and ideas, we may then ask: how can it be represented? A realist may be satisfied with the answer posed by Einstein: "Nature is the realization of the simplest conceivable mathematical ideas."[2] Those who adopt this metaphysical position may be called *mathematical realists*. It is interesting to note, however, that he also acknowledged that "as far as the propositions of mathematics refer to reality, they are not certain; and as far as they are certain, they do not refer to reality."[3]

While there is fundamental dissension among physicists as to interpretations of quantum mechanics, there is widespread agreement concerning its mathematical formalisms. To a mathematical realist this may suggest that a true physical theory is purely mathematical in nature, and any interpretations using physical concepts are beside the point. Nature in its own right cannot be grasped with ideas expressed in the words and grammar of English, German, or any other human language but only with pure mathematical thought.[4] Moreover, declares Einstein, "One reason why mathematics enjoys special esteem, above all other sciences, is that its propositions are absolutely certain and indisputable."[5] Thus, it should come as no surprise that modern concepts of matter, energy, fields, and space-time, which are products of mathematical thought, are not amenable to the nonmathematical imagination.

This metaphysical assumption, like so many others underlying modern physics, traces back to Greek antiquity. The early atomists, like the Pythagoreans, believed that the underlying reality of the physical world is expressible in terms of mathematics.[6] For Plato, mathematics is an intrinsic element of the absolute, unchanging, transcendent realm of Ideas, and the less real physical world can be understood only through the mathematics of the ideal world. Both he and Aristotle agreed, though for different reasons, that mathematical axioms need not be proved, for their truth is unquestionably self-evident. The effort to understand nature through mathematics continued during the Middle Ages, and the chief impetus for this movement was attributed to Euclid's *Elements*.

From Pythagoras, Kepler adopted the approach of treating observed physical phenomena as approximations of mathematically "clean" conceptions; and this has developed into a defining property of physical inquiry. From the sixteenth to the eighteenth centuries mathematicians commonly regarded their work as a religious quest. Descartes, for example, believed that the truths of mathematics are innate to the human mind, having been placed there by God. Galileo went further in stressing the importance of a mathematical description of nature, as opposed to Descartes's emphasis on physical explanation. Both men felt that all of science should be patterned after mathematics, moving from self-evident axioms to logical deductions.

As we have noted previously, Newton was drawn both to the austerity of a mathematical description of physical processes and to the more imaginative goal of physical explanation. He believed that his mathematical principles of mechanics give a true account of phenomena on the grounds that God created the universe in accordance with mathematical principles. Thus, his theology preceded and justified his science. Newton even claims that he wrote his *Principles* with "an eye on such principles as might work with considering men for the belief in a Deity."[7]

During the eighteenth century, religious inspiration for work in mathematics began to decline, and during the following century even belief in God among mathematicians decreased. Such a process of secularization inevitably led to the question: if God did not create nature in accordance with mathematical laws, why should we believe that they are present in physical reality?

In 1753, Denis Diderot was among the first to suggest that mathematics is an artificial convention with no foundation in reality. A major impetus for such questioning was the emergence of geometries using axioms other than those of Euclid. Carl Friedrich Gauss developed his system of non-Euclidean geometry in 1813, and he was the first to suggest the physical applicability of such a system and to question the truth of Euclidean geometry. In 1830, János Bolyai and Nikolay Lobachevsky went a step further in suggesting independently that none of Euclid's postulates are either true or false; they are simply the rules of the game. In 1843, the mathematician William Hamilton devised a new system of physically useful algebra in which the commutative law for multiplication is denied, that is, "a × b" does not equal "b × a." His work was followed by other algebras with still other rules of the game.

Only by the 1870s were mathematicians prepared to acknowledge the ramifications of non-Euclidean geometry. Until then there was a widespread assumption that all knowledge was unitary, and there was hope that all knowledge could attain the absolute, firm footing of Euclidean geometry. This geometry was the exemplar of assertions that are internally consistent, mathematically true, and descriptive of reality, and it was characterized by the inconceivability of its opposite. Alfred North Whitehead comments on this shift of attitude toward Euclidean geometry:

> While mathematics is a convenience in relating certain types of order to our comprehensions, it does not, as used to be supposed, give us any account of their actuality. . . . Euclid's geometry was once supposed to be an exact description of the external world. The only world of which it is an accurate description is the world of Euclidean geometry.[8]

What are the social and intellectual implications of this shift for those people who regard Euclidean geometry as the exemplar for all true knowledge? Mathematicians Philip Davis and Reuben Hersh declare: "All of a sudden, the whole superstructure of ethics, religion and hope for finding true knowledge in the sciences collapses."[9]

Only in the nineteenth century did modern scientists seriously suspect that mathematical axioms may be derived from experience and not from innate reason. Hermann von Helmholtz claimed that the very concept of number stems from experience and that only experience can tell us where the laws of arithmetic apply. For example, if we add one volume of water at forty degrees temperature to an equal volume at fifty degrees, only experience informs us that the temperature of the combined volumes is not ninety degrees.

During this century it began to appear that mathematical axioms are derived, directly or indirectly, from experience and that the physical applicability of arithmetic and other branches of mathematics is determined only by experience. But if this is the case, there is little justification for believing that mathematics contains truth in the sense of laws of physical reality as it exists independent of experience. This possibility was metaphysically so repugnant to nineteenth-century mathematicians, however, that many rejected it out of hand.

Up to the beginning of the sixteenth century, the concepts of mathematics tended to be immediate idealizations of or abstractions from experience. But in the following centuries such mentally originated notions as complex numbers, derivatives, and integrals were introduced that could not be visualized or abstracted from everyday experience. Such mathematical concepts have been devised not for their conceptual simplicity, but for their amenability to useful manipulations and to striking, brilliant arguments.[10] As physical theories came to be formulated in terms of increasingly abstract mathematics, it was inevitable that the physical reality they describe be decreasingly amenable to visualization. Given the abstract formalisms in which quantum theory is couched, the unimaginability of the quantum world, for example, was a foregone conclusion.

In the seventeenth and eighteenth centuries, vagueness and logical gaps in mathematics were usually overlooked due to the success of physical applications of mathematics and the belief that God created a world that operates on mathematical principles. During the eighteenth and nineteenth centuries, however, mathematicians became increasingly concerned with proving the rigorous internal consistency of the entire body of mathematics. Progress toward this goal focused first on calculus, then algebra, complex numbers, irrational numbers, fractions, and finally whole numbers. By 1890 this process of rigorization was widely considered to be complete: the logical foundation for all of mathematics appeared secure. We note, however, that what seemed established was the internal consistency of mathematics, not its truth.

One mathematician who was not so confident about this complete rigorization was David Hilbert. Just as physics in the closing years of the nineteenth century seemed complete, barring a few unsolved anomalies, so did mathematics have a few residual problems in need of solution. Hilbert identified twenty-three such problems, and one of them was a proof that arithmetic is consistent. The mere fact that physics at times seemed to confirm the truth of mathematical principles was recognized by 1900 as being no proof of the consistency of mathematics. As the century progressed, new contradictions in mathematics were produced and old ones revealed by such innovations as the theory of infinite sets. Mathematicians of the early part of this century were faced with the serious problems of resolving present contradictions in their science and of proving its thorough consistency, to ensure that no new contradictions would arise. The assurance in the logical foundations of mathematics at the end of the nineteenth century turned out to be as unfounded as the similar attitude toward physics at that time.

In what sense do mathematical concepts exist? This was the basic, underlying issue in the attempt to establish mathematics on a firm foundation. By 1930, four distinct, conflicting schools of thought had arisen, and the major problem that motivated them—the consistency of mathematics—was not settled at all. Equally competent experts disagreed on the simplest aspects of any reasoning that makes the slightest claim to universality or cogency.

In 1931 the mathematician Kurt Gödel presented a proof that undermined the entire pursuit of consistency for the whole of mathematics.[11] In his incompleteness theorem he demonstrated that if any formal theory adequate to embrace the theory of whole numbers is consistent, it is incomplete. There exist meaningful statements that belong to, but cannot be proved within, those systems. Those statements can be shown to be true or false by nonformal arguments which rely on axioms outside the system.

Until this time, it was widely assumed that a complete set of axioms could be assembled for any given branch of mathematics. Gödel showed, however, that the set proposed in the past for arithmetic was incomplete and that it could not be made complete simply by adding a finite number of axioms to the original list. Thus, any system in which arithmetic can be developed is essentially incomplete. The complete axiomatization of all of mathematics was now seen to be hopeless.

After 1931 subsequent investigations into the foundations of mathematics further frustrated any attempt to determine the nature and validity of mathematical statements. The Löwenhein-Skolem theory, for example, demonstrated that a set of theorems permits many more essentially different interpretations than the one intended. Once again the problem of multiple, incompatible interpretations, which has plagued the foundations of physics, emerges in mathematics as well. Faced with implacable contention among diverse schools of thought, mathematicians have been forced to accept that there is no such thing as an absolute, or universally accepted, proof.

Mathematical axioms, which were traditionally regarded as self-evident truths, are now recognized as conventions. Davis and Hersh comment in this regard: "The axioms are whatever we choose; they are simply playthings. This, you might say, is the spirit of modern mathematics."[12] If a set of axioms for a given system were to be complete, all logical truths based on those axioms would be tautologous. But such a complete set is not possible even for arithmetic. In any arithmetic system, further truths may be established not tautologically, or on the basis of its axioms, but by some form of metamathematical reasoning.

If a system as comparatively simple as arithmetic is not self-contained, we may wonder how a grand unified theory for all of physics could possible have that quality. What is the search for a grand unified theory if not for a complete, consistent theory accounting for all natural phenomena? May it not be that metaphysical reasoning may be necessary to account for certain physical truths, just as metamathematical reasoning establishes certain mathematical truths? If the axioms of arithmetic must remain essentially incomplete, is it not reasonable to expect the same for physical principles?

Just as most contemporary physicists have little interest in or knowledge of the problems lying at the foundations of their science, so is this true of many mathematicians. In both disciplines there are some who are aware of the problems but discount them as being of a philosophical rather than of a scientific nature. As in physics, the fundamental unresolved problems and uncertainties are not generally taught to students; and in this way the myth of the absolute truth of mathematics and of the mathematical nature of independent physical reality is nurtured.

The realist belief that the physical world is the realization of mathematical ideas rests upon the assumption that such ideas are absolutely certain and indisputable. Since this view no longer seems tenable, how is it that so many people still adhere to it? The answer may lie in the way mathematics and science are treated in our educational institutions and popular media. To return to Davis and Hersh:

> Though scientific histories of the past two hundred years have ignored or have been reluctant to admit the association, mathematics has drawn inspiration and nourishment from business, from religion, from law, from war, from politics, from ethics, from gambling, from metaphysics, from mysticism, from ritual, from play . . . and not just from a "sanitized" physical science approved by positivism.[13]

Given this wide array of social influences on the development of mathematics, it is exceedingly difficult to conclude that our mathematical laws and reasoning have somehow been guided to the one true representation of objective truth. Davis and Hersh point out that by means of mathematics we may impose a reality on human affairs which we regard as the objective world. However, it is a reality that does not follow from pure scientific or mathematical inquiry. Furthermore, "it is not unique: one may imagine alternative or rival mathematizations, equally efficacious, and equally fraught with consequences for the human race."[14]

For realists, the above critique may leave unresolved at least one major question, namely: if the objective world is not an expression of timeless mathematical laws, how do we account for the fact that physical measurements do so often lend themselves to such formulations? Certainly no one who has engaged in research in physics can fail to be impressed by the *lawfulness* of much of our observed data. Does this not tell us that the world that we are measuring is subject to those laws? Whitehead comments on this point: "People make the mistake of talking about 'natural laws.' There *are* no natural laws. There are only temporary habits of nature."[15] But even this statement needs to be modified: these "habits of nature" are ones that occur in relation to our systems of measurement. They do not exist "out there" in some realm independent of physical inquiry.

We have already seen the tenuousness of believing that physical concepts and imagery represent anything in the objective world behind the appearance of the senses. Mathematical realism asserts that objective reality is nevertheless represented by mathematics and possibly only by such concepts. But now we have a problem. We may assert that the mathematical lawfulness of our measurements is due to the mathematical nature of the objective world. If we assert that this is the *only* knowledge we have of that world, however, our reasoning becomes circular: knowledge of objective reality is posited on the basis of mathematics, and such knowledge represents objective reality because the world behind appearances is an expression of mathematical ideas, *and that is all we know about it.* The very notion of objective reality thereby simply becomes an empty rack on which to drape the cloak of mathematics.

Bertrand Russell, who devoted much of his life to establishing the consistency of mathematics, eventually was compelled to abandon the view that the axioms of logic are self-evident truths. Moreover, having established that mathematics is derived from logic, he concluded that it, too, is not based on infallible truth. In a famous epigram he remarked that "pure mathematics is the subject in which we do not know what we are talking about, or whether what we are saying is true."[16] Hermann Wehl, another of the foremost mathematicians of this century, made a similar comment in 1940: "In spite, or because, of our disposed critical insight, we are today less sure than at any previous time of the ultimate foundations on which mathematics rests."[17]

Chapter Thirteen

Instrumentalism

Especially during the twentieth century, trends in physics and the philosophy of science have made it increasingly difficult to defend scientific realism. Ernest Rutherford, who presented himself as the epitome of an experimenter and who performed pioneering research in atomic physics, had a virtual contempt for theorizing in physics. The facts of nature, he thought, are to be discovered through experiment, not through theorizing. Yet when he performed an experiment, he liked to have a clear pictorial image of what was going on. Such an image is nothing more than a theoretical model; without it or some other theory, the experiment conveys no information whatever. Rutherford also adhered to metaphysical principles in his work, as illustrated by his reductionist belief that we could predict everything in the universe if we only knew the constitution of atoms. Like so many of the views of his nineteenth-century predecessors in science, Rutherford's unreflective scientific realism became vulnerable under the onslaught of later developments in quantum mechanics.

While the experimentalist Rutherford was impatient with physical theorizing, the theoretician Paul Dirac displayed a similar disinterest in philosophizing or investigating the foundations of physics. As a youth he enjoyed playing with equations and looking for beautiful mathematical relations, regardless of any possible physical meaning that they might have. His formal education was in mathematics and engineering, and for most of his life he found philosophy and the arts nearly incomprehensible.[1] This limitation, however, did not prevent him from becoming one of the chief architects of quantum mechanics, the creator of quantum electrodynamics, and one of the principal founders of quantum field theory. Dirac certainly believed that quantum theory explained processes in the real physical world, and he was concerned that mathematical techniques be physically justifiable. But his comparative lack of training and reflection in philosophy placed him in a difficult position to defend his realist interpretation of modern physics.

Among the generations of physicists following that of the founders of quantum mechanics, interest in the foundations of modern physics has, until quite recently, waned still further. Contemporary theoreticians tend to be less concerned than Dirac with physically justifying their calculations, such as renormalization techniques in quantum electrodynamics. The prevailing view seems to be: if the mathematical theory makes valid predictions, it is to be adopted regardless of any physical justification for it. The end justifies the means. Even in the early years, it was not uncommon for researchers to claim that they wanted to restrict their theories only to quantities they could observe. A movement began to refrain from making statements about physical reality, and this has led to the observation that physicists never understand quantum mechanics, they just learn to use it. David Bohm, for example, comments that in quantum mechanics there is no physical notion of what movement means. Physicists simply use the mathematics of this theory to calculate results, saying that they have no meaning whatsoever other than that.[2]

We recall that Copernicus sought to save the appearances by means of hypotheses that conform to certain physical principles (some of them Aristotelian), and on the grounds of such physical justification he proposed that his theory was true of nature. In contrast, many medieval astronomers demanded of their theories only that they be as simple as possible and that they account for appearances as precisely as possible. By not insisting that their theories be physically justifiable, they relinquished any claim to their being physically true.

Similarly, if particle physicists no longer demand that facets of their mathematical formalisms be physically justified—if only simplicity and accuracy of results are required—they, too, must make no claims of describing and explaining the fundamental components of physical reality. Their concepts must be regarded as instruments for making correct predictions, not as representations of physical entities. Fields and elementary particles must then be regarded as no more real than the equants and epicycles of medieval astronomy. Although the great majority of physicists still adopt the view of scientific realism, this metaphysical stance is now harder than ever to justify.

To adopt scientific realism consciously, we must accept a number of underlying premises: (1) there is a physical world that exists independently of human experience, (2) it can be grasped by human concepts (mathematical or otherwise), (3) among a potentially infinite number of conceptual systems that can account for observed phenomena, only one is true of reality, (4) science is now approaching that one true theory, and (5) scientists will know when they have found it. It seems a safe guess that most people who adopt the view of scientific realism are not aware of the many articles of faith that this view entails. Mathematicians Philip Davis and Reuben Hersh elucidate this point:

> There is a strong craving for permanence, for certainty in a chaotic world, and many people prefer to look for it within a mathematical or scientific rather than a religious context. They are, perhaps, not aware that underlying both mathematics and religion there must be a foundation of faith which the individual must himself supply.[3]

The preceding chapters have attempted to shed light on many of the metaphysical assumptions, leaps of faith, and unresolved problems that are embedded in scientific realism. Over the past one hundred and fifty years, due in part to the advent of non-Euclidean geometry and modern physics, scientists have increasingly been replacing the notion of *theory* with the notion of *model*. We have, for instance, a planetary model of the atom that represents nothing in the physical world but is, nevertheless, a useful tool in teaching. Are our concepts of fields, elementary particles, probability waves, quarks, curved space-time, and superstrings also simply models? In light of the preceding chapters we may find it very difficult to believe that they represent anything in objective reality. If they have no referents in nature, are they anything more than metaphors? As science has gradually dominated our society, many religious assertions about God, angels, heaven, and so forth have come to be regarded as myths. Einstein warns us not to credit religion with statements about truth, but to accept only its moral directives. Religious foundations for morality are, in this view, to be seen as mythical: they serve an important function, but they do not literally represent truth. Can the same now be said of the many theoretical entities and their behavior that are posited in physics? They are certainly useful tools for making predictions and for intelligibly organizing observed phenomena; but are there sufficient grounds for believing that they represent anything in the objective world?

———————◆———————

If physics is in fact capable only of accounting for appearances in a manner similar to that of Ptolemaic astronomy, a realist view of physics is untenable. From an alternative, instrumentalist perspective, a physical theory is valuable for its organizing role in making predictions, but it is not posited as being either true or false. A theory, like any other instrument, may be more or less useful, but the question of its validity simply does not arise. It is regarded as a *leading principle*,[4] in accordance with which conclusions about observable facts may be drawn; but it does not explain why those facts are observed. Accordingly, theoretical entities, such as fields and elementary particles, which are never directly observed, are merely conceptual constructs without any presumed referents in reality.

According to instrumentalism, one theory may still be superior to another if it serves as an effective leading principle for a more inclusive range of inquiries than does another, and if it supplies a method of analysis and representation that makes possible more precise and detailed inferences than another. In short, a good theory is one that is broadly encompassing, simple, and precise in terms of its predictions. Its approximation to reality is not an issue. Thus, Newton's first law of motion is superior to Aristotle's account of the natural motion of bodies because Newton's physics requires fewer ad hoc explanations.

A similar instrumentalist view may be adopted toward mathematics. One may argue that the rules of mathematics are as arbitrary as the grammatical rules of any other human language, and they may vary from one culture to another. Thus its "truths" are simply conventions, and mathematical theories are nothing more than instruments. Many twentieth-century researchers in the foundations of mathematics have such a view: mathematics is justified only by the degree of its success at practical physical application, that is, in giving correct results.

If we find ourselves rejecting scientific realism, instrumentalism might appear to us as a pragmatic and logically invulnerable view of science. Indeed, some realists seem to use it as a safe fallback when their metaphysical assumptions temporarily come under serious attack. Instrumentalism, however, is difficult to defend in any thorough, consistent fashion. How shall we supply a uniform account of the various theoretical entities (for example, electrons and light waves) that are postulated by physics? Are we truly prepared to assert that such terms as *field* and *particle* function only as conceptual links in rules of representation and inference? A consistent instrumentalist must renounce any claim that such theoretical terms have any referents in the physical world at all.

As instrumentalists, we may choose to regard the theoretical entities of physics as mere abstractions; after all, they are never really seen. All we have are observed data that may be accounted for by such entities; but, as we have learned, they may be accounted for by other constructs that are consistent with a different theory. From this viewpoint, particle physics yields no knowledge of the hidden nature of the microworld; it only predicts and organizes directly observable effects in the laboratory. Is such an interpretation of physics truly pragmatic? What experimental physicist would devote a lifetime to research believing that experiments yield no knowledge of physical reality apart from the measurements themselves? If we were convinced that the atomic nucleus is simply a useful concept for organizing data, we might well have no incentive to perform extremely sophisticated, careful experiments to explore its internal structure. Moreover, how could we justify the exorbitant sums spent on such devices as particle accelerators if they simply provide us with data that require the creation of new conceptual constructs? A view of physics that provides little or no incentive for pure experimental research can hardly be called pragmatic.

Is instrumentalism logically unassailable? As we have developed the instrumentalist view thus far, we have made a clear-cut distinction between the speculative, theoretical entities that are postulated in physics and the real phenomena that we actually see. Here we follow a common sense principle: seeing is believing. If we can directly observe a phenomenon, we may feel assured that it corresponds closely to something in the objective world, independent of our concepts. This view, however, ignores the fact that, as Einstein pointed out, it is the theory that determines what can be observed. This insight, while profound, is not a recent one. Kant wrote, "experience is itself a species of knowledge which involves understanding."[5] The facts that we observe have already been subject to interpretation as soon as they have been ascertained.

The truth of this assertion has been borne out by recent research in cognitive psychology and neuroscience. On the basis of his studies of the way we place objects in categories in order to perceive them, psychologist Jerome Bruner declares that "perception is to some unspecifiable degree an instrument of the world as we have structured it by our expectancies. Moreover, it is characteristic of complex perceptual processes that they tend where possible to assimilate whatever is seen or heard to what is expected."[6] The conceptual processing of perception occurs even in terms of what we may regard as the bare data of the senses. Cognitive scientist J. M. Wilding writes in this regard:

> We conclude that the appropriate description for a given input is highly dependent on the way the perceiver chooses to process it, which may vary qualitatively in the way information is interpreted and the degree to which information in memory is tapped, and quantitatively in the number of features extracted from the stimulus and from information in memory associated with it.[7]

It has been experimentally demonstrated that from the moment of an initial stimulus to conscious perception a lapse occurs of about one-tenth of a second. During this time a complex processing of information occurs that has come to light only in the past decade.[8] Thus the very notion of unmediated observation now seems highly questionable. In the light of such discoveries, the phrase "seeing is believing" takes on a new meaning: the very act of observation already entails a belief system that is not based simply on some hypothetical bare data.

If we are to deny the physical reality of theoretical entities that are not amenable to direct observation, we cannot confine such a category to the microworld of particle physics. Many of the physical concepts in astronomy, too, concern objects that are hidden from direct observation. Black holes, for instance, must be relegated to the status of mere concepts bearing no objective physical referents. Consequently, we must renounce any claim of knowing either the microworld of quantum mechanics or the distant, unobservable macroworld of astronomy and cosmology, for all of these sciences are concerned with theoretical entities that are hidden from direct observation.

Logical consistency does not allow instrumentalism to judge merely the sciences of quantum mechanics and cosmology, concerning entities that are either very small or distant in time and space. Electron microscopes, for example, yield observational facts, but these are not unmediated glimpses of the atomic realm. Rather, the observed data ostensibly result from interactions of electrons and atoms as well as other elements of the experimental device. The photographs obtained using such a microscope, therefore, do not show atomic or molecular entities themselves. Rather, such observed results are mediated by the types of measuring instrument that is being used. This is equally true of observations made through an optical microscope. One sees not the investigated subject itself but the effects produced by its bombardment by photons and the influence of the microscope on the reflected light. Microscopes yield visual results, but the theoretical terms of chemistry ostensibly concern objects that exist independently of such visual observations. Thus, from a thoroughgoing instrumentalist viewpoint, the chemical bonds and valences discussed in chemistry must also be relegated to the status of mere concepts with no objective referents in the physical world. Moreover, as Norwood Russell Hanson points out, a trained scientist looking down a microscope will actually see things that are invisible to a layman, and it may take years for them to become visible to a student.

If the visual data obtained through an optical microscope reveal only an interaction between the examined object, photons, and the measuring instrument (processed through a belief system), the same must be true of optical telescopes. In turn, the purportedly physical entities that are posited on the basis of such data in astronomy must also be relegated to the status of mere concepts, and not physical reality. The more closely we examine the process of identifying physical objects, the more we encounter what are in fact theoretical entities. Nowhere do we find phenomena that are observed without the mediation of a system of detection and conceptual processing.

Now, the visual data obtained with microscopes and telescopes are not essentially different from those observed through normal eyeglasses or with the naked eye. In all such cases we detect patterns of light and color, subjective sensory impressions that are not intrinsic characteristics of physical objects. In fact, as Democritus recognized, the color patterns observed by humans are relational attributes that have no existence apart from the human act of observation. This is equally true of all our other sensory impressions of sound, smell, taste, and touch. All such sensations occur as interactions between the sensed objects and our cognitive instruments of detection. Photographs of traces of subatomic particles in a cloud chamber are also interactions between the measured objects and the system of measurement. Thus, if for that reason subatomic particles are regarded purely as theoretical constructs, the same must be said of all the macroobjects that we think we observe in the physical world. If the former lack physical reality, so must the latter. In this case, no observational entities remain in the physical world.

At this point, it might seem that the only observational entities are subjective and mental: at first glance it may appear that we directly detect the sensations derived from our sense faculties, while the presumed real physical world hidden behind such appearances remains as unknowable as the subatomic realm. Sensory and mental events perceived introspectively are, however, just as subject to multiple interpretations as are external physical phenomena. This was confirmed by the Introspectionist School of psychology at the end of the nineteenth century. Moreover, the problems inherent in introspective inquiry—particularly maintaining the standards of objectivity—have led some thinkers to conclude that all such observations are misleading. Some philosophers go so far as to claim that introspective observation of mental events is impossible in principle. If introspective observation of subjective phenomena is possible but mediated by our conceptual frameworks, even such phenomena would not meet the criteria of observational entities. And if subjective phenomena are as inaccessible to introspection as they are to external, mechanical instruments, they would still fail to meet those criteria. Thus, the instrumentalist view results not only in solipsism but in thoroughgoing nihilism, for all the phenomena we observe are filtered through and interpreted in terms of our preconceptions.

Generally speaking, all experiential data obtained by means of our senses, scientific instruments, or introspection must be subject to interpretation before we can make any sense of them. And in all cases, the initial input can be interpreted in diverse ways. The specific interpretations that we choose are not demanded by the initial sensory stimuli but by our metaphysical assumptions and other influences.

Neuroscientists Humberto Maturana and Francisco Varela, having conducted extensive research into the nature of visual perception, conclude that there is not even a direct correlation between the wavelength of light illuminating an object and the subjective experience of color.[9] Thus, even the colors we observe are in some sense theoretical entities.

If we insist on rejecting the physical reality of such theoretical entities as electrons, we may find no justification for believing in the physical reality of anything at all. All of our observations are theory-laden, and none correspond in any straightforward way to objective objects existing in their own right independent of our experience. Thus, the form of instrumentalism that we have explored as an alternative to realism turns out to be a thinly veiled form of solipsism: we know nothing of the physical world existing independently of our senses. All that any individual knows of the world are his or her cognitive sensations.

Galileo, the founder of modern science, designated the physical world independent of our senses as the domain of inquiry of natural science. Quantum mechanics has thoroughly undermined his distinction between primary and secondary attributes of the basic constituents of physical reality. Location, size, shape, and absolute velocity—all regarded as primary physical properties—vanish in the context of individual particles. This leaves us, at least for the quantum world, with relational, secondary properties only. Our senses likewise offer us only relational properties of theoretical entities. As instrumentalists, we may retain our belief in an objective world existing independently of our experience, but we must then concede that such a world remains inaccessible to us.

Chapter Fourteen
Seeking a Middle Way

Einstein held that a belief in a natural world independent of the human mind, yet intelligible to it, lies at the foundation of all natural science. This belief captures the very essence of scientific realism, but upon inspecting the assumptions underlying this view, we may find it very difficult to adopt. If we deny that the theoretical terms of physics refer to real things and events in the physical world, however, we may, following the argument in the preceding chapter, find ourselves with no grounds for claiming knowledge of anything in nature. Scientific realism claims knowledge of objective reality, but its underlying assumptions include articles of faith that many may find hard to accept. Instrumentalism, on the other hand, reduces to a solipsism that can lay claim to no knowledge of the physical world, and when pushed to its logical conclusions, it results in nihilism. If that is our only alternative to scientific realism, Einstein must be correct in insisting that such realism is indispensable to all natural science.

The essential philosophical question is quite simple: can scientific theories represent and make intelligible the natural world as it exists independent of human experience, or can they serve only as instruments for organizing and predicting natural phenomena that are part of our experience? In terms of specific examples we may ask: were quanta and curved space-time objectively existing throughout the evolution of the universe, independent of human concepts, or are they simply theoretical constructs created in this century? Once again, an affirmative response to the first alternative can be reached only with a great leap of faith; yet if we go along with the latter, we implicitly endorse the "know nothing" attitude of solipisism.

Where do we go from here? What is needed is a *centrist view* that avoids the extremes of both scientific realism and instrumentalism, for the former is unfounded and the latter is impotent. As we begin to explore a middle way between these extremes, let us review some of the brilliant insights and reflections of modern physicists. Perhaps these will shed light on the path for us to follow. Let us begin by keeping in mind Heisenberg's statement that what we observe is not nature in itself but nature exposed to our method of questioning. Although this assertion does not encourage us in the belief that we can know the physical world as it exists independent of the human mind, it does allow for knowledge relative to our method of questioning. Einstein sheds further light on this issue with his statement that it is the theory which decides what we can observe, and also that scientific theories are free creations of the human mind. In the scientific context, then, theory and observation are inextricably interrelated, and both are dependent upon the human mind.

Heisenberg, Born, and other physicists promoted the principle of not attributing existence to that which cannot be known even in principle. A major theme that emerges from quantum mechanics is that subatomic entities as they exist in their own right, independent of our systems of measurement, are unknowable. Need we limit this statement to the quantum world alone? Has it not become apparent that the entire universe as it exists in its own nature, independent of human concepts, is unknowable in terms of human thought? This view was certainly expressed by Jules-Henri Poincaré when he declared that a reality completely independent of the mind that conceives it, sees it, or feels it, is an impossibility.

How can we even consider the possibility of renouncing belief in an independent physical world? How else can we account for such things as (1) the coordination of an individual's various sensory perceptions—for example, we can see, touch, smell, and taste the food that we eat; (2) the commonality of different people's experience—people living together share much of their experience of their environment; and (3) the causal interactions that evidently occur in the natural world, regardless of anyone's awareness of them? The assertion of a physical world existing independently of consciousness certainly provides the obvious reason for the above events. And, as with the case of Euclidean geometry, we may find it impossible to conceive of an alternative. The truth of the axioms of Euclidean geometry seems intuitively obvious, and it went virtually unchallenged by even the most brilliant minds of Europe for almost two millennia. But finally, in the nineteenth century, mathematicians explored alternative geometries and thereby helped to revolutionize modern science and mathematics.

There are a few contemporary scientists who are exploring alternatives to the unquestioned belief in an independent physical world. What do we sacrifice if we join in their reflections? The preceding critique of realism casts grave doubt on the belief that science or mathematics has or ever will reveal anything about the nature of this hypothetical objective world. And instrumentalism rejects the possibility of knowing anything about a world independent of experience. Where does this leave us? Kant held that there is an independent world of things in themselves, but that the only thing we can know about it is that it exists. (He also believed that Euclid's axioms are necessarily true.) But what good does this belief do us? Since scientific research has no indubitable access to such a world, it would not be impaired by questioning that belief. Indeed, this assumption rides along with the growth of scientific knowledge like so much useless baggage.

Is it not possible to imagine meaningful alternatives to the metaphysical axiom of an independent physical world? If the above phenomena of commonality of experience and so forth can be reasonably accounted for without this assumption, we can conclude that there is no logical imperative for that belief. We have already encountered arguments that suggest that the contents of such an independent world are unknowable in principle. We now face the deeper question as to whether the very existence of such a world is similarly unknowable. If so, let us follow the lead of Heisenberg and his fellow physicists in not positing the existence of such unknowables.

Let us turn now to some of the alternative perspectives that have been posed by contemporary scientists. Recall physicist John Gribbin's speculation that nuclei and positrons did not exist prior to the twentieth century, since no one before 1900 ever saw one. Here is a radical departure from both scientific realism and instrumentalism. He seems to suggest that atomic nuclei do not exist independently in the objective world, but neither are they purely conceptual constructs having no physical reality. Rather, he implies, they were brought into existence by our conception of them. Note that the term *conception* has been used in both senses of origination and of cogitation. Physicist Bernard d'Espagnat makes a similar point when he writes: "Our existence contributes to causing particles to emerge from a reality, which is an indivisible whole, in a (phenomenal) reality extended in space-time."[1]

This view as we have set it forth thus far entails a serious limitation. If the entities that have been proposed by physicists in this century did not exist before they were conceived, they can hardly be used to explain the origins and evolution of the cosmos. They would suddenly appear, as it were, out of nowhere, bearing no relevance to the physical world prior to their conception. Moreover, if the objects of the macroworld are made up of the very elements that are conceived in physics, they, too, would not exist before they are thought of and labeled. But how can this be if, as cosmology tells us, the universe existed long before the appearance of human beings?

Before rejecting this notion out of hand, let us take a closer look at a concept that is central to this issue, namely time itself. Modern science has adopted a realist view concerning the nature of time, as if it exists in its own nature, apart from experience, with real entities embedded in it like objects carried along by a stream. "Time passes," we say, and things are thought to change and events to occur in the course of time. Although Einstein banished Newton's assumption of absolute time, he still maintained that it exists independently in nature. What we experience, however, is change, and upon close inspection it seems that time is simply a concept that we impute on change. In fact, both time and space appear to be relative not only to specific physical frames of reference but to our experience of them. Surely we know nothing of time or space as they exist independently of our observations. If, in rejecting scientific realism, we disclaim knowledge of an independent physical world, we must also abandon any notion of objective time and space in which that hypothetical world might exist.[2]

What are some of the implications of this view? Theoretical physicist John Wheeler speculates that the whole universe may be a participatory, self-excited circuit. Due to "acts of observer-participancy," he asserts, we may give tangible reality not only to the universe as it exists now but as it was in the beginning: by observing and interpreting the photons of the cosmic background radiation, we thereby "create" the Big Bang and the evolution of the universe.[3] Thus, relative to our twentieth-century scientific perspective, the Big Bang occurred roughly twenty billion years ago, and it was followed by the formation of subatomic elements, atoms, molecules, and so forth that we conceive of today. Conception, in experientially relative time, is therefore retroactive.

Such theories presently contemplated by some physicists are associated with a theme known as the *anthropic principle*. Expressed in different ways by Robert Dicke, Brandon Carter, and John Wheeler, its central message is that our existence determines the design of our universe, and, conversely, the design of the universe makes possible our existence.[4] Astronomer Edward Harrison states this principle succinctly when he writes: "The anthropic principle asserts that the universe is the way it is because we are here."[5]

Some interpretation of the anthropic principle appears as a possible avenue to explore as we seek a middle path between the philosophical extremes of realism and instrumentalism.[6] Realism maintains that although the real world exists independently of our concepts, it can be grasped by them. The anthropic principle, as put forth by the physicists cited above, suggests that the world that we experience can be grasped by thought because it owes its very existence to our concepts. The two are mutually interdependent. The universe that we observe is then a human-oriented world, and it would not exist apart from our presence in it.

Modern science was initiated together with the attempt to banish anthropocentricity from our knowledge of the world. Yet it assumed that the world that exists independently of human thought can be comprehended in terms of human thought. How was this assumption justified? The belief that God created the universe, that He created us in His own image and spoke to us in a language that we can comprehend may have had a lot to do with it. Moreover, the early founders of modern science, such as Descartes and Galileo, believed that God created the world in accordance with mathematical principles. Hence, they felt justified in regarding mathematics as essentially divine. This view encourages the assumption that mathematics somehow transcends mere human language and logic. Note, for instance, Galileo's statement: "We do not learn to demonstrate from the manuals of logic, but from the books which are full of demonstrations, which are the mathematical and not the logical."[7] This view has been challenged by the formulation of non-Euclidean geometries and recent research into the foundations of mathematics, and its justification on theological grounds is not widely claimed within the scientific community. Nevertheless, it is still held by many physicists today. This is illustrated, for example, in this declaration by Richard Feynman: "If you want to learn about nature, to appreciate nature, it is necessary to understand the language that she speaks in. She offers her information only in one form; we are not so unhumble as to demand that she change before we pay attention."[8]

Scientific realism asserts that a universe independent of human concepts is nevertheless understandable in terms of those concepts (mathematical or otherwise). While it displaces humankind from the center of the universe, it grants human concepts the virtually divine capacity to comprehend that universe. The anthropic principle reasserts the essential role of human beings in the universe that is experienced by human beings. This is not to say that the universe, including all other sentient beings, will vanish when we disappear as a race; rather, only the world that we experience will vanish. The universes that are experienced by other conscious beings will continue to exist in relation to them. From this perspective, living creatures play a participatory role in the worlds in which they dwell.

The idea of a participatory universe is in fact not new to Western culture. Philosopher Owen Barfield goes so far as to claim that the whole basis of epistemology from Aristotle to St. Thomas Aquinas assumed participation. Thinkers of that period differed only in terms of the precise manner in which that participation operated.[9] Aquinas, for example, holds that a phenomenon achieves full reality (*actus*) only in being named or thought by man.[10] The concept of a participatory universe thus has roots in both our Greek and Christian heritages. While it was stifled at the birth of modern science in the sixteenth century, recent advances in physics have brought our attention back to this view. Let us investigate some of the problems that face it in our search for a centrist view of scientific knowledge.

Chapter Fifteen

Cosmology and a Participatory Universe

Perhaps the chief objection to the idea of a participatory universe stems from the belief that the mind is an accidental side effect of matter. Some believe that the mind is purely a function of the brain, others seek to equate mental events with neurological processes, and still others speculate that the mind does not exist at all.[1] How then could the mind, which exists at most as a mere epiphenomenon of matter, play such a crucial role in the existence of the cosmos?

This objection can be countered with the argument that Western science simply does not comprehend the nature of the mind. Physical science is based upon the metaphysical assumption that the mind lies outside of nature and plays no active role in it. In the words of physicist Erwin Schrödinger: "Without being aware of it, we exclude the Subject of Cognizance from the domain of nature that we endeavour to understand. We step with our own person back into the part of an onlooker who does not belong to the world, which by this very process becomes an objective world."[2] Schrödinger's own view is that this world is in fact "a construct of our sensations, perceptions, memories."[3]

With its assumption of a mindless universe, physical science has developed no empirical or theoretical tools for understanding the nature of the mind. Its mechanical, quantitative means of research have yielded much information about inanimate physical processes, but they were never meant to be applied to any nonphysical events. As a rule in science, to know what we are measuring, we must know the function of our measuring device. The most fundamental measuring device in physics is the human mind, for without it nothing would be observed at all. Yet physicists are given no training in understanding the nature of this indispensable element of their research.

Western science, in forming physical theories, has frequently made use of Occam's razor to cut away presumably superfluous considerations. But which elements are superfluous? Which data are crucial and which are "garbage"? Once again metaphysical predilection, not nature alone, comes into play. Modern Western science has assumed from the outset that the mind plays no role in nature, and this belief effectively screens out empirical evidence to the contrary. Wielding Occam's razor, materialism carves out a theory of a mindless universe, and physicists conclude that there is no evidence for the existence of any nonphysical, supernatural mind. Since science lacks a coherent theory of the mind, evidence for its active role in nature is generally dismissed as spurious or anecdotal; or it may simply remain unnoticed altogether.

As physicist Eugene Wigner points out, "we do not know of any phenomenon in which one subject is influenced by another without exerting an influence thereupon."[4] Why then should we simply assume that physical phenomena influence the mind without reciprocation? The notion that the mind is nonphysical does not necessarily imply that it lies outside of nature or is supernatural.

Over the history of science, various phenomena have been considered to lie outside the province of science. Until the work of Rutherford in 1911, the interior of the atom was regarded as simply a subject of metaphysical speculation. But new tools of research were developed, it was brought under close scientific scrutiny.

Many contemporary biologists similarly dismiss consciousness from the realm of natural science. Lacking the tools for dealing with it, they discard it as a mere epiphenomenon of the brain. However, rather than nurturing this ignorance of our most basic instrument of research—the human mind—we must develop means to directly, empirically examine its nature.

The idea of a participatory universe may also be opposed on cosmological grounds. The most recent estimates of the age of the universe since the Big Bang are around twenty billion years; and until about three billion years ago, the universe was presumably devoid of consciousness or any life-forms. Since the physical universe preceded the appearance of any sentient beings, how can its existence hinge upon participation by such beings?

Modern cosmology is based upon the assumption that mind and life are simply products of matter and energy, so it was a foregone conclusion that any theory of the cosmos would leave the emergence of consciousness as an accidental afterthought of inert physical processes. This is by no means the only metaphysical assumption that underlies this science. Another central feature of cosmology is known as the *containment principle*, which states that the physical universe contains everything that is physical and nothing else. This principle may be regarded as a mere definition or as a tautology. Any further content of that principle is of a metaphysical, not a scientific, nature.

The Friedmann equation, which is instrumental in determining the age of the universe, applies only to an idealized universe that is entirely free of irregularity. In such a uniform cosmos we are free to study any minute part in space and time and to regard that as representative of the whole.[5] This cosmic assumption is crucial for performing calculations, but on what grounds can we safely conclude that the vast reaches of the universe have such uniformity? This assumption, known as the *cosmological principle*, is acknowledged by astronomers to be "mostly philosophical. It has not been adequately tested, and indeed adequate tests may never be possible."[6]

The problem of multiple, incompatible theories equally accounting for the same empirical evidence is as pertinent in cosmology as it is in particle physics. As Dennis Sciama writes in *Modern Cosmology:* "A rigid theory has not yet been discovered. For instance, general relativity, which is the best theory of space, time and gravitation that has so far been proposed, is, as we shall see, consistent with an infinite number of possibilities, or models, for the history of the Universe."[7] He follows this statement, however, by expressing his realist assumption that not more than one of those models can be correct. There is a great element of faith here that some day a theory will be conceived that uniquely accounts for the phenomena in the one correct way. Such faith persists among realists despite the fact that the entire history of science shows evidence to the contrary.

All interpretations of the empirical data analyzed in cosmology are made upon the basis of premises that lie outside the domain of natural science. In physics these are called principles; the initial assumptions of mathematics are regarded as axioms; philosophy calls them self-evident truths; and religion acknowledges them as articles of faith. Without such assumptions, none of those branches of human understanding would be able to operate at all. But it should be recognized that the principles of cosmology are no more scientific truths than are the principles of scholastic theology. On the surface of a vast ocean of metaphysical assumptions, cosmology spreads a thin film of scientific, quantitative conclusions about the entire evolution of the universe.

The quest for knowledge of the universe from God's perspective—to attain, in effect, divine knowledge—has been a common theme in the history of science. It may be argued that Copernicus was concerned with the movement of the planets not from an earthly, human perspective but from an absolute, divine perspective. Similarly, Galileo considered mathematical knowledge of the physical world to be on a par with divine knowledge. This aspiration for absolute knowledge of absolute reality has persisted even among many physicists who have renounced belief in God. God may not exist, they imply, but His absolute view of reality remains; and it is for scientists to discover that view.

Such an attitude is clearly evident in Einstein's writings. On the one hand, he finds the concept of a personal God utterly incompatible with science, and even declares that such a concept is the major source of conflict between religion and science.[8] On the other hand, he declares his "firm belief, a belief bound up with deep feeling, in a superior mind that reveals itself in the world of experience."[9] This superior mind has an absolute perspective on reality but does not influence natural events in any way. Other physicists go a step further by rejecting any concept of God whatever, yet persisting in their belief in an absolute perspective on nature, sometimes called a view from nowhere.

As we attend to cosmology's description of the evolution of the universe from the Big Bang up to the emergence of life on our planet, a series of images of these events are brought to mind. We may imagine something like a cosmic firecracker at the beginning, red-hot gases expanding in space; the formation of radiant, bright stars; a molten, lifeless planet; and finally nucleotides that mysteriously transform into living, conscious creatures.

Upon reflection, it becomes obvious that none of these images existed in nature, for they are human constructs based upon our conscious, visual experience. While texts on cosmology may display vivid artist's portrayals of the formation of stars and planets, such images may be profoundly misleading. They presumably depict these events as they would have appeared if humans had been on the scene to witness them. But cosmology denies that human consciousness was present, so they never looked like those illustrations. Indeed, in a cosmos devoid of consciousness, they never looked like anything at all. No images are appropriate. Nevertheless, they do come to mind; and the tendency is to reify them, to assume that they existed in a mindless universe all on their own.[10]

Before Copernicus, Western civilization assumed that Earth is physically located at the center of the universe. The Scientific Revolution challenged this view, and since then we have committed ourselves to the opposite extreme: the universe that we perceive and conceive is wholly independent of human existence, and the presence of life and consciousness in the cosmos is merely an accidental by-product of configurations of matter and energy. This materialist view is propounded as a scientific conclusion, thereby shifting a subject—the origin and nature of life and consciousness—from the domains of philosophy and religion to that of science. Indeed, contemporary cosmology increasingly attempts to don the mantle of "divine" scientific knowledge of the fundamental issues of human existence.

Harvard astrophysicist Eric Chaisson's popular book *Cosmic Dawn: The Origins of Matter and Life* is particularly outspoken in its claim to displace philosophical and religious speculation with empirical scientific knowledge. Who are we? Where did we come from? How do we relate to the rest of the universe? What is our destiny? What are the origin and destiny of the earth, the sun and the universe? All of these questions are purportedly being resolved by contemporary scientific research and dramatic technological advances.

What, according to this view, is the nature of human existence? Each of us is a cluster of genes, inherited from our many ancestral life-forms and shaped by our environment. How did life originate? The author presents the two major views of modern scientists: (1) our existence is merely one instance of what is probably a frequent occurrence throughout the cosmos, since life is based on a few of the universe's most common molecules; and (2) "intelligent life on Earth is the product of inconceivably fortunate accidents—astrophysical and biochemical mistakes that are unlikely to occur anywhere else in the Galaxy or the Universe.[11]

Biochemists have indeed formed a consensus that life evolved purely from matter and energy within the special field of study of biochemistry, yet they do not really know how life actually emerged from nonliving substances. In other words, despite this lack of knowledge, there is conformity of belief as to the origin of life in the universe. Chaisson speculates that prebiological substances probably found shelter from solar ultraviolet radiation on earth; and from that point on "biologists can only presume that at least one proteinoid-like amalgam was eventually able to evolve into something everyone would agree is a genuine living cell."[12] He points out, however, that nothing yet discovered in the fossil record documents this pre-life evolutionary phase.

In seeking to understand such events as the origin of life, modern science concerns itself solely with physical evidence, such as fossil records and biochemical processes. Obviously, even before conducting research, twentieth-century scientists had already adopted a uniform metaphysical assumption that the only influences on life's origins were of a physical nature. This consensus is derived directly from the popular mechanistic materialism of the last century, which was no more truly scientific that its present incarnation. Most astonishing of all, biochemists lack both conclusive physical evidence and a compelling coherent theory to account for the emergence of life. Yet we are still led to believe that their musings count as scientific knowledge in place of philosophical and religious speculation.[13] Once again, scientific ignorance describes what probably happened by accident.

The point here is not to place scientific inquiry into the origins of life on the same plane as all theological and philosophical speculation. Such notions by theologians and philosophers are often devoid of any empirical basis accessible to human beings, and they provide no program for further investigation. Scientists theorizing about the origins of life do have some empirical basis—be it ever so partial—and they do have an avenue for further research. The point is that the type of evidence that biochemists seek is already largely determined by their preconceived metaphysical beliefs. While such assumptions suggest some programs for further investigation, they refute the value of others that might be at least as illuminating as the ones they do follow. Those same metaphysical beliefs, then, exert a strong influence on the manner in which empirical evidence is interpreted.

Biology displays a similar ignorance as to the nature of consciousness. This, however, does not prevent Chaisson from stating unequivocally that "the body's nervous system, of which the brain is the paramount part, controls all mental and physical activity. In fact, every thought, feeling or action begins in the brain."[14] He also states that the first animals—the earliest ancestors of humans—appeared less than a billion years ago. Noting this, our interest may quicken as we seek an answer to the origin of consciousness in the universe; for if those first animals were our earliest ancestors, it must have been in them that consciousness first arose. The stupendous, cosmic event—the birth of consciousness—unfortunately slips by unnoticed in Chaisson's account of the universe. The subject is never addressed, and consciousness is vaguely attributed to a certain "complexity" of configurations of matter and energy.[15]

As science has distanced itself from the medieval notion of an anthropocentric universe, it has identified itself with a diametrically opposite metaphysical stance: human existence has no place in the universe at all. Life itself is an insignificant accident in terms of the cosmos as a whole, human existence is a matter of genes dominated by environment, and consciousness has no existence at all apart from certain neurophysiological processes. Chaisson encourages his readers to regard such cosmic evolution as "wonderfully warm and enlightening," and he concludes his book with the proffered hope: "We may eventually gain control of the resources of much of the Universe, redesigning it to suit our purposes and, in effect, ensuring for our civilization a sense of immortality."[16] Many other scientists and nonscientists fail to succumb to the enchantment of such megalomania and are more drawn to the conclusion of physicist Steven Weinberg: "The more the universe seems comprehensible, the more it also seems pointless."[17]

The concept of a participatory universe is fundamentally incompatible not with scientific knowledge of the cosmos but with the mechanistic materialism that is still so prevalent in modern cosmology and science as a whole. Participation implies an interaction between consciousness and its objects, and insight into the nature of such participation requires knowledge of both the mind and the physical world. Natural science has illuminated many facets of physical reality, but it has kept us completely in the dark as to the nature of consciousness. Moreover, in failing to acknowledge its own metaphysical bearings, it proclaims its materialist biases as scientific conclusions and mistakes its ignorance of the nonphysical for knowledge that only the physical exists. A science that claims the entire cosmos as its domain must seek knowledge of all facets of reality. As Edwin Burtt commented in *The Metaphysical Foundations of Modern Physical Science:* "An adequate cosmology will only begin to be written when an adequate philosophy of mind has appeared."[18]

Chapter Sixteen

Concept and Experience

Scientific realism regards science as a means of exploring the universe as it exists from an absolute, objective perspective. For the early founders of modern science, this perspective was that of the omniscient Creator. Though many contemporary scientists have abandoned this belief, the underlying assumption remains: like the Cheshire cat who leaves only his grin behind, God disappears, but His absolute perspective lingers on. Let us now explore a middle way, or a *centrist view* that avoids the pitfalls of both realism and instrumentalism. If in so doing, we follow the principle of unknowability, then we are free to reject the belief in an absolute perspective and in a universe that appears uniquely to it. The centrist view developed in this and the following chapters is based on the Madhyamaka (or "middle") view of Buddhism, as expounded by the Indian contemplatives Nāgārjuna (second century), Candrakīrti (seventh century), and the Tibetan contemplative Tsongkhapa (fourteenth century).

Realism assumes that the objects and events in nature define themselves in ways that can be grasped by the human mind, for example, through the language of mathematics. Einstein expressed this view in his comment that the most incomprehensible thing about nature is that it is comprehensible. A centrist view, on the other hand, challenges the assumption that physical reality defines itself in terms of mathematics or any other human language or concepts. It proposes, rather, that nature does not define itself at all. If objects and events in nature did define themselves—if every entity intrinsically bore its own attributes and were absolutely demarcated from other entities—then all possible languages should, in principle, be able to be mapped precisely onto each other. Definitions of subatomic particles, animals, utensils, and so on would be exclusively determined from the side of those objects. Theory would indeed be derived solely from observation. All the languages of the world, insofar as they accurately represent reality, would have to be composed of terms that were precisely inter-translatable. Any linguist knows that this is not the case. Definitions of terms, grammar, and syntax all vary widely among languages, and often the more distant the origins of two languages, the more pronounced the differences. The axioms, definitions, and rules of mathematics also vary from one system to another, as is true of other systems of human logic.

According to the centrist view, human beings define the objects and events of the world that we experience. Those things do not exist intrinsically, or absolutely, as we define them or conceive of them. They do not exist intrinsically at all. But this is not to say that they do not exist. The entities that we identify exist in relation to us, and they perform the functions that we attribute to them. But their very existence, as we define them, is dependent upon our verbal and conceptual designations. Thus, the world that we experience is related to human language, and the fact that it is humanly comprehensible presents no mystery at all. On this subject Benjamin Lee Whorf writes: "The idea, entirely unfamiliar to the modern world, that nature and language are inwardly akin, was for ages known to various high cultures whose historical continuity on the earth has been enormously longer than that of Western European culture."[1]

Everything in the world that we conceive of and experience is related to the human mind. When that world is reified, however, it appears to exist absolutely, in its own right; and this mental distortion may lead one to wonder how nature can be comprehensible to the human mind. Einstein, who routed absolute space and time from the universe, still clung to an absolute ontology. The centrist view presented here, which might be called *conceptual relativity*, fundamentally challenges the realist ontological assumptions underlying virtually all of Western science. Theory, in the form of conceptual designation, permeates our experience. As theory is not purely determined by some intrinsic nature of reality, there is no one conceptual system that uniquely accounts for the myriad of natural phenomena. Objects exist relative to the theory-laden consciousness that experiences them.

From a centrist perspective, ontological absolutism is based on the mental distortion known as reification. Reification in science is quite similar to the same process in everyday life. This stands to reason, since scientific inquiry itself bears so much in common with ordinary mental activity. Einstein made the following distinction between the two: "The scientific way of forming concepts differs from that which we use in our daily life, not basically, but merely in the more precise definition of concepts and conclusions; more painstaking and systematic choice of experimental material; and greater logical economy."[2]

The process of reification, as we have noted previously, forms the basis for everyday realism, and it is present even in young children. According to the child psychologist Jean Piaget, a child first constructs a concept related to the world and then projects it out into the world. The concept is externalized so that it appears to be a perceptually given object or property, independent of the subject's own mental activity.[3] As we can see from our own experience, the phenomena that we perceive in the external world appear to exist independently of our perceptions and conceptions. Here is perhaps the most fundamental reason for believing in an objective universe independent of consciousness: that is simply how the world appears. But does the world in fact exist the way it appears, or is its mode of existence incongruous with its mode of appearance?

Everyday and scientific realism differ, however, in the types of things that are reified. Whereas the former chiefly reifies objects and properties that appear to our senses, the latter reifies the existence of noumenal entities that lie behind appearances. Thus, subatomic particles, electromagnetic fields, and the zero-point energy of the vacuum are assumed to exist independently of the experimental data on which they are based and independently of the theories in which they are conceived. That is, they really exist "out there" in the objective world, independent of human existence.

The tendency of reification among mathematicians is particularly interesting. Philip Davis and Reuben Hersh comment in their book *Descartes' Dream: The World According to Mathematics* that many modern mathematicians regard their discipline as a system of deductive structures in which deduction moves from axioms to conclusions, and the axioms are "simply playthings." This attitude suggests a formalist view of mathematics, one that Davis and Hersh assert is generally instilled into today's students. Yet in a later chapter, they claim that nearly all mathematicians hold a Platonist conception of mathematics nearly all the time.[4] This view asserts that mathematics exists independently of the world; it exists prior to and apart from the universe, and it will go on even when the cosmos comes to an end. Thus, the world of mathematics exists independently of the mathematician, whose job is to discover and record what is already out there. What is this telling us? It would seem that most mathematicians, when they philosophize about mathematics, profess a formalist view, but the rest of the time (especially when they are actually doing mathematics) they revert to a realist stance. This may well be true of many scientists as well. The natural tendency of reification, which we have had since childhood, is extremely difficult to eradicate from our habits of thinking and perceiving.

Both in scientific research and in everyday experience we ascertain objects that are endowed with certain attributes, and it is by means of the defining characteristics of an object that we identify it. From a centrist perspective, we assert that entities do not determine their own defining characteristics; that is, they are not self-defining. Having recognized a certain object, we say that it has the qualities by which we identify it. Now we may ask: what is the relationship between an object and its various attributes?

If language and concepts were mere superimpositions on preexistent objects objectively discovered through direct observation, then an examination of our language usage would probably not yield any insight into the nature of existence of those objects. If, however, as the centrist view proposes, phenomena are brought into existence through the processes of verbal and conceptual designation, then their very nature is defined by language usage: the relationship between an object and its attributes is determined by the way we speak and think about them. This crucial assumption underlies the following analyses. If it seems at times as if this investigation is placing too much weight on common language usage, consider the alternative: as Wittgenstein pointed out, thinkers who ignore the consensual use of language run the danger of making their own philosophies, not common language, irrelevant to the rest of the world.

Let us focus for the moment on a physical entity and assume, in accordance with the realist view, that it and its attributes exist intrinsically, independent of conceptual designation. Take, for example, an oxygen molecule: It has a certain mass, charge, and size and is made up of two atoms. Is this molecule identical with any one of those qualities or parts? Is it, for instance, identical with its mass? If so, is it really suitable to say that the mass of the molecule has a charge, neutral or otherwise? Might we not equally say that the molecule *is* its charge, and that its charge has a mass? Actually neither statement is true of physical theory. An oxygen molecule has mass and charge, but it is identical with neither. Nor can it be equated with either of its component atoms, for it would be pointless to say that one of its atoms has the other.

We might easily equate the oxygen molecule with the set of all its attributes and parts, for it is true that this set does have all the characteristics of the molecule. However, the qualm arises: is this molecule not endowed with the set of all its attributes? If it has that set of attributes, it is difficult to assert that it *is* that set. How can anything be identical with something that it has? If this were possible, we would have to assert that an oxygen molecule has itself, but this suggests that for every such molecule there would be two molecules: the molecule that has the complete set of its attributes, and the molecule that is the complete set of those attributes.

A second problem is that if something is identical with an oxygen molecule, everything that is true of the latter must be true of the former. Let us take the event of two such molecules colliding. When they do so, one side—let us say the "north side"—of one molecule strikes the "south side" of another. When that happens, we correctly state that one molecule struck another. Is it equally correct to say that the complete set of attributes of one molecule struck the complete set of the other's attributes? The complete set obviously includes all the attributes and components; but it is not true that the "west sides" of both molecules struck one another.

Finally, what is the nature of this complete set of attributes? It is not identical with any one of its components. In fact, it seems to be a prime example of a conceptual designation without any independent referent in physical reality. Thus, if the oxygen molecule is identical with that set, it too must have no independent existence.

Alternatively, we might posit that this molecule is identical with a few of its attributes, such as its mass, charge, and size. These three entities, however, are mutually exclusive: there is nothing that is the mass of a molecule as well as its charge and size. This would be like saying that there is one thing that is the hoof of a camel as well as its tail and its head. Those three entities have very different characteristics, and there is nothing that can be all three. Certainly a camel is not its hoof, any more than a molecule is its mass.

In short, the oxygen molecule cannot be equated with any one or more of its attributes, nor is it identical with the set of all its attributes. It *has* those characteristics, but it *is* none of them. Does such a molecule exist intrinsically apart from all its components? If so, it should be possible to remove all of them, leaving the molecule on its own. But a molecule devoid of mass, charge, size, and so on can hardly be called a molecule, nor can it perform any of the functions of a molecule.

If a molecule does not intrinsically exist either among its parts or separate from them, the inevitable conclusion seems to be that it does not intrinsically exist at all. We must hasten to add that this statement does not imply that molecules and the myriad of atomic and sub-atomic entities described by particle physics have no existence whatever. If such entities can be asserted on experimental grounds and if the theories in which they are proposed are internally consistent, they do exist and are identified by their defining characteristics. But they do not exist independently of the theory in which they are introduced. Rather, they exist in dependence on conceptual designation, and their existence is of a *conventional*, not an *absolute*, nature. According to the centrist view, conventional existence does not imply arbitrariness; rather, it suggests that such existence is contingent upon language and concepts. The notion of absolute existence, on the other hand, implies existence that is independent of all verbal and conceptual designation.

When investigating the relation between scientific theory and reality, we may ask ourselves: is this entity—such as energy, a quark, or a graviton—simply a conceptual construct, or does it exist in the physical world? A common assumption underlying this question is that if something is merely a conceptual construct, it does not exist in nature; and if something actually participates in physical interactions, it must be independent of our concepts. The centrist view we are developing here challenges this assumption by suggesting that the entities conceived by scientists do perform the functions attributed to them in nature, but they do not exist independently of scientific theorizing. Such entities are brought into existence by the process of conceptual designation: we designate certain experimental phenomena as evidence for the existence of energy, quarks, and so on; and as that convention is accepted, the designated entity exists. But had the entity never been conceived, it would not exist at all. Moreover, as suggested previously, the conceptual designation of an object is retroactive: for example, once electrons have been conceived, they can be said to have existed for many billions of years in the past.

A major attribute of modern Western science has been that it has continuously sought to expand and refine our experience of physical reality by means of increasingly sophisticated instruments and experiments. A physical theory based on early experience may not accord with later, more revealing, experimental evidence. How then can we establish that our physical theories accord with experience, when we do not know what future research will bring to light? We can try to recognize the limitations of our present methods of questioning and to be cautious when extrapolating about the physical world as it exists apart from those modes of inquiry and experimentation. In this way our theories can be regarded as conventionally valid within the context of our experience, and they are left open for modification in light of new empirical discoveries.

Despite some claims from the domain of quantum theory, there seem to be no grounds for setting an artificial ontological demarcation between the world of particle physics and the world of everyday experience. A large quantity of particles in a certain configuration certainly may be able to perform functions that the individual particles cannot; but this can hardly imbue them with a more concrete ontological status. If the basic components of the physical world lack intrinsic existence independent of conceptual designation, the same must be true of the physical universe as a whole. Thus, if the elementary particles of which the physical world is composed do not exist independently of conceptual designation, there can be little doubt that macroscopic configurations of such particles similarly lack independent existence.

If one accepts this conclusion, it might be tempting to slip off into a form of idealism, positing mind alone as the absolute reality. Let us see, however, if this view is justified. According to the centrist view, a physical process exists in dependence upon three factors: (1) its own components and attributes, (2) other causally related physical and mental entities, and (3) the mental designation of that process. Similarly, a cognition of a physical process depends upon (1) its own components and attributes, (2) other causally related mental and physical entities, and (3) the mental designation of that cognition. Physical and mental events are mutually dependent, and there is no self-apparent reason for assuming either type of phenomenon to be more real than the other.

The preceding analysis suggests that an oxygen molecule is conceptually designated upon its attributes, and neither the molecule nor its components exists independently in physical reality. The mass of a molecule, for instance, can no more exist independently of the molecule than the molecule can exist apart from it. Moreover, both are also dependent upon the conceptual designations of them. Is the case fundamentally different for a subjective sensation, say a visual image? This sensation, too, has various qualities. Following the same line of reasoning as above, can a visual image be equated with any one or more of its characteristics? The previous analysis still applies. The image cannot be equated with any of its attributes, nor does it exist intrinsically apart from them. It, too, is conceptually designated upon its defining characteristics, and it is neither ascertained, nor does it exist, apart from them. The boundaries that set such sensations apart from other entities are not determined by nature; that is, they are not intrinsic to those entities themselves. Rather, they are imputed by language and concepts. In the words of Benjamin Lee Whorf: "Each language performs this artificial chopping up of the continuous spread and flow of existence in a different way."[5]

Is the situation any different for consciousness itself? The various types of sensory and mental consciousness all have their own characteristics. The awareness, or consciousness, of a visual image, for example, has certain qualities by means of which we recognize it. A continuum of sensory awareness also has parts, being composed of a series of extremely brief moments of cognition. That continuum is not identical with any single instant of awareness. Is this awareness equivalent to the sum of all of them? This cannot be, for the sum total of those moments does not exist at the time of any one of those instants; yet it would be absurd to say that awareness does not exist at the time of any single moment of awareness.

A single finite moment of awareness also has parts: it must have a beginning and an end, otherwise it would have no duration. But it is not identical either to its beginning or its end, nor can it be both, for they exist at different times. A moment of cognition has a beginning and an end, but it is equivalent to neither. Nor does it intrinsically exist apart from its temporal components. As mentioned above, a moment of cognition also has various defining attributes that set it apart from other entities. Without analyzing those specific characteristics, it still holds that such cognition has those properties, and as such is conceptually designated upon them. This suggests that the demarcations between awareness and other entities are not determined by their own intrinsic nature. Rather, the conceptual mind defines such entities and, having done so, imputes them upon their bases of designation. A crucial principle of the centrist view is that a designated entity is never identical with the basis on which it is designated. For example, a burst of anger is an entity designated upon the basis of a complex sequence of emotion, awareness, and thought. The mental events upon which the burst of anger is designated are not identical to that anger, nor does the anger exist independently from them. Moreover, if there were any designated object identical to its basis of designation, the former would not be dependent for its existence upon the designation. The centrist view differs from realism on this point.

Now let us turn to the conceptually designating mind. Does it have a different ontological status from the other entities that it identifies? The centrist would say no, for it, too, has attributes; and it is neither identical with them nor intrinsically separate from them. Take for example a mind that conceives of an electron. The electron that is conceived by it does not exist independently of that mind, nor does that mind exist independently of the electron that it conceives. The relationship between the two is not a causal or sequential one. It is more like the relation between a husband and a wife: a man is not a husband unless he has a wife, and a woman is not a wife unless she has a husband. The states of being husband and wife are mutually dependent, yet this relation is not causally sequential; that is, a man does not become a husband before a woman becomes his wife or vice versa.

Does a mind that conceives of an electron depend upon conceptual designation for its existence? A centrist would say yes. In this case the mind conceiving an electron is itself an object designated by another conceptual mind. This latter mind regards the components or attributes of the former mind and designates it as "a mind that conceives of an electron." As in the cases of all other events, the conceptual mind is imputed upon the basis of its own components. It is the designating mind that demarcates its object from other things and identifies that object as *having* its various attributes and functions.

Having inquired into the ontological status of the physical world and the mind, let us move on to the nature of time. Any instance of time has duration. We may speak of the age of the universe or the time that it takes for light to traverse the diameter of a proton—each segment of time has a duration such that its beginning is not simultaneous with its end. Such a period therefore *has* a beginning and an end. It is not identical with its beginning; otherwise it would not exist at its end, and vice versa. Since it is not its beginning or its end, it cannot be both its beginning and its end. One might hypothesize that it is the same as the complete set of its beginning, middle, and end. In that case, however, it would not exist at its beginning, middle, or end; for that complete set is not present at any of those times. It *has* a beginning, middle, and end, but it does not exist independently of them; otherwise it could exist in their absence.

Once again, the centrist view concludes that any period of time is conceptually designated upon something that is not it. It is not findable under analysis, so we conclude that its existence is purely conventional. Thus, time does not exist absolutely, with respect to either physical or mental events. Time as it is conceived by the human mind does not exist in some independent, objective world; it exists only in relation to the mind that conceives it.

What is the centrist view of space? Any region of space, from the volume of a quark to the expanse of the entire universe, has extension. From any given perspective, it has a front side and a back side, and the two are not the same. Analysis similar to that presented above demonstrates that a region of space is not identical with any of its parts, nor with the complete set of its parts. If it were the same as the complete set of its parts, it would never be possible for a body to enter that space; for it is impossible to enter all its parts simultaneously. The body would have to enter the front before it got to the back. Clearly, it is meaningless to speak of space as independent from all its parts, so we once again conclude that space is not absolute: it exists in dependence upon mental designation.

This conclusion holds equally for the modern concept of space-time. If it has no parts or attributes, it must be forever unknowable, in which case there is no reason to posit its existence. If it does have parts, we can apply the same "whole and parts" analysis, and it leads us to the same conclusion: if space-time does exist as it is conceived in the general theory of relativity, it is a conventional reality only. Ontologically speaking, there is no absolute space, time, or space-time.

Even a casual study of Einstein's relativity theories can leave no doubt that his rejection of absolute space and time is of a different kind than the refutation presented here. In the view that we are now exploring, not only the absolute space and time of classical physics but the absolute space-time of relativistic physics is refuted. Space-time as conceived by Einstein may indeed exist, but as a conventional, not an absolute, reality.

In like fashion, in the case of the zero-point energy of the vacuum—be it of zero, finite, or infinite magnitude—similar analysis can be applied. Such vacuum energy is not one with its parts or attributes, nor is it intrinsically separate from them. If it intrinsically possessed its own parts, the demarcations between it and other entities would exist intrinsically and therefore absolutely. In that case, the centrist view hypothesizes, there could be no interrelation between the vacuum energy and matter, for instance. Being absolutely separate, they would be inherently independent and thus could in no way influence one another.

Thus, if the vacuum energy exists, it is a conventional reality. This by no means implies that its existence is arbitrary, or that its interactions with other events are not subject to physical laws. Physical processes and the natural laws that govern them are of a conventional nature only in the sense that they do not exist independently of conceptual designation. The laws of physics, for example, are precisely determined by means of experiment and observation. They are not simply creations of arbitrary human whim. They have no independent existence, however. Such laws are dependent upon the events with which they are concerned. The gravitational inverse-square law, for instance, has no existence independent of matter; nor does that law, as conceived by human beings, exist independently of human conceptual designation. Its existence is relative, not absolute.[6]

According to the centrist view we are developing here, not only physical laws but the rules of mathematics and logic in general are of a conventional, not an absolute, nature. Once again, it must be emphasized that this does not necessarily mean that they are arbitrary. They occur to the human mind in dependence upon our interactions with our environment. They are not created simply by whim. Thus, both mathematics and qualitative logic can be extraordinarily useful tools in probing the nature of reality; but the truths that they reveal do not exist independently of the intelligence that discovers them. Any philosophical system that devalues the rules of logic as being

purely arbitrary must be self-defeating; for it must have some reasons—and therefore some logic—in support of this position. And any
conclusions that such a system draws must therefore also be regarded
as arbitrary.

———————————◆———————————

We may focus finally on reality as a whole, what Whorf perhaps
had in mind when he wrote of the continuous spread and flow of
existence. Does the whole of reality, without making any distinctions
between mind and matter, matter and energy, or microworld and
macroworld, exist in its own right, independent of conceptual designation? We may ask first: is such a reality posited as having parts or
attributes? Is it made up of all the atoms, minds, galaxies, and space-
time of the universe, or does it exist apart from them? If it is made up
of such components, we may apply the same analysis as above and
arrive at the same conclusion: reality as a whole is also a conceptual
designation. If the whole intrinsically exists apart from all the
components of the known universe, this implies that it would remain
even if the universe as we know it were to vanish. But such a cosmic
totality sounds more like a useless metaphysical appendage to reality
rather than something that bears any meaning for those living in the
universe.

By means of such analysis we can inspect anything that is conceived as being existent, and in each case we find that that entity is
known by certain defining characteristics. It *has* those attributes and
cannot be equated with them. Under such analysis, nothing can be
found that exists in its own nature, independent of conceptual designation. Everything is empty of such an intrinsic identity, and that
emptiness may be regarded as its essential nature. Perhaps the physicist Louis de Broglie had some intimation of this truth when he wrote:
"May it not be universally true that the concepts produced by the
human mind, when formulated in a slightly vague form, are roughly
valid for Reality, but that when extreme precision is aimed at, they
become ideal forms whose real content tends to vanish away? It seems
to me that such is, in fact, the case."[7] When phenomena are not closely
examined, they seem to exist in their own nature, independent of conceptual constructs; but when the preceding type of analysis is applied
to them, they seem to vanish away.

Chapter Seventeen

A Centrist View of Physical Science

According to the centrist view developed here, all things, physical, mental, and otherwise, are devoid of an intrinsic nature; yet they still exist on a relative, or conventional, level, and this is sufficient for them to interact with other entities. Neither physical nor mental events are more real than the other; neither bears an absolute existence; so this centrist view is neither materialist nor idealist. The emptiness of an intrinsic nature of all phenomena is itself not an absolute; it, too, lacks an intrinsic nature; so this view also escapes the extreme of nihilism. The logic by means of which such conclusions are drawn is also not grounded in absolute reality. It is considered to be valid, but its authenticity is of a conventional, not an absolute or an independent nature.

This is perhaps the hardest point to comprehend: although phenomena exist merely conventionally, without any intrinsic identity, they do nevertheless interact with one another. By analyzing an entity in terms of the whole and its parts, it is not so difficult to see that there is no entity in itself existing either apart from or among its attributes. Moreover, as we explore the interactions among mental and physical events, it is apparent that orderly causal relationships do occur in nature. It is far more challenging to recognize the compatibility of these two insights. As we seek a middle way between the extremes of metaphysical realism and nihilism, it may be helpful to ponder the following hypotheses: if phenomena were to exist inherently, they would be utterly immutable and incapable of interactions with anything else. It is only due to the very fact that things lack such an intrinsic identity that they are able to exist in relation to other entities. When, by our insight into the lack of intrinsic existence we see more clearly the manner in which causal relationships take place; and when, by our insight into causal interactions we see more clearly the absence of inherent existence of events—then we are well on the way to experiencing the centrist view that avoids both realism and nihilism.

This centrist view certainly does not accord with either realism or instrumentalism as they have been described in the preceding chapters. Insofar as scientific theories are internally consistent and are based upon experience, the events that they describe are granted conventional reality. They do not exist independently of those theories, but neither are they purely mental creations with no referents in physical reality. Physical realism asserts that physical entities exist independently of the mind, and idealism maintains that they are of the same nature as the mind. The centrist view refutes both positions by declaring that the very dichotomy between physical and mental phenomena has only a conventional existence. On the basis of everyday experience, we do identify both physical and mental events and the distinctions between them. In agreement with worldly convention, the centrist view also acknowledges their existence. Mental events are not subsumed under the physical, nor vice versa.

Physics offers us bodies of experimental evidence which can be consistently interpreted in a variety of ways. We may choose among such competing theories and gradually incorporate our choice into our view of physical reality. Western physics, however, does not offer the only valid possibilities for interpreting the nature of the physical world. It has devised a certain approach to gathering empirical evidence of physical events, namely the use of mechanical instruments. Other cultures, such as those of classical India and Tibet, have devised alternate approaches entailing the refinement of human consciousness as a means of empirically investigating physical reality. The evidence that those cultures have brought to light is quite different from that revealed by Western science, but that does not necessarily mean it is any less valuable. Their approach is chiefly qualitative; that of physics is chiefly quantitative; neither has an exclusive claim to validity. In short, on the basis of evidence not presently known to

Western science, alternative physical theories have been devised; and insofar as they are internally consistent and are based upon experience, they, too, are conventionally valid.[1]

If everything that we believe to exist depends upon mental and verbal designation, it follows that different cultures and even different individuals may dwell in diverse conventional realities. First of all, the experiential evidence that they choose to interpret may be different; and secondly, the manner in which they choose to interpret it may also be different. Nevertheless, when we draw back from such analysis, even if we find it persuasive, we look out upon a world that seems to exist entirely in its own right, independent of conceptual imputation. Although the world lacks intrinsic existence, it certainly appears to exist in its own nature. There is, thus, an incongruity between the mode of existence of phenomena and their mode of appearance. Things appear to have a more concrete, or substantial, existence than they actually have; and in this sense they may be likened to illusions, reflections, and mirages.

Such a statement is regarded by some physicists as being incompatible with Western science.[2] However, if physics, from the time of Copernicus onward, has taught us anything about the physical world, it has told us that sensory experience and the common sense based upon it are not infallible guides to the nature of physical reality. Sensory experience clearly demonstrates that the sun revolves around the earth, but Copernicus challenged such appearances with the heliocentric theory. The infallibility of sensory experience has been most dramatically challenged by twentieth-century physics from relativity theory to quantum theory. The innumerable instances of this hardly need to be recounted here. As we continue to explore a centrist view of reality, we shall have some of our most basic assumptions challenged. If we pursue this investigation with an open but critical attitude, checking new hypotheses with logic and experience, we shall be continuing in the true spirit of science rather than breaking away from it.

From the perspective of the centrist view introduced in the previous chapters, we may readdress the question: what knowledge does physics yield concerning the nature of the universe? As we have noted previously, the program of physics has been to make experiment and observation, together with mathematical analysis, the means for understanding physical reality that lies behind appearances. This approach, which is based on the dualism of Descartes, assumes that nature exists independently of the mind and that it bears little resemblance to the world that we perceive directly. Scientific evidence is thus used as a test to confirm or refute physical theories about the world as it exists in a way that transcends experience. Qualms about this juxtaposition of empiricism and transcendentalism are to be relieved with the conviction that the transcendental world of physics is of a mathematical in nature; and that it is by such analysis that its reality can be grasped.

On this metaphysical basis generations of physicists have devised a myriad of theories, based on mathematics, proposing the existence of such theoretical entities, or noumena, as gravity, energy, ether, electromagnetic fields, space-time, and quarks. For such theories to be deemed scientific, they must yield predictions that can be tested empirically. The closely related assumption is that a theory is confirmed when its predictions are borne out empirically. When physics is taught in the classroom and experiments are done in the laboratory, this assumption is generally taken for granted without further reflection: if one's data correspond to the predicted results, the theory in question is deemed true.

Experienced physicists are well aware, in their more reflective moments, that this is a naive assumption. The fact that multiple, conceptually incompatible theories may equally account for the same phenomena was known by the ancient Greeks; it was recognized by the Church at the time of Galileo; it was acknowledged during the late nineteenth century, at the peak of classical physics; and it is no secret in contemporary physics. When presented with this fact, a realist may respond that verification of a theory on the basis of its ability to predict phenomena does not confirm that it is true; but by a gradual process of elimination, false theories are empirically eliminated, thereby yielding an ever closer approximation of truth.

As demonstrated earlier, such a view is above all an expression of faith that is based not on historical evidence or present scientific grounds but on hope. If our previous critique of scientific realism is valid, empirical science has never been successful in yielding knowledge of a transcendent world independent of experience. Its assertions of the existence of noumena lurking independently behind the veil of appearances are verified neither by direct experience nor inference.

How can we know whether the noumena of modern physical theories exist or not? Shall we conceptually "hold them in custody," in the ontological limbo of being neither existent nor nonexistent? Or, if we find our minds overcrowded with these theoretical suspects, shall we conceptually release them as nonexistent until experiential verification to the contrary is produced? It hardly needs to be said that experiential verification does not occur when a theory that incorporates such noumena yields an empirically confirmed prediction. From a realist perspective, such circumstantial evidence neither confirms nor denies the existence of the noumena proposed in physics, so it must be thrown out of court. Regardless of the quantity of such evidence, it does not justify the conviction that the noumenon in question exists.

We may propose new criteria based upon centrist principles for determining the existence of the noumena of modern physics. Let us begin with Karl Popper's assertion that scientific theories are subject to refutation but not to ultimate verification. From the perspective of scientific realism, this view leaves us in limbo, for science never guarantees that its hypothetical entities exist in the real world. Indeed, theoretical entities may be discarded not only by new scientific insights but by shifts in the zeitgeist of the societies in which science is practiced. How then can we ever say with confidence that any of the theoretical entities exist? Before setting forth our criteria for existence, we must reemphasize the centrist theme that we can know of nothing that exists in its own nature independent of the mind that cognizes it. Scientific research is a participatory act that reveals events in relation to our theoretical and empirical modes of inquiry.

To set forth our criteria for existence, let us return to the example of the zero-point energy of the vacuum. Among the various theories that we explored, recall the interpretation from quantum field theory that the energy of the vacuum (as defined in that system) is of infinite density. This assertion is based upon experience, and it has not been refuted either empirically or theoretically. This condition clearly does not establish its authenticity as opposed to that of other competing assertions, such as the classical theory of Timothy Boyer. According to the centrist view, neither the quantum field theory nor Boyer's theory can be true of the objective physical world as it exists in its own right.

Does an objective physical world exist at all, independently of all conceptual frameworks? To answer this in the affirmative is to assume that the notion of existence is something objectively real, independent of all conceptual systems. But the ideas of existence and nonexistence are defined by humans in a wide variety of ways depending on the contexts in which these human terms are used. Neither existence nor nonexistence is self-defining. Thus, a hypothetical reality that is posited as being independent of all conceptual designations must also be beyond all notions of objective versus subjective or existent versus nonexistent. From this perspective, the task of physics and all other sciences is not to provide a theory that will accurately map onto an independent, external reality but to devise theories that are conventionally valid in the sense of making intelligible conventionally existing events.

If a theory is based upon experience, is conceptually internally consistent, and is not refuted on empirical or rational grounds, the centrist view maintains that it may be deemed valid. In that case, what shall we do with competing, incompatible theories that equally satisfy those criteria? We may of course choose any of them as our conventionally valid theory. In so doing, that theory becomes the reality with which we shall involve ourselves. Moreover, on different occasions we may choose one competing theory over another if we find it more useful for our present purposes. In fact, this is exactly what practicing physicists do in the course of their research and teaching. For example, in one context a simple wave theory of light may be most useful; in another situation we may choose to speak of photons as simple particles of light; and at other times we may need to take account of the wave/particle nature of light. These differing theories are problematic only if we make the realist assumption that light is some independent physical entity that we are attempting to capture within the nets of our conceptual constructs.

In a way we have now come full circle to the standard classroom approach: asserting the correctness of a theory if it is internally consistent and provides accurate predictions. Now, with full awareness of the issue of multiple theories for the same phenomena, we can follow the classroom approach, knowing that we are dealing with relative, conventional truths, not absolute statements about objective reality. Have we gone too far in our philosophical relativism? For example, from the perspective of this centrist view is it ever possible to refute a scientific theory? The answer must certainly be affirmative. If a theory makes predictions about observations that do not hold up, it must be modified or rejected; that is, it is not even conventionally accurate. For example, classical mechanics made assumptions about the behavior of matter moving at extremely rapid velocities and of extremely minute particles of matter. Such assumptions have been contradicted by research done over the past century that has led to the formulation of quantum theory and relativity theory. Those classical assumptions were never correct, and this fallacy was demonstrated by increasingly sophisticated empirical research. Herein lies one of the great boons of science.

A theory may be rejected on the grounds that it is contradicted by experience or reason. Thus, to feel confident in the validity of our present theories, we must be especially cautious in making assumptions about the type of phenomena that would be observed when radically different modes of research or questioning are employed. This would mean that our generalizations about nature must be somewhat less sweeping. A theory may also be rejected for reasons that are not strictly scientific. Recall, for example, that Einstein thought that the concept of the ether was salvageable, but it was nevertheless rejected in twentieth-century physics. Relative to our present perspective, we may say that the ether never existed in any form whatsoever. However, if the ether is reintroduced into physical theory—and there are indications that this may happen—then from that future perspective, it will have existed since the Big Bang (if it is dated that far back).

In conceptually designating an entity, such as the ether, we bring it into existence, and from that perspective its existence is retroactive: it is a natural event interrelated with other events that are incorporated in our theory. If all such entities are contingent upon the specific methods of research that brought them to our attention, what hope is there of devising a grand unified theory that encompasses all of nature? This may be impossible even in principle. Different experimental procedures may reveal incompatible attributes of a single entity such as light, and it may be no more possible to produce a single theory that coherently accounts for all such attributes than it is to produce a single experimental procedure that reveals all of those attributes. Finally, we may have to acknowledge that we are stuck with plurality. Then we may be in a position to explore the full depth and breadth of experience that can be opened up by such plurality.

Chapter Eighteen

A Centrist View of Contemplative Science

In our discussion thus far we have focused on problems in the interpretation of Western science. The fundamental issues with which we have been grappling, however, were also a major concern in the civilization of classical India. The centrist view of Buddhism is primarily concerned with questions of ontology—the essential mode of existence of things. However, in order to investigate the fundamental nature of the human body and mind, for example, one must first clearly ascertain their phenomenal characteristics. Buddhist contemplative science has, thus, long been concerned with the phenomenological study of physical and mental events. Although the five senses and the mind's capacity for thinking are certainly used in this pursuit, this science has developed other mental faculties that are crucial for such investigation. Methods, some of them predating Buddhism in India, have been discovered for profoundly stabilizing and clarifying mental awareness.[1]

Different contemplative traditions do proclaim varying theories concerning topics ranging from human physiology and psychology to cosmology. In many areas, however, there appears to be a conformity of experience.[2] To begin to understand the differences, we must apply Heisenberg's assertion that what we observe is not nature in itself but nature exposed to our method of questioning. Hindu and Buddhist contemplatives question nature in somewhat different ways, so it is to be expected that their observations will vary to some extent. The contemplative mode of questioning is strikingly different from that of technological science, and the types of understanding gained from the two approaches differ correspondingly. Such contrary theories do not necessarily invalidate one another; they may be complementary.

The notion that Eastern contemplative science may complement Western technological science may strike many people as bizarre. Physicist Stephen Hawking is an outspoken critic of any such meeting of Eastern and Western knowledge. In an interview with philosopher Renée Weber, he explains his dislike of what he calls mysticism on the grounds that it clouds issues with obscurity and does not provide good theories in Karl Popper's sense of making definite predictions that can be falsified.[3]

In responding to this objection by a great scientist, we must first acknowledge that much of what passes for mysticism is to Eastern contemplative knowledge what scientism is to scientific knowledge. There is a large market in the West for both phony mysticism and phony science, and both are equally seductive to the dilettante. It requires informed discrimination to glean authentic information from the popular literature, and mastery of the writings of professional contemplatives and professional scientists requires years of intensive training. It is most unfortunate to discard either body of knowledge as worthless simply because one has not bothered to separate the wheat from the chaff.

Much of the professional literature of Buddhist contemplative science is extraordinarily precise, lucid, and logically coherent. This should come as no surprise, for intellectual training in the Buddhist monastic colleges and universities of such countries as Sri Lanka and Tibet is long and demanding.[4] Hawking's comment that people turn to mysticism because they find theoretical physics and mathematics too hard may be true of a few Western dilettantes. But such people would find that serious study and practice of Buddhist contemplative science is at least as challenging as the study of theoretical and experimental physics.

Does Buddhist contemplative science produce theories that make definite predictions that can be falsified? The answer is definitely yes. The primary focus of interest of Buddhist contemplatives, however, has traditionally been quite different than that of physicists. The former have been pragmatically concerned chiefly with the nature and prob-

lems of human existence and the untapped resources of consciousness. Their writings abound with precise explanations of techniques
for refining awareness, balancing the mind, and unveiling its latent
powers. Such documents give definite predictions concerning the
types of experiences that will arise when those methods have been
properly executed; and many generations of contemplatives claim to
have confirmed them experientially.

Such research has revealed a number of cognitive laws of the universe that are said to have been discovered and verified experientially. Buddhist contemplatives have been far less concerned with
physical laws concerning such things as gravity and electricity, so their
writings contain few references to purely physical predictions. This
does not mean that the forms of heightened awareness that can be
cultivated using Buddhist methods cannot be used to explore subtle
physical events and the laws that govern them. It simply means
that such contemplatives have found other fields of research more
compelling.

One who is accustomed to the worldview of modern Western science will likely be very skeptical of the specific Buddhist and Hindu
claims of heightened awareness and other mental powers. This is a
natural response, for such potentials of the human mind have been
largely overlooked in Western civilization, especially since the Scientific Revolution. Productive skepticism, however, does more than complacently rest in the conclusion that such claims must be unfounded.
They must be put to the test of experience. If one travels to India or to
communities of Tibetans in Asia[5] and patiently seeks out experienced
contemplatives, one may find those who possess extraordinary mental powers; but one may first meet with a number of charlatans.

A greater challenge is to test such claims by engaging oneself in
Buddhist or Hindu methods of mental training and testing experientially the predicted results. Even modest efforts in this field, when
performed correctly under competent guidance, can yield significant
results. The task of becoming a professional contemplative and profoundly transforming the mind is naturally far more demanding and
time-consuming.

Inevitably, some skeptics will complacently nurture their disbelief
in knowledge gained using unfamiliar methods, without taking
any steps experientially to settle the matter for themselves. Galileo
encountered such people when he proclaimed his astronomical
discoveries using a primitive telescope. His findings contradicted

Aristotelian physics, which was widely accepted by the intellectuals of his day; and some of his opponents reportedly refused to look for themselves through his telescope at such things as lunar craters. Such things simply could not exist, for the prevailing view of the heavens disallowed their presence. Even if craters were visible through the telescope, these adversaries were already convinced that such apparitions were due only to distortions in the lenses. They were apparently not sufficiently motivated to study optics and the technology of grinding lenses to see whether their assumptions were substantiated. These critics thereby removed themselves from participation in the Scientific Revolution, and they were to see their worldview steadily eroded by the science that they chose to ignore.[6]

Similar skepticism has been expressed with regard to contemplative discoveries when they cannot be verified by other means. The most frequent charge is that events observed as a result of contemplative training are creations of the observer's imagination. In fact, many claims of supernatural visions by self-proclaimed mystics can be discarded as fantasies—such dilettantes and charlatans abound in the East and the West. But the prevalence of frauds does not refute the existence of others who have gained profound contemplative experience of various facets of reality.

Buddhist contemplatives claim that upon accomplishing high degrees of mental refinement, it is possible to direct one's heightened awareness not only to gross physical and mental events here and now, but to events that are extremely subtle or distant in time and space. The great fifth-century Indian Buddhist sage Buddhaghosa lists in his *Path of Purification* five types of heightened awareness, some of which can be of great use in the exploration of nature.[7] He also describes various mental powers of "psychic technology," which may be of interest to people seeking a thorough understanding of the natural laws of the universe (including both physical and mental laws).[8] On the basis of the Buddha's teachings, Buddhaghosa also explains in detail how each of these types of heightened awareness and mental powers is achieved.

Many of these mental abilities are not unique to Buddhist contemplative science. The great Indian Hindu contemplative Patañjali (possibly a contemporary of Buddhaghosa) also presented methods for developing a wide range of supernormal powers.[9] These techniques, which Patañjali mostly compiled from the discoveries of earlier contemplatives, are different from those set forth by Buddhaghosa;

but many of the results appear to be essentially the same. There is certainly widespread agreement among these contemplative traditions as to the immense potential of human consciousness, as an instrument for both investigating and transforming reality.

The accomplishment of such abilities, however, does not necessarily imply that one who wields them is an infallible judge of reality. In Western society, if a scientific theory makes a prediction that is verified by experience, naive devotees of science are wont to believe that the entire theory is true. Similarly, in traditional Indian society, if a contemplative makes accurate predictions about the future, naive devotees are prone to regard that person as an infallible source of wisdom. Technological wonders also may, at first glance, suggest a profound understanding of nature, just as displays of psychic powers may overawe their beholders. In both cases the ability to manipulate phenomena does not necessarily imply an understanding of the more subtle processes involved.

In Buddhist mental training, great emphasis is placed from the outset on distinguishing between the fantasizing mind and verifying cognition. Indeed, the tendency of the human mind to assume the existence of things that are in fact nonentities is considered to lie at the root of a broad range of unnecessary conflicts and miseries. The most basic expression of this mental distortion is the reification of oneself as an intrinsically existent personal identity. Having reified oneself, it is inevitable that one reifies others in the same way, and this sets up absolute demarcations between self and other. One naturally also reifies one's natural environment as intrinsically existent, and therefore as absolutely other.

When such a view is put into action, the program is set for establishing one's own well-being as opposed to, and possibly at the expense of, that of other people. And one's environment, seen—like other people—as unrelated to oneself, is manipulated toward one's own ends. Such reification encourages the view that one can ravage other sentient beings and one's environment with impunity: people are to be exploited, and nature is to be conquered.

The centrist view acknowledges the obvious truth that one person is different from another and that they are different from their inanimate environment. But such distinctions are of a conventional, not an absolute, nature. This does not mean that such demarcations are arbitrary. Rather, the centrist view asserts that they exist in dependence upon conceptual designation. Every sentient being and every inanimate object thus exists as a dependently related event. Earlier in this chapter we discussed the manner in which the theoretical entities of physics are brought into existence by the process of mental designation. Recall, moreover, from even earlier discussions that any demarcation between theoretical and observable entities is arbitrary. The ontological assertions that were made concerning events described in physics are equally true of everyday experience: we are continually in the process of creating our world, both as individuals and as a society.

Ignorance of this essential truth gives rise to other mental distortions as well. In dependence upon the sense of an absolute self as opposed to absolute others, there arises selfish desire for objects (sentient and otherwise) that are regarded as being conducive to one's own well-being. Similarly, there arises hostility toward objects that appear to threaten one's well-being and that stand in the way of the fulfillment of one's desires. When people who are subject to such mental afflictions interact with one another, conflict, frustration, and pain are inevitable.

Modern Western science is based on the reification of the objective world. It initially adopted the Cartesian decision to reify subjective consciousness and to displace it from the reified world of nature. Over the ensuing centuries, the mind has fallen to the epiphenomenal status of a function of the brain; it is assumed to have originated from chance configurations of unconscious matter and energy. Physical science has, in the meantime, discovered many of the laws of nature; and some physicists, including Stephen Hawking, speculate that within twenty years, a complete unified theory may well be established. Hawking is reasonably confident that Western science knows the history of the universe back to a tiny fraction of a second after the Big Bang. That initial fraction of a second, he acknowledges, is still something of a mystery; but if it does become understood with certainty, "we'd really know everything. . . . We'd have solved all the problems and it would be rather dull."[10]

It is hardly a secret that some of the most prominent physicists at the end of the nineteenth century were equally confident that knowledge of the universe was virtually complete. That, of course, was just a few years before the modern revolution in physics, entailing the emergence of relativity theory and quantum mechanics. Can a complete understanding of the universe be gained in principle, if not in detail, while ignoring the role of consciousness? The centrist view clearly denies this possibility. The distinction between the subjective mind and the objective world is a conventional one, existing in dependence upon conceptual designation. Thus, if physical events do not exist independently of mental events, understanding of the former can hardly be complete, even in principle, without accounting for the latter.

Unlike education in physics, Buddhist contemplative training entails a strong emphasis on moral responsibility. Before attempting to gain profound states of heightened awareness or extraordinary mental powers, the aspirant must attenuate such mental distortions such as selfish desire and hostility. As one ascends to increasingly advanced states of contemplative awareness, one must complement such progress with the cultivation of such virtues as loving-kindness, generosity, and patience. Insofar as the powers that one gains are guided by wisdom and motivated by compassion, they are of benefit to oneself and others. In Buddhist mental training one strives for such balanced development.

This is not to suggest that Western science be discarded in favor of Eastern contemplative science. The former has yielded benefits that the latter has not. Nor should the two be set in competition with each other in a misguided attempt to determine which is better. Each has its unique advantages and drawbacks, and it is a civilization's loss to discard either. At present we are in a position to draw from the wisdom of the East and the West. The problems that face humankind are severe, and any lesser solution may be insufficient.

Chapter Nineteen

Experiencing a Centrist View

The centrist view sketched in the preceding chapters declares that everything that exists lacks an intrinsic nature or identity. How then do things exist? All entities are viewed as dependently related events, and none bears a self-defining, independent existence. Events are dependent for their very existence upon the power of the mind and convention that designates them, and even the mind itself bears only such a conventional identity.

When a subatomic particle, for instance, is first discovered, it is conceptually designated as existing with a certain set of attributes. If that designation is consistent within the theory in which it is incorporated and is not invalidated by experience, it is deemed valid, and the particle may be said to exist. If, in time, the accepted subatomic theory changes so that the particle no longer has a place in it, the particle no longer exists relative to that later time. Thus, if we declare that a certain subatomic entity exists, we must at least implicitly identify the conventional system in which it plays a part. The conventional realities of two simultaneous, diverse cultures may be significantly different; this is also true of the realities of a single culture over a period of centuries, and even of a single individual who experiences a fundamental change in worldview.

Composite entities are also viewed as dependently related events in that they occur in dependence upon causes and conditions. Moreover, all things are dependently related events in the sense that they depend upon their own components or attributes. They are not identical with their properties, nor are they independent of them; rather, they depend upon them for their existence.

The centrist view may be regarded chiefly as an ontological theory; and, as a metaphysical view, we might assume that its truth or falsity is beyond the reach of experience. The treatment of this view in the preceding pages has been based upon the Madhyamaka, or centrist view, of Buddhist philosophy. In its native context, it is presented as a system of intellectual inquiry as a means for experiencing reality in a profoundly different way.

This approach of employing philosophical theory as a means of refining and deepening one's personal experience of reality is not alien to Western civilization. The Greek word for theory (*theoria*) meant "contemplation"; and it is the term used in Aristotle's psychology to designate the moment of fully conscious participation, in which the soul's potential knowledge becomes manifest. Only then can the individual at last claim to be "awake."[1]

Western civilization has unfortunately allowed this dimension of theory to atrophy in the context of modern scientific and philosophical systems of thought. Insofar as its religions have divorced themselves from their contemplative or mystical wellsprings, religious doctrine, too, is often not recognized as a means of profoundly deepening one's experience of reality.

The assumption that intellectual insight must remain divorced from personal experience is certainly challenged in classical Greek thought. Plato recognized three levels of knowledge. The first of these is derived from simple observation, such as the observation of the movements of the stars, sun, moon, and planets. The second level deals in geometry, by means of which one devises orderly, mathematical accounts for the apparently arbitrary movements of the planets. This level of knowledge includes the science of astronomy. The third level entails an unobscured participation in the divine Mind, or Word; and such knowledge cannot be gained without profoundly transforming one's own mode of experience, or awareness. It is not accessible to logic alone. For Plato this third level of true knowledge was not of a transcendent, mystical nature, but rather an experience of ordinary reality unobscured by the veils of bewildering mutability.

Contemporary Western civilization has apparently forgotten how to cultivate this third level of personally transformative knowledge, as it has forgotten the deeper meaning of *theory*. The direct means for deepening and raising our level of awareness calls for a qualitative, contemplative science. Such a science would yield insight not only into the nature of the mind but into the physical world as well. At present we lack such a science in the West, but it would be rash to conclude that it has been developed nowhere else.

Western civilization has created philosophy as a discipline separate from empirical science, and it has artificially divorced both from religion. In contrast to philosophy and religion, science has progressed largely due to the fact that it has devised means of empirically testing its theories. In so doing, it has brought us much conceptual understanding of and power over the physical world. But it has shed little light on the nature of consciousness as one of the fundamental constituents of the universe together with space, matter, and energy. Nor has it shown us how to transform our way of directly experiencing reality in accord with its deepening insights.

Buddhist civilizations of classical India, East Asia, and Tibet did not develop the triad of science, philosophy, and religion as autonomous disciplines. Each of these avenues of understanding was indeed cultivated in their own ways, but they were traditionally regarded as fundamentally interrelated. In these cultures qualitative, contemplative sciences were created and developed over two and a half millennia. Their fundamental aim is to transform personal experience such that one gains direct insight into reality. Buddhists maintain that this goal has been realized not just once by the historical Buddha, but thousands of times by later contemplatives. Indeed, Buddhist contemplatives today continue to apply themselves to these practical methods, testing their value by means of their own experience.

The empirical methods of "contemplative research" presented as part of the centrist view in Buddhism lead one to a direct realization of the nature of phenomena as dependently related events. This approach does not entail quantitative analysis or theory couched in mathematical terms, but it does, nevertheless, address many of the fundamental ontological issues that are being investigated in the context of the foundations of modern physics. For this reason there may be meaningful dialogue between scientists concerned with such questions and those who have gained conceptual and experiential insight into the centrist view.

--------◆--------

Among the contemplative traditions of classical Indian culture, many mutually incompatible theories are promoted concerning the fundamental nature of reality. This suggests that there are many levels of insight that arise from contemplative practice; and the manner in which those insights are interpreted may vary greatly. Different techniques may lead to the same experience; a single technique may lead to a variety of experiences in accordance with the different backgrounds of those who practice it; and it can also happen that the same experience may be interpreted in different ways. As one engages in contemplative research, it is very possible for one to regard an experience as ultimate, feeling that one has realized the essential nature of reality; whereas in fact there may be far deeper insights to be gained.

Even among Buddhist treatises several mutually incompatible ontological theories are taught. Tibetan Buddhism utilizes these theories in monastic training in a sequential way. In many Tibetan monastic universities, students are first introduced to a form of dualistic realism in which real, intrinsic existence is attributed to both cognitive and physical events.[2] Strong emphasis is placed on logical analysis and on the study of the causal interrelations among such phenomena. Following this phase of the training, students are introduced to a form of Buddhist idealism,[3] which challenges the existence of a physical world independent of consciousness, while asserting the absolute, intrinsic existence of the mind. As their understanding is refined by such training, they enter the study of the centrist view, which denies the intrinsic existence of both cognitive and physical events.

All of these ontological views are traced back to the Buddha's own teachings. Each one is used to dispel certain levels of ignorance, especially involving reification. Thus, the student ideally engages in one of these philosophical systems both theoretically and contemplatively until the insights that it was designed to yield have been gained, and then naturally proceeds to a deeper view. The most profound ontological theory is considered to be the centrist view; and when one's mind is freed from all obscuring reification, the conceptual apparatus of this system, too, is left behind. It was designed as an instrument for gaining direct experience of reality, and when that is achieved, it has served its purpose. In this sense, Buddhist philosophy is above all pragmatic.

————————◆————————

Buddhist contemplative science contains hundreds of methods for investigating not only the ultimate nature of phenomena but the conventional or relative nature of physical, mental, and other types of entities. Even in terms of exploring the ultimate mode of existence of phenomena there are a wide variety of techniques. Here we shall briefly look into just one of these methods.

As mentioned previously, the centrist view regards the emptiness of an intrinsic nature to be the ultimate, or essential, mode of existence of phenomena. The truth of this is established first of all through observation, study, and logical analysis.[4] When conceptual insight is gained in this way, one proceeds to seek experiential realization by means of meditation. One could begin by empirically exploring the fundamental mode of existence of space, matter, consciousness, or any other entity; but the preferred approach in Buddhist practice is to begin exploring one's own essential nature.

While devoid of an independent identity, the self does exist as a dependently related event; and it exists in dependence upon mental imputation. Similar investigation is brought to bear on the mind, the body, and other entities, and the conclusion is the same: all of these are empty of an independent, intrinsic nature, but they do exist as dependently related events. As one gains deeper experiential insight, it becomes apparent that for the very reason that entities do exist as dependently related events, they cannot possibly bear intrinsic identities. Because they are empty of a self-defining nature, they are able to enter into dependent relationships with other phenomena.

The meditations on emptiness employ rational thought, but they result in a penetrating awareness that transcends concept and verbal description. Initial insight into the nature of emptiness is mixed with the idea of emptiness, but as experience deepens, a nonconceptual, direct realization of this truth is experienced. In that state, one no longer has any sense of a subject/object dichotomy, nor any differentiation between "this" as opposed to "that." According to firsthand accounts of highly advanced contemplatives, it is possible to experience a reality that transcends all conceptual frameworks once one's mind is freed from all conceptualization. When first abiding in such a realization, one has no awareness of conventional reality at all. As one proceeds to full awakening, the challenge is to integrate this profound insight with one's experience of relative truth, in all its diversity.

Such meditative practice is extraordinarily subtle. If the mind is not previously refined by means of meditation, one may still gain a glimpse of this ultimate nature, but its impact upon one's consciousness will be very limited. Thus, in traditional Buddhist practice, such insight training is preceded by methods for stabilizing and refining one's awareness. In this regard, the minimum prerequisite for fully effective insight training is the attainment of meditative quiescence. With this accomplishment the mind can be focused single-pointedly, without distraction and without effort, for hours on end, with vivid clarity.

Such a refinement of awareness obviously entails a major transformation of consciousness, and this is not easily brought about. In general it can be achieved only by months of continuous mental training usually pursued in solitude, free from the distractions of ordinary daily life. If one engages in such practice correctly, with skillful guidance, it results in an unprecedented state of mental and physical buoyancy and well-being. If one enters such intense training prematurely, it can lead to serious mental and/or physical imbalance.

Because of this danger, such an endeavor is properly preceded by a thorough training in generally refining the quality of one's awareness in active daily life. A mind that is frequently subject to hostility, sensual craving, lethargy, confusion, and semi-conscious, conceptual rambling is unfit for serious training in meditative quiescence. A wide variety of methods are employed on a day-to-day basis for subduing these mental distortions. In the process, one's general emotional and mental condition improves, and one's physical health may also be enhanced.

In Buddhist contemplative science, the initial, fundamental concern is not with the ontological status of atoms but with the human condition of suffering and discontent. Why are we subject to unhappiness, so much of it apparently unnecessary and fruitless? Certainly external conditions can be found that lead to physical and mental pain, and it is appropriate to seek external means of dealing with them.

Medicine, improved agricultural techniques, and other aspects of modern technology can all be effective means in this regard. But despite the awesome powers that modern science has brought to us, such external measures have not proven effective in bringing about inner contentment or well-being.

Buddhist contemplative science turns then to the inner sources of conflict, strife, and misery. Certain types of physical, verbal, and mental activity are recognized as leading to suffering for oneself and others, and these are regarded as unwholesome. The roots of such behavior have been empirically identified to be such distortions of the mind as hostility, craving, and confusion. Buddhist practice therefore focuses from the outset on diminishing the power of such distortions and their resultant unwholesome behavior. The fundamental mental affliction is confusion, and this refers specifically to the tendency of reifying oneself, others, and the world at large. A confused mind conceives of people and everything else as intrinsic, absolute entities. This mental distortion lies at the root of all other mental afflictions.

The individual does not exist as an isolated, independent entity, intrinsically cut off from other sentient beings and the rest of the universe. Rather, each person exists as a dependently related event: neither our existence nor our degree of well-being is independent from the rest of our environment. Recognizing this, a Buddhist contemplative who aspires to full spiritual awakening strives not only for individual enlightenment but for the awakening of all sentient beings.

With such a motivation one refines the quality of one's standard of living, that is, the quality of one's life, not the standard of one's physical prosperity. By following practices to diminish mental distortions and unwholesome behavior in active daily life, one approaches the degree of inner purity that is required for effective training in meditative quiescence. This is the next major step of contemplative practice, and upon mastering it, one properly moves on to insight training focused on gaining realization of ultimate truth—the emptiness of intrinsic existence of all phenomena.

Chapter Twenty

Realizing Personal Identitylessness

As we look out on the world around us, external things and events appear to exist by their own intrinsic nature, independent of any conceptual designation. When we explore uncharted terrain, the things we observe seem to be lying in wait for us to discover them: they appear to be self-defining phenomena, and the process of discovery seems to be a relatively passive one. The preceding chapters suggest that the mode of existence of such phenomena is actually contrary to the way they appear to us. Physicist Nick Herbert addresses this problem when he writes:

> The source of all quantum paradoxes appears to lie in the fact that human perceptions create a world of unique actualities—our experience is inevitably "classical"—while quantum reality is simply not that way at all. . . . Since physics assures us that our lives are embedded in a thoroughly quantum world, is it so obvious that our experience must remain forever classical?[1]

The Buddhist centrist view addresses this problem by setting forth means for penetrating appearances and gaining experiential insight into the fundamental manner in which the world exists. The first step is to understand how the world appears to us. Just as we naturally see our environment as intrinsically existent, so do we regard ourselves and other individuals as existing independently of verbal and conceptual designation. With this innate sense of personal identity, we separate ourselves absolutely from the rest of the world. The division of self and other is seen not as a conventional distinction but as an absolute gap in the fabric of reality. Having reified our own personal identity, we reify that of others, setting them absolutely apart from us; and we similarly objectify our inanimate environment.

Another aspect of our existence is that we experience pleasure and pain. Each sentient being strives for the former and seeks to avoid the latter. Our pleasure and pain are often associated with observed events which we therefore identify as attractive or repellent. Failing once again to recognize the interrelation between subject and object, we may regard the feelings that we experience as originating from those events on their own. While already clinging to the intrinsic existence of those events, we now further reify their attractive and repellent qualities. This way of experiencing the world exerts a profound influence on our sense of values. What is worth doing? This worldview answers: acquire pleasurable objects and avoid disagreeable ones, for therein lies the key to happiness and freedom from pain.

As our worldview strongly influences our values, so do our values largely determine the way we live our lives. With this value system we are set to conquer the world, manipulating our animate and inanimate environment to our own ends. History and our own personal experience demonstrate, however, that such a program quickly creates conflict and pain. Relationships among external events—one could call them the laws of nature—are often beyond our power to control. We may exert our will upon our environment, shaping it according to our desires, only to find that the desirable conditions that we created are inexorably eroded by time. Moreover, our goal of dominating our environment may also be frustrated by others' desires, for we cannot avoid interaction with other individuals for whom we are the "other." We find ourselves as part of their animate environment which they are trying to shape to their own ends. Self and other are therefore on a collision course: it is only a matter of time before two or more individuals find that each is striving for exclusive acquisition of an object that they all have reified as being intrinsically desirable. Other people now appear as adversaries. Those others are now reified as disagreeable objects and must be dealt with accordingly. They must be either conquered or destroyed.

This innate sense of the intrinsic existence of ourselves, others, and our environment leads to frustration, conflict, strife, and misery. Other individuals are impersonalized as agreeable or disagreeable objects, and human relationships are thereby impoverished. The centrist view declares that such a situation stems from a misapprehension of reality, namely grasping onto intrinsic existence. This mental distortion is not itself intrinsic to the human mind, nor is it inevitable that we continue to be afflicted by it. How may we free ourselves of this distorted way of viewing reality? Not by faith alone, nor by belief, nor is a purely intellectual grasp of the centrist philosophy sufficient. Rather, such ignorance can be dispelled only through investigating reality for ourselves, with complete intellectual integrity. The message is an ancient one: the truth shall make us free.

As we engage in a contemplative investigation of the fundamental nature of reality, we may focus either on our own essential mode of existence or on phenomena other than the self. The former approach leads to a realization of personal identitylessness, while the latter yields insight into phenomenal identitylessness. There is no difference in subtlety between these two; the difference lies only in the type of entity whose mode of existence is being investigated.

In the Buddhist tradition one is generally encouraged to focus initially on the question of personal identity. It is sometimes said that the absence of an intrinsic personal identity is easier to realize than the noninherent nature of other physical and cognitive phenomena. Because of the central role of one's sense of self, any fundamental misconception about one's own identity is bound to exert a strong disruptive influence on one's life. Thus, for very practical reasons one is well advised to focus first of all on the nature of one's own identity.

The first step in this practice is to scrutinize the manner in which we already conceive of ourselves. In this first phase of the inquiry, it is crucial that we attend to the manner in which we actually conceive of ourselves in the course of our daily lives, and not begin with some metaphysical hypothesis concerning some purportedly true nature of the self. The centrist philosophy declares that people who have not gained a direct experience of ultimate reality conceive of themselves basically in two ways. On many occasions we may think of ourselves and others in a manner that does not distinguish between an intrinsic or nonintrinsic self. For example, I may walk in the door of my home and call out, "Hello! I'm home," and in so doing there may be no sense of an inherent personal identity that has walked through the door. Or I may casually remark, "John is sitting on the couch," without attributing intrinsic existence to him. In this case, the label "John" is simply designated upon his body, and there may be no sense of a person existing apart from that simple designation. Likewise, when commenting, "I'm glad you're here," the "I" may be simply imputed upon the mental feeling of gladness, while the "you" is designated upon your body. There is no fallacy in such designation or identification of self and other.

The centrist philosophy also maintains, however, that we have an innate tendency to reify this conventionally existent "I," such that we grasp onto it as if exists inherently. Rather than accepting this philosophy as a matter of dogma, the contemplative is challenged to investigate this issue: how do I naturally conceive of myself, before bringing in philosophical views from Buddhism or elsewhere? In what manner am I related to my body and mind?

This type of contemplative practice requires not merely subtle philosophical reasoning, but extremely acute introspective alertness. It is to be pursued not only in solitude but while conversing with others and carrying on an active life in the world. The investigation is a demanding one, and it needs to be practiced during times of excitement and lassitude, joy and grief, indignation and delight. An immediate objection to such a practice might be that it disengages one from wholehearted interaction with other people and one's environment. It might even be regarded as an unhealthy form of self-absorption.

Whether or not this judgment is justified depends largely on the motivation of the contemplative. Many people are engrossed in their own desires, feelings, hopes, and fears. They perceive other people and their environment only through a thick mesh of self-oriented conceptualization. Such a way of life is a symptom of the affliction of grasping onto one's own intrinsic personal identity. The Buddhist contemplative practice discussed here is a remedy for that affliction. When such introspection is pursued correctly, it leads to greater insight into the fundamental interrelationship between self and others; and in this way one is freed from a distorted, self-centered view of the world.

Identifying one's sense of personal identity is difficult. While sitting quietly in meditation, one may look inward; but as one does so, one's sense of "I" seems to fade away. For this reason, the beginning practitioner is encouraged to pursue this contemplation especially in times of strong emotion or passion. If while driving on a highway, another driver suddenly pulls out in front of me, endangering both our lives, there may be a sudden mental response: "Didn't you see me coming?! You could have gotten me killed!" Now the sense of "I" is clearly pronounced, and because of its grossness it is fairly easy to examine.

Similarly, in times of great delight and anguish the sense of "I am" arises quite forcefully together with the emotion: "I am thrilled with the prospect of this new job," or "I am crushed with the loss of my dearest friend." In such cases the contemplative is encouraged to observe the nature of the self that is grasped by the mind. Is this self conceived as existing by its own nature, bearing its own intrinsic identity? Perhaps the most obvious case in which such a sense of "I" arises is when one is vehemently accused of a wrong that one did not commit. If someone points a finger at me and in the presence of others declares, "You have been filching money from our community fund!" there may arise a strong sense of the "I" that has been wrongly accused and who must now be vindicated. Even hours after such an episode there may be a lingering thought, "How could he have thought that of *me*?" The contemplative takes this situation as a precious opportunity to investigate the question of personal identity. The mundanely self-absorbed person, in contrast, tends rather to wallow in self-pity and in indignant thoughts of retaliation.

———————◆———————

The initial task, then, is to identify the self that is grasped as being intrinsically existent. As soon as this is done, the contemplative analyzes this self to determine whether or not it exists. A clear distinction must be drawn between the mind that conceives of such an "I" and the intrinsic self that such a mind grasps. The centrist philosophy declares that the former does indeed exist and that this distorted cognition radically influences one's behavior. The self that is grasped by such a cognition, on the other hand, has no existence whatever, conventional or otherwise. That an intrinsic self is imagined by the mind does not endow it with existence. Again, it is insufficient for the contemplative simply to believe such a tenet; one must ascertain its truth.

While holding this presumed intrinsic self before the mind's eye, one may analyze it as follows: if there is an entity corresponding to this appearance of an intrinsic personal identity, it must be as real as my body and mind. Is it then the same as my body or my mind, or is it separate from them? If this self were the same as my body, it would be meaningless to say, "I am disappointed," for this would imply that my body is disappointed, and this is gibberish. Moreover, the phrase "my body" also becomes problematic, for it would be tantamount to saying "body's body." Intuitively I feel that I have a body, but it is absurd to claim that the body has a body.

Might it, on the other hand, be true that this intrinsic self is the same as my mind? If this were the case, the statement "You are pushing me!" becomes absurd, for the mind, being without form, cannot be pushed by anything. It would also be impossible for other people to see me, for they cannot perceive my mind. And, as in the above case, the phrase "my mind" becomes as untenable as "the mind's mind." I cognize things with my mind, but I am not the same as my mind.

Is the intrinsic self the same as the combination of my body and mind? If this were so, the statements "I am disappointed" and "You are pushing me!" would still be inaccurate, for the mind-body combination can be neither disappointed nor pushed by a physical object. Moreover, I would still be invisible to my friends, for none of them has seen the combination of my body and mind. Finally, while accepting the common notion that the body and mind are two distinct types of phenomena, we are here introducing a third single entity that we have called the combination of those two. Since we are identifying this combination with the intrinsic self, it, too, must have intrinsic existence. If so, we should apply the same analysis to it: is it truly separate from its two components, or is it the same as them? The combination obviously cannot be the same as either of its components. Can it be the same as both of them? The body is made up entirely of mass and energy, which gives it physical dimension and location, while the mind lacks those components and attributes. Thus, it would follow that a single entity cannot be both body and mind; otherwise, it would have to be and yet not be entirely composed of mass and energy.

Is the intrinsic combination of the body and mind truly distinct from both of its components? If this were so, the three entities in question—the body, mind, and their combination—should be as separate as a cow, a horse, and a goat in a field. In the absence of the cow and the horse, the goat remains on its own. Similarly, in the absence of the body and the mind, the combination of the two should persist. This is obviously not the case. Now if that intrinsic combination is neither the same as the body, the mind, or both, and it is not distinct from them, it must have no existence whatever. Thus, it is pointless to equate this nonentity with one's own personal identity.

If the intrinsic "I" is not the same as the body, the mind, or their combination, and if it does exist, it must be truly separate from any and all of its components. For a third time the statements "I am disappointed" and "You are pushing me!" lose meaning; for disappointment is a state of mind and being pushed is a condition of the body; and the self is now presumed to be separate from both. And I am still invisible to my friends, for none of them has seen an "I" apart from my body and mind. Moreover, as in the above argument, this intrinsically separate personal identity should persist even in the absence of the body and the mind. Such a self performs no function, for everything a person does is performed with the body, the mind, or both. In short, an intrinsic self that is separate from the body and the mind is illogical, unknowable, and functionless. If we were to insist on its existence despite these shortcomings, we might as well admit into reality all manner of absurd fantasies. This, of course, would mean abandoning the quest for truth.

If the intrinsic self exists neither as the same as the body, the mind, or the combination of the two, nor as separate from them, it logically follows that it does not exist at all. Recoiling from this conclusion, one might object that the question of personal identity transcends the domain of logic: what is refuted by the conventional use of language and reason is not necessarily refuted by reality. If language and reason are inappropriate tools for investigating the nature of the self, there would seem to be little justification for using them to probe any other aspect of reality: why should the self have a transcendent status while mind, body, and the rest of the cosmos do not? It goes without saying that there is no reasonable way to refute the use of logic: its value cannot be refuted by absurd reasoning; nor can it be dismissed with sound reasoning—for it is the usefulness of sound reasoning that is being called into question.

One may, of course, simply believe that the nature of personal identity cannot be explored by logical means, just as one may dismiss the use of logic from the entire domain of contemplative practice. One can hardly dispense with the use of language and one's best approximation to rationality, however, while actively relating to the rest of the world. By banishing language and clear thinking from contemplative practice, one sets up a fundamental rift between such practice and the rest of one's life. Such a disjointed, fragmented way of life can hardly be conducive to the quest for an integrated understanding and experience of reality.

This investigation of the nature of the self requires a refined ability in introspective awareness and in philosophical analysis. With this ability the contemplative finds that the intrinsic "I" that appears to the mind is an impossibility. Upon recognizing the nonexistence of such a personal identity either in the body or the mind or apart from them, one focuses the mind on that mere absence. At this point, one disengages the mind from all ideation. Without grasping onto any conceptual constructs, the awareness is allowed to rest without modification or conceptual structuring. The simple negation of an intrinsic "I" is known as *emptiness* with respect to the self. This emptiness is the ultimate mode of existence of the self, and the experience of that emptiness dispels the false sense of an intrinsic personal identity.

Due to one's long habituation to grasping onto the false self, a single experience of emptiness will not completely dispel that misconception. As the contemplative directs the mind to this emptiness, it gradually fades, and one is left with a vague sense of vacuity. At this time the mind may be free of thought, and it may not have a clear object. Such a nebulous state of mind is unprofitable and the contemplative is not encouraged to indulge in it. Rather, once the awareness of the emptiness of an intrinsic self has waned, one should return to the introspective and analytical practice outlined above. In this way one repeatedly experiences emptiness with increasing clarity, depth, and duration; and here lies the means of dispelling completely the false sense of an intrinsic self.

The above "parts and whole" analysis is but one of many analytical approaches to realizing emptiness. Another type of analysis concerns the arising and cessation of entities.[2] If the self were intrinsically existent, then it would need no causes for its creation, now or at conception. It would stand on its own, immutable, uninfluenced, and inactive for all time. But such a concept of an "I" bears nothing in common with the "I" of daily life. On the other hand, if one asserts that before conception in the womb the intrinsic self did not exist, then nothing in the world could bring it from absolute nonexistence to absolute existence. This is as true of the self as it is of any other entity that is assumed to exist intrinsically. In short, creation and cessation become impossible.

———————◆———————

The nonexistence of an intrinsic personal identity does not imply that the self does not exist at all. The "I" is verbally and conceptually designated upon the body and/or the mind. Although it is unfindable upon analysis, this "I" nevertheless bears a conventional existence; and as such it can be influenced by events and actively respond to them. As the body and mind are interrelated continua, so is the self an ever-changing continuum. It is not a physical, psychic, or spiritual substance propelled through time; rather it is a sequence of dependently related events. It is dependent upon the body and the mind that are its basis of designation, upon other causes and conditions that give rise to the present state of its continuum, and upon the mental designation of the self. There remains a difference between self and other, but this distinction is of a conventional, not an absolute, nature. The Buddha expressed this point as follows: "For these are merely names, expressions, turns of speech, designations in common use in the world. Of these he who has won truth makes use indeed, but is not led astray by them."[3]

By realizing the emptiness of an intrinsic personal identity, one comes to experience the essential interrelatedness of oneself and others. The sense of absolute isolation from the rest of the world is banished. The arising of joy and of sorrow may also be seen as dependently related events, and this insight leads to the cessation of selfish craving and aggression. In the absence of these mental distortions one can explore ways of life that are in accord with reality rather than at odds with it. And such a way of life yields greater harmony and well-being for oneself and the rest of the world. If grasping onto intrinsic existence is the fundamental mental affliction, realization of emptiness is the fundamental cure.

Chapter Twenty-one

A Contemplative View of the Body

In the contemplative practice described in the preceding chapter, one investigates the nature of the self, in particular its essential mode of existence. For this practice to be fully effective in yielding direct realization of emptiness, one must clearly understand the nature of the body and mind. Let us focus initially on the human body.

Modern medical science has presented us with extensive knowledge of the components of the body and their various functions. This view of the body has been developed on the basis of the conceptual constructs and philosophical assumptions of Western science. Moreover, the type of data we have obtained concerning the body is necessarily related to the type of instruments that have been used. Medical science, especially in this century, has increasingly used the technology provided by physics; and it has sought quantitative data to which the laws of physics can be applied. Indeed, many physicians have adopted the metaphysical assumption promoted in physics that every function of a human being can be understood from the point of view that a person is composed of atoms acting according to the laws of physics.

This physics-based approach to understanding the human body has produced great quantities of information about the body and the ways in which it malfunctions. Insofar as the body fits the description of an organic machine, this knowledge has been very useful in curing certain ailments and suppressing the symptoms of many others. Western medical science shines its brightest when it displays its technical dexterity in removing and at times replacing malfunctioning parts of the body and in mechanically repairing others. It seems to glow its dimmest, however, when it confronts systemic imbalances, especially those in which physical and psychological afflictions are obviously interrelated. In this mystery-shrouded domain, reducing the human being to a complex of atoms governed entirely by the laws of physics seems an article of faith rather than a scientific fact.

The profound interaction between subjectively experienced mental states and the objective human body is an awkward area of research for a physics-based medical science. The simple reason is that physics has provided it with means for exploring the body but not the mind. Especially since the nineteenth century, Western medicine has been deeply influenced by mechanistic materialism. With the bias of assuming that only physical entities are real, it has, until recently, treated the interaction of body and mind as a one-way street: physical states influence subjective experience, but not vice versa. Recent research in such areas as biofeedback and the placebo effect challenge this view, but materialists interpret such interactions solely in terms of brain functioning.[1]

The problem of mind-body interaction is an unavoidable one for modern medicine, and in seeking to investigate this subject, researchers turn naturally to the data-gathering devices provided by physics. In this area, however, the human organism is strikingly unlike the nonliving configurations of mass and energy that the theory and methods of physics were designed to investigate. The medical researcher examines a human subject and in this way acquires quantitative data from the instruments provided by technology and qualitative information from questioning the subject. Neither approach provides direct experience of the subject's mind or the mind-body interactions that may be taking place. Both the mind and such interactions remain in a black box as far as medical science is concerned.

Recognizing the relative, conventional nature of the Western scientific description of the human organism, we may well wonder if there are other descriptions that are derived by modes of questioning unknown in the West. The answer to this question is certainly yes. We shall now focus on another view of the human body: that of the Buddhist contemplative. Unlike the Western scientist, the contemplative does not rely on the instruments of technology for gathering information about the body. Rather, the mind is honed into a fine in-strument which is used for direct, introspective exploration of the body and its interrelationship with the mind.

In Western thought it is commonly assumed that the sole access to reality is by means of the five senses and thought: the senses gather information, and the intellect processes it. The various contemplative traditions of the world have found means of refining mental, as dis-tinct from sensory, consciousness so that it can be used in the direct, empirical investigation of reality. Although existent in Western con-templative traditions, the cultivation of such heightened awareness has unfortunately atrophied in this civilization. For centuries it has played only a minor role in Christianity and Judaism; for centuries it does not appear to have been a major concern for Western philoso-phers; and natural science has ignored it altogether. In the domain of contemplative science, then, Western society seems to be compara-tively backward and undeveloped. When Westerners judge other peoples by the standards in which they especially excel, namely in objective science and technology, they do not recognize this.

Using their highly trained, refined awareness as an instrument of investigation, Buddhist contemplatives have been able to examine the body, the mind, and the interrelationship between the two as they are immediately experienced. This does not mean, however, that their observations are not theory-laden. Indeed, a Tibetan contemplative, before beginning advanced practices for the transformation of the mind-body, normally first receives theoretical instruction on subtle human physiology and mind-body interactions. Such theory plays a strong role in the subsequent meditative practices.

With the aid of a given theory, the contemplative observes a subtle network of vital energies coursing through the body, performing a variety of specialized functions. These vital energies (Sanskrit *prāṇa*, often translated as *winds*) are thought to be responsible for all physiological processes. They are also intimately associated with all forms of sensory and mental consciousness. In fact, each of the five principal types of vital energy is connected to a specific group of func-tions that are described in detail in the literature of contemplative physiology.

These vital energies have no intrinsic existence in the body, and the observation of them by contemplatives is clearly theory-laden. Having studied Tibetan medical theory, a Tibetan physician learns techniques for empirically identifying the functioning of each of the types of vital energy, and this knowledge is put to practical use in healing. On a deeper level, a Tibetan contemplative first becomes acquainted with such theory and, by means of refining the mind through meditative discipline, actually perceives these energies within the body. Vital energy, for an advanced contemplative, is not merely a conceptual abstraction but an element of perceptual experience. Western scientific methods have yielded much knowledge about energy as it was discussed earlier in this book, but it is often pointed out that they have produced no evidence for such vital energies. It is highly questionable whether such methods using inorganic instruments of research will ever shed light on vital energies that are essentially related to life. This in no way refutes the conventional existence of vital energies that are accessible to contemplative research.

According to Buddhist contemplative theory, these various energies course through channels in the body, known in Sanskrit as *nāḍis*. There are tens of thousands of these channels throughout the body, but the three main ones run together from midforehead up over the crown of the head down to the base of the spine and then under the trunk of the body to the tip of the sexual organ.[2] Along these three main channels are centers, known in Sanskrit as *cakras*, or wheels. They are so called because smaller channels branch out from them like the spokes of a wheel. They are located at the top of the head, the forehead, throat, heart, solar plexus, base of the spine, and sexual organ. At these centers the left and right channels wrap around the central one, constricting the flow of energy through it.[3]

The explanation of the winds, channels, and wheels is part of a broader understanding of human anatomy and physiology that derives largely from contemplative investigation of the body. Like Western medical knowledge of the human organism, it plays a major role in diagnosing and treating illness. Tibetan medicine, for instance, which stems largely from the Buddhist contemplative science of classical India, diagnoses and treats many psychophysiological imbalances in relation to the various winds. The medical training of traditional Tibet included detailed studies of anatomy, both on the subtle levels as described here and on the grosser levels. Part of that training entailed inspecting the gross physical organs by opening up and examining corpses. The channels, wheels, and other subtle elements of the human anatomy, however, were recognized as being invisible to the eye; they are accessible only to refined contemplative observation.

Within the vast body of Buddhist literature on the subtle human anatomy, various discussions can be found that differ on relatively minor points. Hindu contemplative science diverges more significantly from Buddhist views, and traditional Chinese medical theory differs even more from those of India and Tibet. The realist may respond to such diversity by either discounting all such theories as speculative fictions, or may try to determine which of the above presentations is objectively true. In the realist view if one explanation of the body is deemed true, then other theories can be deemed valid only insofar as they agree with that explanation. All of the above contemplative systems, like modern Western medicine, have their strong and weak points, so their truth cannot be determined pragmatically, simply on the basis of their effectiveness. So the realist is in a quandary.

A centrist recognizes that the human body has no intrinsic, purely objective nature, so no medical theory can claim an exclusively correct understanding of the body. Just as human anatomy and physiology will be understood differently when examined by physical science and by contemplative science, so are different theories devised on the basis of the diverse contemplative practices of India, Tibet, and China. Insofar as these theories are based upon experience and are internally consistent, they are conventionally true in relation to their various modes of inquiry. It is not at all certain, however, that traditional Chinese medical theory can be translated into the context of Hindu or Buddhist medicine. It is even more questionable whether contemplative-based medicine can be understood within the concepts of modern Western science, or vice versa.

Each of the above systems of medical theory and practice treats certain afflictions more effectively than the other systems do. Once this is recognized, it becomes pointless to dwell on the question as to which system is the best. One may as well ask which food or vitamin is best. Each system should be examined on its own merits, and the human population will be best served if it draws from the strong points of each one. In this light, these different ways of understanding and healing are seen as complementary, rather than as incompatible.

Throughout one's life, the functioning of the various winds is intimately related to mental states. If the winds are in imbalance, this invariably affects one's psyche adversely, and if they are in proper balance, one experiences an inner sense of well-being. Gross physical factors such as food, environment, behavior, and the functioning of the internal organs influence the subtle winds; and these in turn affect the mind. But the avenue of influence runs both ways: states of consciousness—including thoughts, emotions, and desires—affect the subtle winds, which in turn influence one's gross physical metabolism and behavior. Indeed, the interrelation between the subtle winds and consciousness is so intimate that the former cannot be properly understood apart from the latter. Let us therefore turn now to the nature of the mind as it is understood in Buddhist contemplative science.

Chapter Twenty-two

Subjective Experience and Objective Science

In the following discussion let us use the word *mind* as an umbrella term covering the broad range of cognitive phenomena including perceptions, inferences, feelings, thoughts, recollections, fantasies, and consciousnesses. Before looking into a Buddhist contemplative view of this subject, it is worth looking into the manner in which Western natural science has dealt with—or failed to deal with—the mind.

Let us first recall Descartes's seminal division of the world into the physical realm as the proper field of study for natural science, and the cognitive realm, which he granted to philosophy. The objective world, in his view, is composed of particles of matter bearing shape, size and motion. The soul, while having no physical dimensions or location, influences the body—and indirectly the physical environment of the body—via the pineal gland. Yet he asserted that the particles making up the objective physical world can be fully explained without introducing nonmechanical agents. While he acknowledged that the mind influences matter, his followers replaced his idea with the notion that there is no interaction between mind and matter. This is not such a big step once one has asserted that the mind is a nonmechanical agent and that the physical world can be understood thoroughly without resorting to such influences. Thus, Descartes's followers denied consciousness and all other mental events any active role in the physical universe, introducing this view as a point of metaphysical dogma, not as a scientifically demonstrated conclusion.

Over the next three centuries, scientific knowledge appeared to make rapid, logical, and universally acknowledged advances. In the meantime, successive generations of philosophers devised elaborate theories encompassing such widely divergent fields as ethics, epistemology, ontology, and aesthetics. But, unlike their scientific colleagues, these philosophers were able to arrive at few generally accepted conclusions, and no universally acclaimed progress was in evidence. As a result, by the closing decades of the nineteenth century, speculative metaphysics was widely held in low esteem. In the eyes of many people, the only authentic approach to understanding the real world seemed to be that of science.

In one sense this point is well made: scientists had over the centuries developed increasingly refined and ingenious instruments for exploring nature, and their mathematical tools of analysis had likewise become more and more sophisticated. Philosophers, on the other hand, had developed no new means of empirically investigating their given domain—the mind and subjective experience in general—nor did the pervasive dissension among them suggest that they had devised new forms of logical analysis that all were compelled to accept as valid. While scientists draw from experiment, theorize, and return to further experimentation, philosophers characteristically draw from books, theorize, and return to further reading.

Recall that a dominant ontological view among scientists from the time of Descartes to the present is scientific realism. This theory asserts that the real physical world exists "behind appearances," and that it is knowable by means of precise quantitative experimentation, observation, and mathematical analysis. The basic constituents of reality—elementary particles, fields, energy—therefore exist in a black box forever veiled from direct experience but knowable through mathematical inference. Many philosophers have adopted a similar stance concerning the mind: reasoning that the mind cannot observe itself, just as the eye cannot see itself, they conclude that the cognitive realm can be known only inferentially. In this case, both the objective and the subjective world seem in danger of disappearing into a black box. By the time this view is joined with the theological assertion that matters of revelation—the nature of the soul, God, salvation, and so on—are beyond the domain of experience, we may have allowed the whole of reality to slip into a cosmic black box.

When Descartes set forth his division of the objective and subjective world, such terms as color, heat, light, and smell were regarded as belonging to the realm of subjective experience. It was then the challenge of natural science to explain the independent, objective processes in nature that account for such sensations, processes that are hidden from experience and are revealed through mathematical reasoning. Although the causal physical events and the resultant subjective experiences of color, heat, and so on are asserted as two entirely different types of entities, the subjective terms were applied to the objective processes. *Light*, for example, is now understood as referring to a rapidly alternating electromagnetic field traveling through space in the form of waves. This statement is based on experiment and mathematical analysis, and it thoroughly removes knowledge of light from the domain of ordinary visual experience. The physicist's black box of nature contains even light itself, safely removed from the prying eyes of the nonscientist.

Precise observation, quantitative reasoning, and the benefits of technology had, by the close of the nineteenth century, given natural science enormous prestige and authority. Metaphysics, on the other hand, had proven unable to test its theories by means of experiment; its subject matter did not lend itself to quantitative analysis, and its practical benefits for the general public seemed meager at best. Physicists, with their commitment to scientific realism, felt confident that mathematics allowed them intellectual access to the physical world behind appearances. But if mental events cannot be measured quantitatively, and if they are hidden in a subjective black box, how can they possibly be known?

With the enormous success of natural science in comparison with the comparative absence of progress in philosophy, many people have been led to the conclusion that science is our sole means of knowledge: if something is inaccessible to the methods of science, it is unknowable. This may further suggest that whatever is unknowable is irrelevant. And this may imply that whatever is unknowable and irrelevant does not exist. If we are to salvage the realm of mental events from the refuse bin of unknowability, irrelevance, and nonexistence, we must, according to this view, learn to study it scientifically.

The discipline that has been created in response to this call is, of course, psychology; and one of its most influential branches in the twentieth century has been behaviorism. This approach follows the trend of the physical sciences by concerning itself with measurable phenomena subject to quantitative analysis. It is noteworthy that behaviorism initially developed during the opening decades of this century, when instrumentalism and logical positivism were gaining popularity. Physicists of this philosophical persuasion sought to concern themselves solely with measured phenomena as opposed to presumed noumena in the black box of nature. Similarly, there was a trend in behaviorism to focus entirely on observable behavior, without indulging in speculations about the noumenal mental processes behind such behavior. The American behaviorist John B. Watson wrote in 1913 that "the time has come when psychology must discard all reference to consciousness.... Its sole task is the prediction and control of behavior; and introspection can form no part of its method."[1] Fifteen years later he even more emphatically declared that the behaviorist must exclude from his scientific vocabulary "all subjective terms such as sensation, perception, image, desire, purpose, and even thinking and emotion as they are subjectively defined."[2]

With this decree, all mental events are banished from the realm of science. From the time of Descartes they were prohibited from any active engagement with the physical world and thus were ignored by the physical sciences. The life sciences have found the nature of the mind so elusive that there seems to be no hope of including it in the natural sciences. Francis Crick, a Nobel laureate in biology, writes, for example, that "the ultimate aim of the modern movement in biology is to explain all biology in terms of physics and chemistry."[3] Finally, according to Watson, mental events are excommunicated even from the discipline of psychology, which William James defined as the description and explanation of states of consciousness.

Exiled from the domains of all the sciences, banned even from scientific discussion, the very existence of the mind seemed by midcentury to be open to attack. And attack there was, by one of the most influential behaviorists of the twentieth century—Harvard University's B. F. Skinner. In 1953 Skinner let the axe fall when he asserted that mind and ideas are nonexistent entities, "invented for the sole purpose of providing spurious explanations.... Since mental or psychic events are asserted to lack the dimensions of physical science, we have an additional reason for rejecting them."[4]

All scientific theory consists of ideas together with mental images that form our models of natural events. As the radical behaviorists somehow come to the decision that mind and ideas do not exist, they expel from existence both their own decision-making process and the ensuing theory. The theory of behaviorism together with the rest of science assumes the status of a nonentity; and we may be left wondering: how can a nonentity refute its own existence?

———◆———

Even during the heyday of behaviorism, there were other schools of psychology that continued to try to describe and explain states of consciousness. Even among the adherents of these schools, however, there was widespread belief that mental events could not be scientifically investigated firsthand. Rather, they could be known only through inference, while leaving the entire mental realm in an experiential black box. Whereas the behaviorist would study stimuli and responses and ignore any mental processes that occurred in between, other psychologists sought to infer the nature and contents of the mind by questioning their subjects and performing experiments that would yield observable results. This black-box approach, however, has the same drawbacks when applied to the mind as to the physical world. In the words of Francis Crick:

> The difficulty with the black-box approach is that unless the box is inherently very simple a stage is soon reached where several rival theories all explain the observed results equally well. Attempts to decide among them often prove unsuccessful because as more experiments are done more complexities are revealed. At that point there is no choice but to poke inside the box if the matter is to be settled one way or the other.[5]

By the mid-1960s, the shortcomings of behaviorism were becoming increasingly apparent. Many of its notions were found to be largely sterile, particularly in terms of understanding human behavior. Given the complexity of human responses, behaviorists had been obliged to focus their studies on rats and pigeons; but the implications of such research on human behavior were less than obvious. Moreover, simple elements of daily experience, such as the fact of being hungry, were denied any meaningful content since no observable stimulus and response are present. A move was on to reinstate subjective experience back into the black box stationed between stimulus and response. But how, given the materialist trend of contemporary science, was the mind to be allowed back into reality?

One theory proposes that mental states are equivalent to behavioral dispositions; if a hungry man is presented with food, he will eat. His disposition to eat is equated with his subjective experience of hunger. This theory is simplistic in that it ignores other possible restraints on behavior—perhaps the hungry man is on a diet—and it is sterile in that it provides no information about the actual nature of mental events. It acknowledges the reality of mental events, but only nominally.

Another approach to admitting the existence of the mind is to equate all mental events with neurophysiological processes. The mind/body duality is thereby discarded by reducing the mind to the body, and the body to inanimate chemical and physical components. When a proponent of this view, such as Francis Crick, speaks of "poking inside the black box" between stimulus and response, he refers not to observing mental states by means of introspection but to exploring the brain. Having dispensed with mental events in this fashion, a neuroscientist may assert, for example, that pain travels in nerve cells on the way to the brain in the form of electrical impulses, activating the release of a chemical carrier (neurotransmitter) at a synapse between two nerve cells. The subjective experience of pain is thus granted existence, but purely as an electrical and chemical phenomenon.

We have already noted how physics has explained the objects of the five senses—color, sound, and so forth—in terms of black-box events that are inaccessible to direct experience. Now neuroscience completes this process by seeking to explain all mental events in a manner abstracted from experience. Crick writes in this regard that "the evidence of introspection should never be accepted at face value. It should be explained in terms other than just its own."[6] Individual personal experience now counts for virtually nothing in our quest for truth, for the actual nature of all physical and mental events is presumed to lie behind experience. The black box of the mind has been discarded, only to be replaced by the black box of chemistry and physics.

Some of the shortcomings of the black-box approach have been discussed in previous chapters dealing with the foundations of physics. These problems are all the more acute when one devalues not only sensory experience but all other mental states. The dogma of mechanistic materialism insists that all of reality be explained by the laws of physics. That subjective sensory experience is related to physical stimuli is not in question; nor are there any grounds for doubting that other mental events, such as pain, desire, and awareness, are related to neurological processes. But on what grounds, and at what expense, shall we reduce subjective experience to objective, physical events? Research into electrical impulses, neurotransmitters, and synapses may indeed provide us with valuable insight into the physical basis for the experience of pain. But on what scientific grounds shall we assert that pain is nothing more than those physical processes?

By reducing all subjective experience to physical processes, this approach provides no further knowledge about the physical events that it investigates, and it closes the door on any possible empirical, introspective investigation into the nature of the mind. If one were to identify neurological events simply as the physical basis for subjective experience rather than equating the two, the value of such physical research would be in no way diminished, and the door would remain open to introspective research that may yield its own unique insights.

In short, the reduction of the mind to the brain is scientifically unjustified and pragmatically disastrous. What are the effects of conceiving all our emotions, hopes, ideas, and perceptions—indeed our very personal identity—as coemergent properties of chemicals and electrical circuitry? By adopting such a view, people may feel that the source of all psychological afflictions lies fundamentally in the neural system. As a result, they may reasonably seek only material remedies for such problems, such as drugs and tranquilizers. Similarly, issues of a spiritual nature dealing with the fundamental questions of our existence are also reduced to physics and chemistry, closing the door on any truly spiritual quest for truth and personal fulfillment. We have paid a severe price for the materialist ideal of reducing life and mind to matter, and we have received very little in return.

The existence of the mind has clearly proved a quandary for natural science. Radical behaviorists sought to deny it altogether. Other cognitive scientists, reacting to the absurd sterility of that conclusion, nominally reinstated mental states as dispositions, without shedding

any further light on the actual nature of the mind. Physical reductionists acknowledge the existence of mental events only by reducing them
to physical processes—once again offering no knowledge apart from
the physical basis of subjective experience. Yet another response is to
assert that mental events do indeed exist and are themselves of a nonphysical nature. The duality of the body and mind is thereby resur-
rected, returning us, at least in principle, to Descartes. In this view,
however, mental events are granted only an epiphenomenal status as
functions of the brain. They are not equated with any configuration
of neurological events but rather are regarded as mere functions of
them. Thus, the brain thinks, feels, perceives, decides, and imagines
much as a computer calculates and analyzes.

Adherents of this *functionalist* view seem to overlook the anomalous nature of these purported emergent functions of the brain. In all
other cases of emergent properties of natural phenomena, both the
phenomenon itself and its emergent properties (including its functions) can be seen simultaneously using a single mode of observation. When instruments detect the brain and its various electrochemi-
cal functions, however, they do not detect mental events; and when
we introspectively observe mental events, we do not detect the brain
or its functions. Despite this problem, the functionalist view might
have some credibility if it entailed a clear understanding of the manner in which the brain or any other physical system produces conscious and unconscious mental events. But in fact, modern neuroscience has no idea how the brain gives rise to the purported emergent property of consciousness. Proponents of this view frequently
acknowledge this fact, but they call upon others to join them in their
faith that such scientific knowledge will soon be forthcoming.

The functionalist view, like that of physical reductionism, has not
been empirically or scientifically demonstrated. Rather, it is simply
one more expression of a metaphysical predilection. Like the Cartesian view, it wishes to acknowledge the mind/body duality, while
allowing the mind no active role in nature. While appearing very
modern, particularly when discussed in terms of brain/computer com-
parisons, the basic functionalist hypothesis was devised long before
the advent of Western science. Perhaps its earliest expression was in
the tenets of the Cārvāka philosophical school of ancient India.

There is compelling scientific evidence in support of the view that
neurological processes contribute to the creation of mental events. That
such physical and mental events are causally related is beyond dis-

pute. Proponents of both physical reductionism and functionalism, however, often ignore the empirical fact that these causal relations work both ways. Research that is performed on the brain shows how neurological events influence the mind. But such ordinary experiences as voluntary movement provide ample evidence that the mind influences the brain as well. Such common events are not adequately explained by these theories, and the manner in which subjective experience influences the body remains unknown.

It appears, then, that the functionalist view provides a mere semblance of understanding of mental states, without justifying its conclusions or shedding any further light on the actual nature of the mind. This hypothesis and the others mentioned above cannot explicate the unique character of mental events, they offer no knowledge of the origins of consciousness, they fail to elucidate the obvious interaction of mental and physical events, and they provide no method for empirically investigating mental states as opposed to their physical bases. In the concluding remarks of his article "The Mind-Body Problem," Jerry Fodor writes: "There is probably no better way to decide what is methodologically permissible in science than by investigating what successful science requires."[7] If we apply this criterion, we must conclude that while modern science has valuable methods for exploring neurological events that are associated with subjective experience, it is less successful in explaining the nature of mental events themselves. Its measuring devices, experimental techniques, and mathematical tools are well designed to increase our knowledge of the physical world; but their use is limited when it comes to the investigation of subjectively experienced mental states.

Crick writes that much of philosophy has been barren for more than two thousand years because we have been able to report only a minute fraction of the events taking place in the brain. Introspection, he claims, must be retained, but, as mentioned previously, the evidence gained thereby must in his view be explained in terms other than just its own. If we accept the premise that much of Western philosophy has been barren, need we accept this explanation for its shortcomings? Since the time of Aristotle, objective science has made enormous strides in devising finer and finer instruments of measurement, experimental techniques, and mathematical tools. These advances have been largely responsible for our achievements in exploring the objective world. What comparable progress have we made in refining our means of empirically investigating and analyzing the subjective world of the mind and experience? Have philosophers or scientists made remarkable breakthroughs in improving our introspective abilities? For these, after all, are our sole means of directly exploring mental events as opposed to their physical bases in the brain.

Clearly our civilization has developed no means for scientifically investigating subjective experience that in any way compare to the methods of objective science. Physical reductionists value introspection only insofar as it enables them to identify neurological events with subjective experience. But the level of introspection required for such identification thus far has been crude and unrefined. If neuroscience is to employ its own methods with maximum effectiveness, it should be conjoined with a level of disciplined introspection that is comparable to its own degree of sophistication. This is an enormous challenge, for modern neuroscience employs methods of physics, chemistry, and biology that have been gradually developed over centuries. How, then, in terms of an introspective science, are we to make up for the lack of progress in this field over the past two millennia?

The answer to this dilemma lies in the recognition that ours is not the only civilization that has seriously concerned itself with verifiable, empirical research into the nature of reality. We have excelled in the field of objective science, but our introspective achievements are so primitive that they are hardly worth mentioning. The ancient cultures of India, China, and Tibet did not match our objective science, but they developed contemplative sciences far in advance of our own marginal efforts. Each civilization will be enhanced by drawing from the other's hard-earned experience; and by the integration of the deepest insights of the ancient and the modern, of the East and the West, an unprecedented natural science may appear that embraces the entirety of nature, including mind, matter, and energy.

Chapter Twenty-three

A Contemplative View of the Mind

When we inquire into our personal experience of physical and mental events, we find that we encounter two types of phenomena that bear distinct differences. Material objects characteristically have location and may have mass, velocity, and physical dimensions. Thus, they lend themselves to quantitative measurement and analysis. Some mental events, such as physical pain, may be located in specific areas in the body, but for others the notion of location seems inappropriate. Where, for example, is affection located; or where are the recollections of one's childhood? It is possible to locate neurophysiological processes that are associated with certain mental states, but science has in no way demonstrated that the two are equivalent. It is possible to trigger specific mental events by electrically stimulating areas of the brain and to trigger specific neurological events by subjectively stimulating the mind. This proves neither that the mental events can be reduced to the physical nor the opposite. It is just as reasonable to explain the evidence of introspection in its own subjective terms as it is to explain the findings of objective science in its terms.

The concepts of mass, velocity, and physical dimension are all inappropriate when discussing the whole range of mental events; nor do they lend themselves to precise quantitative measurement. Just as physical phenomena have their own unique attributes, so do mental events have theirs. The dominant property of mental states is awareness. To define consciousness, we need not engage in mental gymnastics, nor in abstract, philosophical speculation: it is that very event of knowing, with which we are all familiar. The mental gymnastics come in only when we try to define this firsthand event in terms of noncognitive physical processes, configurations of matter, abstract behavioral dispositions, emergent properties of the brain, and so on.

Mental events are modes of awareness, and it is this property that distinguishes them from physical entities. Unless we allow our introspective faculty to atrophy (for example, by subjecting ourselves to the dictates of physical reductionism, which takes us away from experience, not deeper into it) we must readily acknowledge that mental events are every bit as real as physical events. Our thoughts, intentions, and emotional states maneuver our bodies and thereby other physical objects; likewise, material things are constantly influencing our mental states. Subjective empirical examination of mental and physical events indicates that both types of phenomena are in a constant state of flux, both act as causal agents, and both are influenced by causes that are themselves physical and mental.

Adherents of mechanistic materialism, with their insistence on quantitative knowledge, may easily overlook these otherwise evident facts of our experience. We may recall Einstein's comment that it is the theory that determines what can be experienced. In the light of this insight, it is apparent that physical reductionism blinds its proponents to realms of experience that are easily available to those unafflicted by this view.

Just as the materialist is bent on expressing the evidence of introspection in terms of physical science and reducing all of existence to mass and energy, so does the idealist seek to reduce the physical world to an emanation of the mind. Idealists are not content to acknowledge the existence of objective physical events. Turning Francis Crick's admonition on its head, they might well state: "The evidence of objective science should never be accepted at face value. It should be explained in terms other than just its own, namely in terms of the one absolute reality—the mind."

Idealists may further claim that we have no empirical access to a physical world apart from the mind; therefore objective physical events cannot be explored or discussed in a truly scientific manner. Any scientific explanation of physical phenomena must be couched in terms of the one type of phenomenon that is immediately accessible to direct observation, namely mental events. Just as materialists deprive themselves of the possibility of profoundly exploring the mind and manifesting its deepest potentials, so do the idealists turn their backs on careful investigation of the physical world and the development of technology.

The Buddhist centrist view regards both materialism and idealism as extremes. The objective physical world is empirically knowable in relation to our modes of experience, as is the subjective cognitive world. The terms *subject* and *object* are used, but they denote a mere conventional duality, rather than the absolute duality that we encounter in Cartesian-based Western thinking. For example, in scientific dualism it is common to posit photons or electromagnetic waves as objective conditions for the visual experience, and such physical phenomena are considered to exist independently of perception. According to the Buddhist centrist view, the objective condition for a visual perception of the color of a rose is the very color that we perceive; and it exists in relation to our perception of it.

Thus, from the perspective of the centrist view, the object of that perception is not photons, a certain set of frequencies of electromagnetic waves, or any other event existing inherently in some independent, objective, and invisible world. Both subject and object exist in interdependence, both are evident to experience, and the distinction between them is conventional, not intrinsic.

To elucidate this point further, let us take another example: the conceptual cognition of electromagnetic waves. Let us assume that such waves do in fact exist. In this case, the cognized event—electromagnetic waves—exists in relation to the conceptual awareness of it; and that conceptual awareness exists in relation to that event. That cognition contacts its object via a generic idea of such waves, and that idea also exists only in a mutually dependent relationship with the corresponding conceptual awareness. We may also conceive of things that have no existence whatever. The absolute space of classical physics provides one example. Absolute space does not exist, either conventionally or intrinsically, so it does not exist in relation to the conceptual cognition of it. The generic idea of absolute space does exist, however, and it is mutually interdependent with the belief in such space.

Physical and mental events occur in mutual interaction and are therefore interdependent. Thus, neither can be considered absolute in the sense of being independent; nor is one more real than the other. Our verbal and conceptual constructs determine the manner in which we commonly experience physical and mental phenomena;

and the events that we perceive do not exist independently of those constructs. Even the very distinctions between subject and object, mental and physical, do not exist apart from conceptual designation; so neither class of phenomena could possibly exist intrinsically and independently.

The centrist view casts off the limitations of experience imposed by materialism and idealism. It encourages us to explore the natural world in its entirety, including the physical and the mental domains, and to tap these resources to their fullest. Western civilization is justifiably proud of its enormous achievements in objective science and technology. A major challenge facing it now is to acknowledge the possibility that other civilizations may have made their own astonishing discoveries and accomplishments in terms of their contemplative science and technology.

———————◆———————

Let us reexamine the nature of mental events in relation to the physical world. Nowadays, perhaps the most sophisticated scientific cognitive theory states that mental events are equivalent to patternings or configurations of mass/energy. Most people who adopt this view assume that mass/energy exists independently of consciousness. Thus, the Cartesian duality of mind versus matter is overcome by identifying the mind with epiphenomenal patternings of physical events. There is solid evidence for stating that mental events are related to such patternings, but the grounds for equating the two seem inconclusive. The experience of heat is normally related to the random kinetic energy of molecules; the perception of colors is associated with certain frequencies of electromagnetic radiation; the experience of taste is usually related to the chemical structure of the tasted substance. But in all the above cases, close inspection has shown that there is no one-to-one correspondence between the subjective experience and the objective phenomena posited by modern science. No such uniform correspondence has been demonstrated between mental events and patternings of mass/energy, and it is questionable whether any such equivalence will ever be established empirically. Even if such a correspondence were eventually proven, this by itself would not necessarily imply that mental events are themselves patternings of mass/energy.

Scientific convention uses the term *light* in reference to the conceived phenomena of electromagnetic waves, whereas in common parlance it refers to a visually perceived phenomenon. Similarly, science may use subjective terms such as *pain, perception,* and *memory* in reference to configurations of mass/energy. Such conventions are malleable, but they should not lead us to believe that mental events are equivalent to patternings of mass/energy, any more than the appearance of light is identical with electromagnetic waves.

Everyday experience provides us with a general mode of observation of such sensory objects as the color of a rose and such mental events as feelings, desires, and mental imagery. This mode of observation is regarded as subjective. It allows us to describe these events in accordance with our personal experience. Western science has developed another general mode of research which uses the phenomena presented to our awareness as grounds for constructing a physical world that purportedly exists independently of the events that we perceive and yet accounts for them. These two modes of inquiry are profoundly different, and in many respects they are incompatible. Neither unveils reality itself as it exists apart from our perceptions and conceptions. Both illuminate elements of conventional reality that exist in relation to those modes of inquiry. Thus, the grounds for equating elements of the physical world constructed by Western science with elements of everyday personal experience are extremely tenuous.

It makes just as little sense to try to equate quantum phenomena with those of classical physics. It is usually not the case that classical and quantum mechanics observe the same phenomena in different but complementary ways. Rather, due to their differing modes of inquiry, they reveal different aspects of the physical world. Similarly, modern neuroscience and Buddhist contemplative science do not usually examine the same phenomena in different ways. Rather, they observe different types of events that exist in relation to their contrasting modes of investigation. The powerful urge to include all phenomena within a single unified theory—while ignoring the profound distinctions between the modes of questioning that resulted in the observation of those phenomena—is based upon the deep-rooted assumption that the universe we experience exists independently of our perceptions and ideas. It is this assumption that is questioned by the Buddhist centrist view.

Let us now proceed to explore the nature of mental events in relation to contemplative research, which may be regarded as refined everyday experience. Modern physical science has discovered a principle of nature that has become perhaps its most central tenet: namely, the conservation of energy. Although mass/energy may undergo radical transformations, it is never created from absolutely nothing, nor does it ever totally vanish from existence. Might there be a comparable principle when dealing with consciousness?

Before addressing this question, we must take a position concerning the relation between mental and physical events. We have seen that the grounds for reducing mental events to physical phenomena of any kind, including patternings of mass/energy, are inconclusive. The Buddhist centrist view finds equally untenable the reduction of the physical world to configurations or emergent properties of consciousness. Mental events deserve to be examined and analyzed in terms of their own characteristics, just as science does with physical phenomena. Let us regard the mind from the contemplative viewpoint and provisionally use the hypothesis that mental events exist as a different class of phenomena than the physical. We thereby accept a dualism of a conventional sort, not of an absolute, Cartesian variety.

Using the above hypothesis, we are now in a position to ask: whence do mental events arise? Is mass/energy the stuff out of which they are created, or do they originate from some other type of phenomenon? Let us examine the hypothesis that awareness, as an example of a mental event, arises from mass/energy. According to the principle of conservation of energy, if any new physical entity, such as the heat from a fire, is created, some other form of mass/energy must have been used up in the process. That heat may have originated from some of the stored energy of wood, which is released in the process of combustion.

It therefore follows that if some physical entity—say, a component of the brain—is to be identified as the origin of awareness, that physical entity must be used up in the process of producing the awareness. The physical component would be transformed into the mental phenomenon, just as the energy in the wood is transformed into heat. The difference in our hypothetical production of awareness is that the physical component would be transformed into a nonphysical phenomenon. Now physics has discovered a vast body of evidence to support the principle that physical phenomena are conserved through all known transformations. To be conserved means, for the physicist, that they retain their physical status as forms of mass/energy.

Thus, the hypothesis that any physical component or process in the brain transforms into a nonphysical mental event would be vigorously denied on the grounds of energy conservation. Given our initial hypothesis that mental events are nonphysical, events in the brain certainly influence mental phenomena, but the former cannot be the source of the latter.

Does the whole range of mental entities arise from nothing at all? In this case, processes in the brain would assist in the continual production of mental events, but those nonphysical phenomena would essentially arise from nothing. Nowhere else in the whole of nature does an entity originate from simply nothing, so it seems implausible that this process should be posited for mental events. Even in principle it seems to fly in the face of logic to suppose that events in the brain could influence nothing to become something.

If mental events do not originate either from mass/energy or from nothing, whence do they arise? Buddhist contemplative science responds that they originate from preceding mental events. Mental states arise from previous mental states in an unbroken continuum, much as physical entities arise from preceding physical entities. The aspects of those mental events may change dramatically, but consciousness is essentially conserved. Physical events modify and condition mental processes without transforming into them; and, conversely, mental events modify and condition physical processes without transforming into them.

Modern physics claims that mass/energy can never be utterly destroyed: in the physical realm something cannot transform into nothing. Does a similar principle hold true for consciousness? Buddhist contemplatives respond that the essential stream of consciousness of any sentient being—human or otherwise—cannot be utterly destroyed. The contemplative principle of the conservation of consciousness holds, both in the process of creation and in that of cessation. As this is the case during the course of an individual's life, so is it true at conception and at death.

Tibetan Buddhist contemplatives assert that during the death process, the various forms of vital energy in the body retract into the very subtle life-sustaining energy. During this same process the five forms of sensory awareness as well as one's conceptualizing faculties retract into the very subtle consciousness. At the final, clear light stage of the death process, this very subtle energy and nonconceptual awareness remain; and when they depart from the body, death occurs. This subtle continuum of vital energy and consciousness can never be destroyed, nor can the two ever be separated.[1] Indeed, it may be more accurate to think of a single entity—the continuum—bearing physical and mental attributes. It is at this level that the duality of physical and mental events disappears.

The very subtle continuum of energy/consciousness can also never be freshly created. It is the entrance of this continuum into the union of the sperm and egg that enables the zygote to grow into a fetus. Consciousness is therefore present from the moment of conception onward; and during the development of a human fetus, the five types of sensory awareness and conceptual cognitions arise from that initial consciousness. Similarly, during the growth of the fetus, various derivative forms of vital energy arise from the original very subtle life-sustaining energy. Modern neuroscience regards human sensory and mental cognitions as being emergent properties of the brain. Buddhist contemplative science, in contrast, regards them as emergent properties of the very subtle energy/mind.

According to Tibetan Buddhist contemplatives, there is an unbroken continuum of consciousness throughout life, the death process, an intermediate state, and on to the next life.[2] These transitions are ordinarily so traumatic, however, that the individual quickly loses any recollection of this experience; and by the time an infant can speak, memory of its time in the womb and before then may be inaccessible. This should hardly come as a surprise, since most adults can remember very little even of their early childhood. The more recent events of one's life intervene, and earlier memories withdraw into a latent state. The continuum of consciousness itself flows on, unbroken, but because one's memory is lost at these crucial transitions, one loses this sense of continuity. On what, then, do Buddhist contemplatives base their highly detailed accounts of the sequence of death, intermediate state, and rebirth?

These contemplatives employ ancient meditative practices that enable the adept to refine and stabilize the mind so that an unbroken clarity of awareness is maintained throughout all these events. Here is a mode of research that could hardly differ more drastically from the methods of modern Western science. The observed events, too, are bound to be profoundly different from those known by Western science. The events witnessed by a Buddhist contemplative, however, are no more intrinsically real than those observed by a neuroscientist. Nor do Buddhist, any more than scientific, theories describe the way things "really are," unrelated to the mode of research upon which those theories are based.

Tibetan contemplatives also create facsimiles of the death, intermediate state, and rebirth process through their powers of meditation, enabling them to transform these actual experiences to the enhancement of their spiritual growth.[3] It is believed that such advanced contemplatives die, take rebirth, and as young children often remember many of the events of their previous lives as well as experiences following their recent deaths. Such children are called *tulkus* in Tibetan, and for centuries it has been the tradition in that culture to seek out such spiritually advanced children so that they can quickly recommence their contemplative training.[4]

Other young children, often up to the age of four or five, may also recall events in their previous life, particularly if they had died in a sudden, violent way. There are numerous documented cases of this occurrence on several continents, and the most plausible explanation seems to be the simplest: for each individual there exists a continuum of life, intermediate state, and rebirth.[5]

If one seriously considers this assertion of the continuity of consciousness, a number of qualms may arise. How, for example, does this theory account for the fact that the human population on the planet is increasing if no new continua of consciousness are created? And how can the population decrease in times of war or famine if consciousnesses cannot be destroyed? Buddhist and other contemplatives commonly assert that the rebirth process can carry over from human to nonhuman forms of life and vice versa. Moreover, there is no reason in principle why a conscious continuum must invariably reincarnate on our planet. According to the Buddhist worldview, there are countless other worlds inhabited by human and nonhuman forms of life; and a being that dies in one world may be reborn in another.

We may further wonder whether there are meaningful causal relationships among the sequence of lives connected by an individual's continuum of subtle energy/mind. Buddhist contemplatives respond that such relationships are indeed present. The quality of our present life profoundly influences the type of future births that we will take: some types of rebirth are favorable, both for one's well-being and in terms of one's further spiritual maturation; and the type of behavior that yields such rebirth is deemed wholesome. Unwholesome behavior leads to misery in future lives and to situations in which the opportunities for spiritual growth are extremely limited.

On this basis a system of ethics is developed that is asserted to be grounded in natural relationships between actions and their results from life to life. The laws of karma concern just those relationships. The Buddhist spiritual path entails the cultivation of wholesome behavior and the attenuation of the unwholesome. In this way one comes to live increasingly in accordance with reality, in which all things exist as dependently related events. Unwholesome action, on the other hand, is motivated by mental distortions, primarily ignorance. By increasingly living in accordance with reality, one gains ever-deepening experiential insight into the nature of that reality.

As we follow the implications of this worldview, we may ask: how did consciousness first originate in the evolution of the cosmos? If no stream of consciousness is freshly created, this would imply that each continuum has no conceivable beginning! This is precisely the conclusion of Buddhist contemplatives. At the same time, Buddhist cosmology does posit a beginning to the present cycle that the cosmos is evolving through, though its history thus far is thought to be much longer than the twenty billion years suggested by modern cosmology. At the beginning of this cycle, there was only empty space, composed—according to one Buddhist theory known as the Wheel of Time—of space-particles. These particles were stimulated by the actions of the sentient beings who were to inhabit this cosmos, giving rise to a movement of energy. This in turn resulted in the production of heat, which led to the formation of liquids and solids.

In the early stages of this evolution, the cosmos was uninhabitable for human and animal life. However, highly advanced Buddhist and Hindu contemplatives speak of experiencing other realms, or dimensions, of existence that transcend this gross sensual realm, which they call the *kāmadhātu*. They report the existence of the *rūpadhātu*, a form realm that is unperturbed by many of the changes in the gross physical cosmos. And beyond this is the *arūpyadhātu*, a formless realm that is completely unaffected by the stages of cosmic evolution. All three of these realms are said to be inhabited by sentient beings. Indeed, when the sensual or gross physical dimension of a cosmos is uninhabitable, most sentient beings are thought to dwell in the form and formless realms or in other inhabitable cosmoses. Humans cannot dwell in the form and formless realms, although they are considered to be accessible to a human mind that has been highly refined through the practice of meditation.

According to Buddhist contemplative science, ours is not the only world that is undergoing these stages of evolution. The universe is composed of clusters of worlds, each containing on the order of a billion systems, and many of them are inhabited.[6] In short, we dwell in a limitless universe inhabited by countless sentient beings. Neither the universe nor its conscious inhabitants can be traced to an ultimate beginning, nor are we destined for ultimate annihilation.

Tibetan Buddhism asserts that our experiences of our environment come about as manifestations (might one say emergent properties?) of imprints placed upon our mental continua due to previous actions. Such imprints are sometimes called *karmic seeds*, and the world that each of us experiences arises from those seeds. Some of our actions are committed in relative isolation, while others are committed in participation with others. As the imprints from those actions manifest, we experience events individually and in common with others, respectively. In short, participatory action yields participatory experience, while solitary individual action yields solitary experience.

According to this view, multiple worlds coexist in an interpenetrating fashion. One might liken this to different frequencies of electromagnetic energy occupying the same space: the band of frequencies that one detects depends upon how one's receiver is tuned. This allows for a tremendous malleability of experience for a single individual, depending on how the mind is transformed. The type of events that we experience is a function of our conceptual conditioning. And numerous Buddhist contemplatives have verified that in the utter absence of even the most subtle conceptualization all appearances vanish, and only emptiness is experienced.

The theory of emptiness is relatively simple, whereas the Buddhist theory of karma, or of actions and their results from life to life, is extremely complex. A satisfactory understanding of the process underlying the commonality of our experience and of the causal interactions among phenomena can be gained only through prolonged study and contemplative inquiry. As one's insight into emptiness deepens, understanding of the interdependent nature of events is enhanced. And as one investigates more closely the interactions among phenomena, their lack of inherent existence becomes increasingly apparent.

Upon first encountering this contemplative view of the mind and the cosmos, our initial reaction may be: this worldview, while rather interesting, can only be the product of the imaginations of Eastern mystics. Using only the human mind as one's means of investigation, how could one ever know of the existence of past and future lives, the relationships between actions and their effects from life to life, and the history and breadth of the universe? This entire worldview must be relegated to the status of religious mythology and not be confused with sound scientific discovery.

This response is based on the assumption that the mind is incapable of such direct empirical investigation of physical and mental reality. Buddhist contemplatives would swiftly agree that anyone who is not highly experienced in advanced meditative discipline can only speculate on these matters. But a central facet of Buddhist cultures over the past twenty-five hundred years has been precisely to keep this contemplative tradition alive. If modern scientists find it unbelievable that Buddhist contemplatives can explore physical reality and higher dimensions directly with their minds, so do traditional Tibetans find it amazing that modern cosmologists have gained so much progress using only mechanical instruments, mathematics, and imagination.

Although many of the assertions of modern cosmology seem abstract and speculative, scientists are able to show the evidence on which they base their claims; and their mathematical reasoning is accessible for those of sufficient intelligence and training. Can Buddhist contemplatives likewise give a precise account of the empirical manner in which they arrive at their view of the nature of the mind and its role in the universe? And are these types of training accessible to us today as a living discipline? If so, their theories stand the scientific test of being subject to empirical refutation, perhaps even more so than scientific theories concerning entities in the black box of nature.

When first encountering a theory that differs radically from one's accustomed views, skepticism is bound to arise, whether in a classical physicist upon first hearing about quantum theory, or in a neuroscientist upon first learning of Buddhist contemplative theory. It is most useful to transform simple skepticism into critical investigation, and the first step is to identify the specific object of one's doubts. In the creation of an empirically based theory, three phases deserve special attention: (1) the method of research or experimentation, (2) the reporting of the observed phenomena, and (3) the conclusions drawn from those observations.

If a theory is based upon research methods that lack credibility, the contents of the theory may be dismissed. One example would be a physical theory that is based upon a poorly conducted experiment. Similarly, if certain contemplative methods do not refine human awareness but simply lead to states of trance and hallucinations, we need not concern ourselves with the theories that arise from them. We must be convinced of the usefulness of a research method and its reliability in yielding sound data.

Secondly, we may question the reporting of the observed phenomena. This is essentially a question of accuracy and honesty. In Western science high standards of integrity have normally been maintained in this regard, and the same is true in the Buddhist tradition. Nevertheless, out of reverence for outstanding scientists and contemplatives, their followers may attribute to them discoveries and accomplishments that they never claimed. Thus, care needs to be taken to check out the source and veracity of such accounts.

The third phase is most subtle, especially when we bear in mind that both the method of research and the reporting of results are theory-laden. The essential question here is: is the theory justified given the nature of the empirical evidence? Are the conclusions drawn in a reasonable fashion, or do they appear farfetched? Here is the issue of interpretation, and—as we have seen in the case of the Casimir effect—it is a complex one. It should certainly be evident that more than one theory may appear justified in light of the evidence; that is, the observed phenomena alone do not determine how they are to be interpreted.

In the preceding discussion of Buddhist theories frequent reference has been made to the views of Tibetan contemplatives. It would be misleading to leave the reader with the impression that all Tibetan contemplatives hold the same views and speak with one voice. While there is widespread agreement among them concerning many of the essential aspects of Buddhist theory, there is also a diversity of methods that they favor, as well as differing modes of interpretation.

Buddhism does offer various means for experiencing ultimate reality in a manner that transcends language and concept. Concepts, however, are used in the training leading to such experience, and differing theories are created around it. Moreover, some modes of contemplative investigation are more penetrating than others, and some theories make intelligible a broader range of phenomena. For those reasons, one contemplative theory may be regarded as being superior to another.

Various incompatible theories concerning conventional phenomena can also be found in Buddhist literature. Different contemplative techniques yield different results, and the interpretation of those results also varies. For example, discussions of the types and functions of vital energy differ from one Tibetan Buddhist system to another. Further distinctions are found in discussions of this topic by Hindu and Taoist contemplatives. All of these contemplative traditions, however, recognize the existence of vital energies and emphasize the advantages of mastering them. Recognizing that no type of vital energy exists inherently in nature, we may focus more on the usefulness of a given theory, rather than on its presumed representation of any objective truth. For the search for the one true theory of vital energies is futile.

As stated previously, an empirically based theory deserves our attention only if the research methods upon which it is based appear useful and credible. Thus, let us turn now to a closer inspection of some of the methods used in Buddhist contemplative science.

Chapter Twenty-four

Refining Human Consciousness

Western scientific research has led to a number of theoretical conclusions similar to the tenets of the Buddhist centrist view. For example, there is now a widespread belief among contemporary psychologists that refutes the existence of a homunculus, a little person in the mind/brain that controls all conscious mental functions. Much insight has also been gained concerning the pervasive role of language and concept in our experience. And scientists in various fields have begun to seriously ponder the possible relation between conceptual designation and reality itself.

Such insights, however, usually remain abstracted from daily life. They often remain on the level of an intellectual conviction without making a profound impact on the individual's personal experience. For example, one may be intellectually certain that an individual is not endowed with a substantial, autonomous personal identity; yet one may still strongly *feel* that one exists with such an ego. Especially in moments of strong ambition, passion, or arrogance this sense of personal identity may arise forcefully. Similarly, one's theories about the role of conceptualization in human experience and the nature of reality may be very acute, and yet one's day-to-day experience may be virtually untouched by those theories.

In a previous chapter we investigated methods of realizing personal identitylessness. The modes of analysis that were presented made frequent use of the terms *body* and *mind*. Now if one's knowledge of the nature of one's own body and mind is largely abstract and intellectual, inquiry into the relation between the self and the body/mind is unlikely to penetrate to a deeper level. It will simply lead to further theoretical conclusions that have little power to transform one's experience of reality. Thus, as a basis for such analysis it is most useful to examine closely the nature and functioning of one's body (and sensory experience in general), feelings, mental states, and other mental contents.

One's own mind is potentially the most penetrating instrument for examining each of these four types of phenomena from moment to moment. Do they exist as static things, or do they exist in a continual state of flux? Is the experience of them essentially pleasurable, indifferent, or unsatisfactory? Do any of these phenomena exhibit qualities of "I" or "mine" in their own nature, or do they simply arise into consciousness and pass from it as mere impersonal events? A major challenge of this method of inquiry is to distinguish what seems to be presented to one's awareness as opposed to the preconceived judgments that we project upon those appearances.

Upon investigating these phenomena from moment to moment, one proceeds to examine the sequential, causal relationships among these physical and mental events. As one witnesses with relative passivity the interactions among sensory experiences, feelings, desires, intentions, and so on, one may further question the existence of any controlling ego that lies outside the fields of one's experience. Even when that sense of personal identity is restrained from active manipulation of one's body/mind, it may be found that mental and physical interactions continue to take place. In this way one may experientially realize that no substantial, autonomous "I" is to be found within the experienced body/mind. And one may further realize that there is no evidence of mental and physical events being controlled by an ego that lies outside of one's experience. The "experiencer" itself can be identified as mental consciousness, which is devoid of "I" or "mine."[1]

Such empirical insights can have an extremely profound effect upon one's intuitive sense of personal identity. This in turn makes a major impact on one's emotions, one's way of regarding other people, and the manner in which one responds to them. Such familiarity with the physical and mental phenomena that form the basis of designation for the self provides a firm foundation for yet deeper investigation from the perspective of the centrist view. The techniques outlined above are very challenging. They are examples of Buddhist "insight" meditation. Insight in this context is attained through a general and detailed examination of reality and the systematic application of intellectual discrimination.[2] The sole instrument for that research is one's own mind, and if its attention span is brief and its powers of observation heavily clouded with compulsive conceptualization, such inquiry is bound to be unreliable. Most of us may well find that our own present mental stability and clarity for such research are very limited.

To test this statement, let us pause to engage in a brief experiment to test the present level of these faculties. Sit comfortably in a chair, with the feet firmly resting on the floor. One's back should be reasonably erect, the eyes may be closed, and the muscles of the face, eyes, neck, and shoulders should be relaxed. Maintaining normal unforced respiration, direct the attention to the tactile sensations of the expansion and contraction of the diaphragm during inhalation and exhalation. Allow the mind to remain conceptually silent: quietly direct the awareness to these sensations associated with the breath, with the mind remaining in a passive, witnessing mode. Do not take the respiration as an object for conceptual analysis or cogitation, but simply perceive the tactile sensations, moment by moment, with a continuity of clear, stable mindfulness. Maintain this conceptually silent, yet lucid and wakeful state of awareness for five minutes, without mental wandering or torpor.

It is quite possible that in all your years of education, you have never been trained to cultivate this simple form of quiescent, stable, lucid awareness. If so, you probably found that much of that five-minute period was spent in conceptual distraction, and even when the attention was on the breath, it lacked clarity and continuity. Such an undisciplined mind is a very poor instrument for empirically investigating the nature of mental or physical events. This unrefined state of consciousness also makes us prone to unnecessary suffering when the mind is dominated by such emotions as fear, resentment, guilt, and aggression.

The disadvantages of an undisciplined mind were widely recognized in India during the time of the Buddha, twenty-five hundred years ago. Individuals who earnestly sought truth were therefore naturally encouraged first to refine the quality of their lives and to train their minds through contemplative practices. Traditionally, the initial emphasis in Buddhist meditative discipline is on stabilizing the mind.

Such training requires very demanding preparation and sustained, undistracted commitment to meditative discipline, and it is fraught with physical and psychological perils. These are some of the reasons why this training is not frequently given nowadays, especially in the West, despite the obvious need for mental stability and clarity as a firm foundation for contemplative insight.

One may, of course, devote one's contemplative practice entirely to the cultivation of insight, without specifically seeking to stabilize the mind as a discipline in its own right. Such training can still yield many insights, but if one's awareness is unstable, such moments of realization are bound to be brief and intermittent at best, and limited in their transformative power to eliminate suffering and the mental afflictions that produce anxiety and grief. The emphasis in traditional Buddhist practice is on saturating the mind in the realization of the absence of a substantial personal identity and in the realization of emptiness. It is only by repeated and prolonged experience of those truths that one is freed from the mental distortion of ignorance. In principle, it is possible to develop mental stability in the very process of exploring the nature of reality. But as long as one's attention is moving from one object to another, deep stability is not gained.

In the Buddha's teachings recorded in the Pali language, forty techniques are set forth that lead to mental stabilization.[3] Among them, specific methods are indicated for aspirants of various temperaments and inclinations. Among those forty methods, only one is appropriate for people with a strong tendency toward conceptualization and imagination: mindfulness of the respiration.[4] A wide variety of other techniques are presented in Sanskrit and Tibetan contemplative literature. Visualization of the Buddha, for example, is one commonly taught method,[5] while focusing one's awareness on the mind itself is another potent method for achieving quiescence.[6] Numerous other means are set forth in more advanced systems of Buddhist meditation.[7]

Given the fact that so many people brought up in modern Western society are prone to intense, compulsive conceptualization, it may be helpful to introduce briefly the technique of mindfulness of the respiration. In this practice one sits with the torso erect in a posture that is both stable and relaxed. At the beginning of an inhalation, the attention is focused on the apertures of the nostrils. Then throughout the inhalation, one follows the course of the sensations of the breath into the nose, down the throat, and down the torso to the level of the navel. The object of the awareness is the tactile sensations associated with the inhalation, rather than the actual movement of the air into the lungs. At the beginning of the exhalation, one focuses on the tactile sensations at the level of the navel, and then follows the sensations in the reverse direction back to the apertures of the nostrils. This practice entails a passive witnessing of those sensations, without conceptual elaboration.

The mental qualities to be cultivated here are clarity, stability, and relaxation. All of us have experienced periods of mental clarity and intense alertness, but at such times the mind is not usually very stable or relaxed. Such moments may occur, for example, while watching a thrilling movie or engaging in a fast-paced, competitive sport. We can also recall times when our minds were stable and calm—for example, after vigorous exercise or just before sleep—but on those occasions vivid mental clarity is rarely experienced. Thus, the emphasis in this training is to strive first of all for mental stability in which the mind is not being compulsively bombarded by conceptual distractions. As such stability is acquired, one then seeks to heighten one's mental clarity. The first of those qualities allows one to remain focused on the chosen object without being pulled away by conceptual or sensory distractions. The second allows one to examine the fine details of the object.

The integration of stability and clarity is very challenging, and the tendency among beginning trainees is to try to accomplish that goal by means of sheer determination and effort. Such an approach, however, leads to mental and physical exhaustion, and if one still perseveres, damage to the body and mind results. Effort must certainly be given to the cultivation of stability and clarity, but it must be skillfully applied. If the effort is too slack, the mind quickly succumbs to unrestrained conceptual wandering or to an increasingly dull stupor. If the effort is too tight, nervous exhaustion and physical discomfort are the result. When one skillfully combines the qualities of stability, clarity, and relaxation, the quality of one's effort becomes increasingly refined. At the beginning of the training, one encounters gross levels of conceptual agitation and mental laxity, and a relatively gross type of effort is needed to counter this. But as those obstacles become more subtle, the appropriate effort in the practice also becomes refined.

When mindfulness can be maintained with continuity on the tactile sensations of the breath from the apertures of the nostrils to the level of the navel, one is ready for the next stage of this practice. One now focuses on the tactile sensations of the inhalation and exhalation where the breath strikes the apertures of the nostrils or the skin above the upper lip. Whereas previously one's attention moved through the body, now it is fixed at a single point. As one proceeds in this training, the mind and the breath are gradually calmed. As the object of one's awareness—the breath—is neither attractive nor repulsive, it stimulates neither craving nor aversion. The calmed mind that is not afflicted by those impulses experiences a relative emotional equilibrium, and from this arises an unprecedented state of mental and physical suppleness and well-being. In the early stages of the practice these qualities arise only intermittently, but as one progresses suppleness and joy are experienced with increasing frequency, intensity, and duration.

As one continues to apply oneself to the practice, there eventually arises an acquired sign.[8] To some this sign appears to the mind's eye like a star, whereas for others it is seen as a cluster of gems or pearls or as various other forms.[9] This sign may arise when one can remain focused on the breath for roughly an hour with only a few brief conceptual distractions. It arises spontaneously and is not to be intentionally visualized. When the sign appears regularly and with continuity, one directs the attention away from the tactile sensations of the breath and now focuses entirely on this purely mental image. With this as the object, mental stability and clarity are developed further until eventually one experiences the counterpart sign,[10] which is far more refined than the earlier sign. This new sign is a purely mental representation of the primary quality of the breath, and, like the acquired sign, it varies from one individual to another. When this sign arises, one attains a meditative state known as *quiescence*.[11] Just prior to its attainment one experiences a marked increase in mental and physical suppleness and unprecedented mental and physical joy.

At this point the mind is endowed with intense clarity and stability during meditation that can be maintained effortlessly for hours on end. Throughout this time, one's awareness is untainted by even subtle distraction or dullness. Even upon arising from meditation, one's mental and physical pliancy is enhanced, and it is very difficult for such afflictions as craving and hostility to arise and dominate the mind.[12]

Upon attaining quiescence, it is said that one may engage in further training to develop various types of extrasensory perception. For example, Buddhist tradition asserts that one may attain the ability to hear sounds that occur far beyond the range of normal hearing. Such distant sounds are heard not with the ears but purely with mental awareness. Likewise one may develop clairvoyance that enables one to perceive events far distant in space and time, including a limited ability to witness future events. The abilities to penetrate others' minds and to know one's own and others' past life experiences can also be developed upon the basis of the attainment of quiescence. Exact procedures for developing such types of extrasensory perception are clearly set forth in Buddhist meditation manuals.[13]

Other paranormal powers are also said to be attainable upon the basis of quiescence. The techniques for developing them are also described in Buddhist treatises,[14] and there are many accounts in the history of Buddhism in India, Tibet, and elsewhere of people displaying such abilities. Some of the powers that are cited are the ability to cause one's body to vanish and reappear, to move physically through solid objects, and to create a "double" of one's physical body. These and other powers that are claimed by Buddhist contemplatives clearly break the laws of physics as we presently know them. Many of the technological abilities that we in the West take for granted today, however, would be regarded as miraculous in terms of the laws of nineteenth-century physics. This fact does not suggest that we should gullibly accept all claims of supernormal powers that are made by other cultures. At the same time, our civilization knows virtually nothing of the contemplative methods that lead to those abilities or of the theories that explain them. This fact makes it unreasonable for us to reject such claims without investigating their validity. In Buddhism such powers are not regarded as supernatural. Rather, they are explained in terms of theories that probe deeply into the potentials of refining consciousness and the vital energies within the body. If we wish to test whether such abilities can be developed, we may seek out those rare contemporary individuals who have attained them; or, better yet, we may engage in the mental training ourselves and thereby empirically test the results.

Regardless of the specific method that one chooses in the cultivation of quiescence, it is necessary to overcome the five obscurations of (1) sensual desire, (2) malice, (3) laxity and lethargy, (4) excitation and remorse, and (5) skeptical doubt.[15] The essentially pure nature of the mind may be likened to a clear pool of water. Following this analogy, sensual desire is like a red dye in the water; malice is like boiling water; torpor and drowsiness are like algae and weeds that darken the water; restlessness and regret are like windswept waves; and skeptical doubt is like water that is clear but in darkness.

Upon the attainment of quiescence, the mind is temporarily free from the five obscurations. At this point one follows one of two paths of contemplative development. Individuals who are of a passionate nature, who have entered spiritual practice through strong faith, may benefit by stabilizing their minds to a higher degree before turning to the more essential cultivation of insight. People who are of a more intellectual and skeptical disposition and who are philosophically inclined may proceed directly from this attainment to the pursuit of insight.[16] Such a state of quiescence is the minimum prerequisite for engaging in insight meditation with full effectiveness. It is only with this degree of mental stability and clarity that one gains access to "understanding arising from meditation."[17] Certainly much understanding may arise prior to this attainment, but such insight will be able to attenuate only temporarily the distortions of the mind.

Upon first learning of mental states described in traditions outside of one's own, there is a natural tendency to seek counterparts in one's own background or in the knowledge of one's native culture. For many people it is difficult to acknowledge the possibility that the attainment of quiescence may have no counterpart in Western civilization, that the contemplative science of ancient India made advances that the West has not duplicated. Especially over the past five hundred years, the West has made tremendous advances in developing physical instruments to aid us in exploring the world. Such research instruments have enabled us to probe deeply into the nature of physical phenomena, but they offer no direct access to mental events. The mind is the only instrument capable of examining all types of natural events—including both the physical and the mental. But in terms of refining human awareness in the development of stability and clarity as described above, Western civilization has made no progress since the Scientific Revolution. In this field of contemplative science ours is a backward, undeveloped culture. If we wish to explore these Buddhist theories and practices further, we are well advised to proceed not with blind faith, but with our full powers of critical intelligence. In so doing we follow the advice that the Buddha gave to his monks when he counseled:

> O monks, sages accept my words after examining them well—like gold after it has been melted, cut, and rubbed—but not out of devotion [for me].[18]

Chapter Twenty-five

Worlds in Harmony

In the Buddhist tradition the chief purpose of refining and stabilizing the mind is to cultivate wisdom and compassion. A mind that has been trained in concentration and clarity is a superb tool for investigating the nature of reality—of the self, consciousness, the physical world, and so on. This instrument can be an effective one for developing the insight needed to eliminate the fundamental distortions of the mind—ignorance, craving, and hostility. The healing of the mind from these afflictions, and the cultivation of wisdom and compassion for all living creatures are the greatest miracle. When mental powers are developed within that spiritual context, their use is guided by wisdom and motivated by compassion. They are used in the service of others, and the danger associated with them is thereby avoided.

Objective scientists must take great care to keep their research equipment in excellent running order, both during and between the times that it is being used. Otherwise the results that such instruments yield in experiments would be unreliable, and the research would be pointless. However, the scientists' own minds—their most basic research equipment—do not necessarily receive such care. They may be subject to such distortions as craving, selfishness, hostility, absent-mindedness, and egotism; but the attenuation of such afflictions usually plays no explicit role in scientific education. There may be a similar lack of attention to examining motives for scientific research. Some scientists feel no qualms about using our most advanced knowledge for devising state-of-the-art methods of polluting our planet with radiation and biological and chemical poisons. Powers that become available through scientific research are swiftly put to use for the destruction of life and the stimulation of fear. Clearly the use of such research is not simply determined by scientists—politicians and the people who put them in power are largely responsible. But it must also be said that much research done by scientists is explicitly aimed at destroying life on earth. We may feel little sympathy for the possible response that scientists devoting themselves to such work are simply following the orders of their employers. The development of such weapons is considered by many people as the only realistic way to preserve peace in the modern world. Peace of mind, however, seems to be a necessary casualty, regardless of the external semblance of peace that may be achieved with that program.

The ground of Buddhist practice is the cultivation of an ethical way of life in thought, speech, and deed. The essence of this foundation of spiritual growth is the avoidance of harm to others. Buddhist contemplatives recognize their own minds as the essential instrument for research. Thus, the use of any type of intoxicants at any time is strongly discouraged, as is indulgence in other activities that stimulate unwholesome mental states. Contemplative practice is not a profession in the sense of an activity that is pursued for limited portions of the workday, with weekends and holidays off. It is a vocation that properly consumes all one's waking hours and even modifies one's sleep. There is no task more demanding, none requiring greater courage, and none more rewarding.

Apart from actual sessions of meditation, the contemplative is encouraged to follow four disciplines in daily life.[1] The first of these is restraint of the senses. This entails guarding one's five senses from focusing on objects that arouse the mental distortions of craving and hostility. It also includes restraining one's thoughts from indulging in reflection on such objects. Craving and anger weaken the mind; they make it gross and unfit for the cultivation of refined, stabilized awareness.

The second of the daily contemplative disciplines is to act with mindfulness and introspection. Such awareness is to be directed not only to one's own mental states but to the ever-changing situations in one's environment. It is applied, for example, while engaging in the five activities of walking, seeing, extending and retracting the limbs, using utensils and clothing, and eating and drinking.

The third discipline concerns eating. The contemplative is encouraged to follow a wholesome diet, eating neither too little nor too much. Food is eaten with the attitude of taking medicine: it is for the benefit of the body, to maintain one's health for the sake of spiritual practice. If one experiences craving for food, specific techniques of meditation are employed to remedy that obstacle.

The fourth discipline has to do with sleep. The contemplative is encouraged to sleep during the hours around midnight, lying on the right side. As one falls asleep, one seeks to maintain a lightness of mind, and to cultivate mindfulness and introspection, with the anticipation of awakening with mind and body fully refreshed.

As one enters into intensive, sustained contemplative practice, one is bound to meet with numerous external and internal obstacles. And responding to them in a wholesome, intelligent manner is a major element of the training. Nevertheless, it is advantageous to avoid unnecessary hindrances, particularly those that may seriously hamper one's efforts. To complement one's training in mental stabilization, for example, one is strongly encouraged to cultivate other wholesome attitudes. None are more important than loving-kindness, compassion, sympathetic joy, and equanimity.

These four are known in Buddhism as the four *divine states*,[2] and they are of enormous benefit in attenuating a broad range of mental distortions and in providing protection from external hindrances. The first of these, loving-kindness, arises from linking others with oneself in affection, and it entails the wish for others' welfare. It is an indispensable antidote to malice and hostility. The cultivation of loving-kindness is especially important for those who seek to stabilize and empower their minds. One of the Buddhist discourses states that people who have attained mental powers through stabilization but have not yet cultivated loving-kindness can destroy others by the mere disturbance of their minds through anger.[3]

The first step in the practice of loving-kindness is to reflect upon the disadvantages of hatred—both for oneself and others—and upon the advantages of forbearance. One then cultivates loving-kindness for oneself, taking oneself as an example that one relates to others. This step further antidotes feelings of self-contempt or self-depreciation that would be an obstacle to this practice. Here one cultivates the wish: may I be without enmity, affliction, and anxiety, and may I live happily. One then turns one's attention to a friend, but not a person with whom one is intimately involved. Attending to the fundamental similarity of oneself and this friend as living beings, one wishes for this person's well-being, just as for one's own. The next step is to cultivate loving-kindness for people for whom one feels indifference. And, finally, such affection is cultivated even toward one's enemies. After each stage of the meditation, it is helpful to direct loving-kindness to all sentient beings—human and otherwise—in all directions. The goal of this practice is to develop this attitude of friendliness so that it extends to all beings, without discrimination and without limit.

The second divine state is compassion, which arises from sensing the helplessness of those who suffer. Entailing the wish to relieve others from misery, it acts to attenuate the mental distortion of cruelty. Compassion is developed sequentially, focusing first on the evils of unkindness and upon the blessings of kindness. One then directs one's attention to those who suffer misfortune, sorrow, or pain, and with a feeling of compassion yearns that they may be free of this suffering and its source. Compassion is also directed to those who are prosperous and happy but who engage in evil, for they sow the seeds of future misfortune either in this or future lives.

The third divine state, sympathetic joy, arises from the sight of other's prosperity, and it acts to eliminate envy. Here one focuses first on a friend, then on others whom one regards less, and one takes delight in these persons' happiness. As in the case of the other three practices, this attitude is to be developed not only in the quietude of solitary meditation but in daily life: observing another person's good fortune or well-being, one pauses and truly takes delight in this person's joy.

The fourth divine state is equanimity, which arises from a clear understanding of the natural laws concerning the manner in which joy and sorrow arise, from life to life, due to wholesome and unwholesome deeds. These are the laws of karma, and an awareness of them frees one from feelings of aversion and partiality toward others. When equanimity is fully developed, one no longer cherishes oneself more than others, nor does one regard some beings with attraction and others with repulsion. A perversion of this attitude is callous and unintelligent indifference—this is incompatible with any spiritual practice, Buddhist or otherwise. When equanimity is properly cultivated, it too leads to a sense of kinship with all beings and forms the foundation for boundless love and compassion without reservation.

———————◆———————

The central purpose of Buddhist practice is to eliminate all distortions and obscurations of the mind and to bring to fulfillment all wholesome qualities. The contemplative training outlined in the preceding chapters leads to a direct realization of the manner in which the world consists of dependently related events. Physics was originally designed to explore the essential nature of reality, and it is precisely to such insight that Buddhist contemplative practice leads.

In the preceding chapters, we have examined a variety of theories from both Western science and Buddhist teachings. Upon close examination it appears that no theory is true in the sense of describing or explaining reality as it exists in its own inherent nature. Nor is such an ultimately true theory to be found in any eventual integration of scientific and contemplative insights. If we grasp onto any theory as being true in the above sense, we may become satisfied with that conceptual construct of reality, and that impedes the quest for truth, which finally transcends all concepts. We may avoid this obstacle by asking not whether a theory is true, but by inquiring to see how meaningful it is.

The term *meaningful* may suggest two aspects of a theory. First of all, a theory is meaningful insofar as it makes intelligible a domain of phenomena. One theory is more meaningful than another if it accounts for and explains a broader range of events. This quality is closely related to its capacity for yielding accurate predictions about those events. In Western science and among contemplative traditions some conceptual systems are clearly more meaningful than others in that regard. In accounting for a body of phenomena, we also expect a theory to be internally consistent, and this raises the question of mathematical and other logical systems. The centrist view denies that any logic is inherently true. We can nevertheless inquire as to how meaningful a logical system is in terms of organizing and making intelligible our knowledge of the world. One system may be generally more meaningful than another, or it may happen that one system is more meaningful in one specific area of experience, while another logic is of greater value in another field.

Secondly, we can inquire as to the usefulness of a theory. This immediately stimulates the question: useful for what? The pursuit of knowledge and understanding is fundamentally motivated by a yearning that we share with all sentient beings: the wish to experience happiness and contentment and to be free of pain and discontent. Given this universal condition, we can demand of our systems of knowledge that they be useful in relieving physical pain and mental grief throughout the world. This is a second criterion for judging the meaningfulness of a theory. In this regard, if a body of knowledge brings satisfaction only to a select few scientists or contemplatives, its meaningfulness is very limited.

On a broad scale, scientific knowledge has yielded innumerable benefits to humankind in terms of relieving physical suffering and in making life materially more comfortable. Further, in an unprecedented fashion it has enabled people around the world to share their ideas and experiences, thereby broadening everyone's horizons. Largely due to the present ease of travel and communication, the world is in a position to recognize its condition of being a global village. In this regard, scientific knowledge has proven itself extremely meaningful. In terms of relieving mental distress, anxiety, and discontent, however, such knowledge has been of little value. It is precisely in this realm of experience that contemplative knowledge has proven itself extremely beneficial. The great contemplative traditions of the world focus on the essential concerns of human existence, which are not addressed by physical science. The meaningfulness of scientific and contemplative knowledge is therefore complementary. In the absence of either, the world is impoverished.

In all of human experience two types of aspiration bear an integrity and nobility beyond all others: the yearning for understanding and spiritual awakening, and the longing to be of service to others, to dispel suffering and bring joy. Modern science, as developed and expressed by the greatest of its exponents, is motivated by both these aspirations. Intellectually and practically it stands, at its best, as a model of freedom of inquiry and ingenuity; and if put into active balance with religion and philosophy, it may well serve us long into the future.

Both aspirations play a fundamental role in Buddhist contemplative science as well. The contemplative, with complete intellectual integrity, seeks an ever-deepening experience of reality, while living in accord with that reality through the cultivation of loving-kindness and compassion. In Buddhist practice there are times for sustained periods of solitary reflection and meditation, and there are times for active service and interaction with others. In solitude one follows a life of simplicity and clarity, seeking to confront the basic elements of one's existence. The insights and spiritual awakening experienced in solitude are then brought to bear as one reenters society and offers one's life in service to the world.

It is possible to integrate one's yearning for truth with one's wish to help others so that they become one's abiding motivation in solitary and active life. This is achieved through the cultivation of a "spirit of awakening":[4] the aspiration to attain full spiritual awakening in order to be of most effective service to others. This longing may lead one into the deepest states of contemplation as well as the most active ways of service. It implicitly acknowledges the interdependence of self and others and the kinship of all that lives, and is the sole motivation with which one can attain the full spiritual awakening of a Buddha. Just as it is the supreme motivation for spiritual practice, so is it the finest incentive for scientific research. As physics and Buddhism encounter one another in the modern world, it may be in this spirit of awakening that they find their deepest affinity and sense of integration.

Notes

Chapter 1. Worlds Apart

1. Alfred North Whitehead, *Dialogues of Alfred North Whitehead: As Recorded by Lucien Price* (New York: New American Library, 1956), 109.

2. Ibid., 277.

3. Werner Heisenberg, *Physics and Philosophy: The Revolution in Modern Science* (New York: Harper and Row, 1962), 58.

Chapter 2. Exploring the Nature of Empty Space

1. In Planck's 1911 theory, he proposed that the emission of radiation always takes place discontinuously in quanta, whereas absorption is a continuous process which takes place according to the laws of classical theory. In 1914, he abandoned this theory in favor of the idea that both emission and absorption of energy by the oscillators in the cavity are continuous; but he discarded that theory a year later.

2. Claude Itzykson and Jean-Bernard Zuber, *Quantum Field Theory* (New York: McGraw-Hill, 1980), 139.

3. I. J. R. Aitchison, "Nothing's Plenty: The Vacuum in Modern Quantum Field Theory," *Contemporary Physics* 26.4 (1985): 343.

4. E. A. Power, *Introductory Quantum Electrodynamics*, (New York: American Elsevier, 1964), 32.

5. Ibid., 33.

6. Such calculations were first done by H. G. B. Casimir and D. Polder, "The Influence of Retardation on the London-van der Waals Forces," *Physical Review* 73 (1948): 360.

7. Julian Schwinger, "Casimir Effect in Source Theory," *Letters in Mathematical Physics* 1 (1975): 43.

8. See Julian Schwinger, *Particles, Sources and Fields* (Reading, MA: Addison-Wesley, 1973).

9. For a historical account of the development of his theory, see E. T. Whittaker's *A History of the Theories of Aether and Electricity: Modern Theories 1900-1926* (New York: Philosophical Library, 1954), chap. 3.

10. Timothy H. Boyer, "Classical Statistical Thermodynamics and Electromagnetic Zero-Point Radiation," *Physical Review* 186.5 (1969): 1313.

11. Ibid.

12. Ibid., 1304.

Chapter 3. The Conception and Preservation of Energy

1. Gottfried Wilhelm Leibniz, Reply to Catelan (1687), *Philos. Schriften* 3: 45-46; cited in P. M. Harman, *Metaphysics and Natural Philosophy* (Totowa, NJ: Barnes & Noble, 1982), 37.

2. Gerald Holton, *Introduction to Concepts and Theories in Physical Science*, 2nd ed. (Reading, MA: Addison-Wesley, 1973), 283.

3. Ibid., 272.

4. Cf. "Energy Conservation as an Example of Simultaneous Discovery" in Thomas Kuhn, *The Essential Tension: Selected Studies in Scientific Tradition and Change* (Chicago: University of Chicago Press, 1977), 94.

5. P. M. Harman, *Energy, Force and Matter: The Conceptual Development of Nineteenth-Century Physics* (Cambridge: Cambridge University Press, 1982), 43.

Chapter 4. Views of Science and Reality through History

1. Norwood Russell Hanson, *The Concept of the Positron: A Philosophical Analysis* (London: Cambridge University Press, 1963), 44.

2. For a more extensive account of the history of this ontological debate, see Pierre Duhem, *To Save the Phenomena: An Essay on the Idea of Physical Theory from Plato to Galileo*, trans. E. Doland and C. Maschler. (Chicago: University of Chicago Press, 1969). In the following discussion the terms *realism* and *instrumentalism* are applied to the views of thinkers going all the way back to Eudoxus. I have thereby

taken certain liberties in using these modern terms, but I believe this is justifiable in order to accentuate recurrent themes in the foundations of physical theory.

3. Plato may have encouraged an instrumentalist view concerning the project that he set for his astronomy students, but he can in no way be regarded as a thoroughgoing instrumentalist. On the contrary, many of his views are clearly those of a realist.

4. Owen Barfield, *Saving the Appearances: A Study in Idolatry* (London: Faber and Faber, 1957), 49.

5. Duhem, *Phenomena*, 109.

6. Philipp Melanchthon, "Initia doctrinae physicae dictata," in *Academia Vuitebergensi*, 2nd ed. (Wittenberg: Johannes Lufft, 1550), fols. 39-42; cited in Duhem, *Phenomena*, 88.

7. Arthur Koestler, *The Sleepwalkers: A History of Man's Changing Vision of the Universe* (New York: MacMillan, 1959), 357.

8. Robert Cardinal Bellarmine, private letter, cited in Koestler, *The Sleepwalkers*, 447.

9. See Hanson, *The Concept of the Positron*, 34.

10. For a more detailed discussion of this mechanical philosophy see Richard S. Westfall, *The Construction of Modern Science: Mechanisms and Mechanics* (Cambridge: Cambridge University Press, 1977), chap. 2.

11. Edwin A. Burtt, *The Metaphysical Foundations of Modern Physical Science* (New York: Harcourt, Brace, 1927), 80.

12. See Ludwig Büchner, *Force and Matter, or Principles of the Natural Order of the Universe* (London: Asher, 1884).

13. See Hermann von Helmholtz, *Popular Lectures on Scientific Subjects*, trans. E. Atkinson, 2nd series (New York: Appleton, 1881).

14. Jules-Henri Poincaré, *The Value of Science* (New York: Science Press, 1907).

15. Albert Einstein, "On the Method of Theoretical Physics," *Ideas and Opinions*, trans. and rev. Sonya Bangmann (New York: Crown, 1954), 273.

16. Albert Einstein, "Physics and Reality," *Out of My Later Years* (New York: Philosophical Library, 1950), 96.

17. See Albert Einstein, "Autobiographical Notes," *Albert Einstein: Philosopher-Scientist*, ed. Paul A. Schilpp (La Salle, IL: Open Court, 1969), 5.

18. Einstein, "Science and Religion," *Out of My Later Years*, 25.

19. Einstein, "Religion and Science," *Ideas and Opinions*, 40.

20. Einstein, "The Religious Spirit of Science," *Ideas and Opinions*, 40.

21. See Niels Bohr, *Atomic Theory and Description of Nature* (London: Cambridge University Press, 1961).

22. Cited in Hanson, *The Concept of the Positron*, 86.

Chapter 5. Scientific Realism Today

1. Pythagoras and Plato also took a realist view of the physical world, and their writings formed the basis of later mathematical realism as adopted by Kepler.

2. Norwood Russell Hanson, *Patterns of Discovery: An Inquiry into the Conceptual Foundations of Science* (Cambridge: Cambridge University Press, 1958),158.

3. Einstein, "Physics and Reality," *Out of My Later Years*, 59.

Chapter 6. Assumptions of Scientific Realism

1. See Bernard d'Espagnat, "The Quantum Theory and Reality," *Scientific American* 241.5 (November 1979).

2. Richard P. Feynman, R. B. Leighton, M. Sands, *The Feynman Lectures on Physics* (Reading, MA: Addison-Wesley, 1963), 1.

3. Ibid., 4.

4. Sir Arthur Eddington, "The Domain of Physical Science," *Science, Religion and Reality*, ed. Joseph Needham (rpt. New York: Braziller, 1955), 217.

5. Albert Einstein and Leopold Infeld, *The Evolution of Physics* (New York: Simon & Schuster, 1966), 197.

6. Cited in Nick Herbert, *Quantum Reality: Beyond the New Physics* (Garden City, NY: Anchor Press/Doubleday, 1985), 12.

7. Bernard d'Espagnat, *In Search of Reality* (New York: Springer-Verlag, 1981), 84.

8. John Gribbin, *In Search of Schrödinger's Cat: Quantum Physics and Reality* (New York: Bantam, 1984), 259.

9. Edward R. Harrison, *Cosmology: The Science of the Universe* (New York: Cambridge University Press, 1981), 148.

10. Ibid., 162.

11. Cited in Paul Davies, *Superforce* (New York: Simon and Schuster, 1985), 49.

12. Cited in Herbert, *Quantum Reality*, 22.

13. Ibid., 22.

14. Cited in Davies, *Superforce*, 54.

15. Einstein, "Physics and Reality," *Out of My Later Years*, 72.

16. Hanson, *Patterns of Discovery*, 153.

17. Einstein, "Physics and Reality," *Out of My Later Years*, 78.

18. Cited in Herbert, *Quantum Reality*, 7.

19. Sir Oliver Lodge, *Ether and Reality* (New York: Doran, 1925), 91.

20. Einstein and Infeld, *The Evolution of Physics*, 175. In view of the reductionist assumption that living beings can be understood thoroughly in terms of their component atoms, we may ask: what insights has this theory yielded concerning the nature of the mind? Neuroscientists, adhering to the belief that the mind is simply a coemergent property of the nervous system, have certainly provided us with valuable knowledge about the physical basis of subjective experience. But in terms of understanding the subjective phenomenon of human consciousness, we might echo the above statement: this metaphysical assumption has led nowhere!

21. See "Ether and the Theory of Relativity," in Albert Einstein, *Sidelights on Relativity*, trans. G. B. Jeffrey and W. Perrett (New York: Dover, 1983).

Chapter 7. Theory and Discovery in Physical Science

1. Cited in Werner Heisenberg, Physics and Beyond: *Encounters and Conversations* (New York: Harper and Row, 1971), 63.

2. Bohr, *Atomic Theory*, 1.

3. Peter Medawar, *Pluto's Republic*, 117.

4. Friedrich Nietzsche, *The Will to Power*, trans. Walter Kaufmann and R. J. Hollingdale (New York: Random House, 1967), 263-64.

5. See Hanson, *The Concept of the Positron*.

6. See Hanson, *Patterns of Discovery* (Cambridge: Cambridge University Press, 1958), 30.

7. See *Language, Thought, and Reality: Selected Writings of Benjamin Lee Whorf*, ed. John B. Carroll (Cambridge, MA: MIT Press, Cambridge, 1966).

8. A more detailed critique of mathematical realism is presented in chapter 12. See also Philip J. Davis and Reuben Hersh, *Descartes' Dream: The World According to Mathematics* (New York: Harcourt Brace Jovanovich, 1986).

9. Heisenberg, *Physics and Philosophy*, 58.

10. Albert Einstein, B. Poldolsky, and N. Rosen, "Can Quantum-Mechanical Description of Reality be Considered Complete?" *Physical Review* 47 (1935): 777.

11. Niels Bohr, "Quantum Mechanics and Physical Reality," *Nature* 136 (1935): 65.

12. *Symmetries and Reflections: Scientific Essays of Eugene P. Wigner* (Bloomington: Indiana University Press, 1967), 197.

Chapter 8. The Hypothetical Realities of Physics

1. Hanson, *Patterns of Discovery,* 86.

2. Ibid., 109.

3. This analogy is drawn from a lecture on the foundations of physics by the theoretical physicist Hanspeter Seipp at Amherst College, April 23, 1986.

4. Cited in Medawar, *Pluto's Republic,* 120.

Chapter 9. Quantum Reality

1. Herbert, *Quantum Reality,* 46.

2. Cited in Herbert, *Quantum Reality,* 26.

3. Heisenberg, *Physics and Philosophy,* 181, 186.

4. It should be emphasized that, mathematically speaking, the collapse of the wave function is straightforward. It is when one tries to associate the mathematics with physical reality that problems are encountered.

5. See J. A. Wheeler and W. H. Zurek, eds., *Quantum Theory and Measurement* (Princeton, NJ: Princeton University Press, 1983).

Chapter 10. Uncertainty in the Quantum World

1. Cited in D. Wilson, *Rutherford: Simple Genius* (Cambridge, MA: MIT Press, 1983), 391. See also R. P. Crease and C. C. Mann, *The Second Creation: Makers of the Revolution in Twentieth-Century Physics* (New York: MacMillan, 1986), 32.

2. Harrison, *Cosmology,* 359.

3. Einstein, Podolsky, and Rosen, "Quantum-Mechanical Description," 777. See also A. Pais, *Subtle Is the Lord: The Science and the Life of Albert Einstein* (New York: Oxford University Press, 1982), 454-57.

4. Einstein, "The Fundaments of Theoretical Physics," *Out of My Later Years,* 110.

5. John Bell, "On the Einstein Podolsky Rosen Paradox," *Physics* 1 (1964): 195.

6. N. David Mermin, "Is the Moon There When Nobody Looks? Reality and Quantum Theory," *Physics Today* (April 1985), 38.

7. A. Aspect, P. Grangier, and G. Roger, "Experimental Tests of Realistic Local Theories via Bell's Theorem," *Physical Review Letters* 47 (1981): 460.

8. T. Mike Corwin and Dale Wachowiak, "Experiment and the Nature of Quantum Reality," *Physics Teacher* (October 1984): 425.

9. N. C. Petroni and J. P. Vigier, "Dirac's Ether in Relativistic Quantum Mechanics," in *Quantum, Space, and Time—The Quest Continues*, ed. A. O. Barut, A. van der Merwe, and Jean-Pierre Vigier (New York: Cambridge University Press, 1984), 522, 526.

10. W. Duch and D. Aerts, "Microphysical Reality," *Physics Today* (June 1986), 14.

Chapter 11. Scientific Realism in Review

1. Kant, *Prolegomena to Any Future Metaphysics*, vol. 1. Cited in Frederick Charles Copelston, *A History of Philosophy* (London: Search Press, 1946), 1: 3.

2. Alfred North Whitehead, *Process and Reality* (New York: Free Press, 1978), 14.

3. Einstein, "The Fundaments of Theoretical Physics," *Out of My Later Years*, 110.

Chapter 12. Mathematical Realism

1. Interview with David Bohm, *The Holographic Paradigm and Other Paradoxes: Exploring the Leading Edge of Science*, ed. Ken Wilber (Boston: Shambhala Press, 1985), 52.

2. Einstein, "On the Method of Theoretical Physics," *Ideas and Opinions*, 274.

3. Einstein, "Geometry and Experience," *Ideas and Opinions*, 233.

4. Einstein, "On the Method of Theoretical Physics," *Ideas and Opinions*, 274.

5. Einstein, "Geometry and Experience," *Ideas and Opinions*, 232.

6. This historical discussion is based largely on Morris Kline's provocative book *Mathematics: The Loss of Certainty* (New York: Oxford University Press, 1980).

7. Sir Isaac Newton, letter to Rev. Richard Bentley, 10 December 1692; cited in Kline, *Mathematics*, 59.

8. Whitehead, *Dialogues*, 175.

9. Davis and Hersh, *Descartes' Dream*, 207.

10. Eugene P. Wigner, "The Unreasonable Effectiveness of Mathematics in the Natural Sciences," *Communications of Pure and Applied Mathematics* 13 (1960): 7.

11. See Ernest Nagel and James. R. Newman, *Gödel's Proof* (New York: New York University Press, 1964).

12. Davis and Hersh, *Descartes' Dream*, 209.

13. Ibid., 304.

14. Ibid., 276.

15. Whitehead, *Dialogues*, 289.

16. Cited in Nagel and Newman, *Gödel's Proof*, 13.

17. Cited in Kline, *Mathematics*, 319.

Chapter 13. Instrumentalism

1. Crease and Mann, *The Second Creation*, 76.

2. Wilber, *The Holographic Paradigm*, 52.

3. Davis and Hersh, *Descartes' Dream*, 235.

4. Ernest Nagel, *The Structure of Science* (Indianapolis, IN: Hacket, 1979), 130.

5. Immanuel Kant, *The Critique of Pure Reason*, trans. N. Kemp Smith, 2nd ed. (London: MacMillan, 1933), 22.

6. Jerome S. Bruner, *Actual Minds, Possible Worlds* (Cambridge, MA: Harvard Universiity Press, 1986), 46.

7. J. M. Wilding, *Perception: From Sense to Object* (London: Hutchinson,1982), 100.

8. This general topic is discussed very lucidly in Jeremy W. Hayward, *Shifting Worlds, Changing Minds: Where the Sciences and Buddhism Meet* (Boston: Shambhala, 1987).

9. Humberto Maturana and Francisco Varela, *The Tree of Knowledge: The Biological Roots of Human Understanding* (Boston: Shambhala, 1987).

Chapter 14. Seeking a Middle Way

1. d'Espagnat, *In Search of Reality,* 97.

2. See "Time and Nowness," in Hayward, *Shifting Worlds, Changing Minds*.

3. Gribbin, *Schrödinger's Cat*, 212.

4. There are a variety of interpretations of the anthropic principle, not all of which attribute any fundamental importance to the human mind. Wheeler's theory, for instance, asserts that any computer-generated measurement would suffice. This, however, raises the philosophical issue of the nature of a measurement. If a stick falls parallel to a yardstick, is it thereby measured? If one rock rebounds off another, is the momentum of either thereby measured? Do the revolutions of an uninhabited planet about a distant star measure time? It would appear in each case that the term *measurement* is meaningful only if cited in relation to a conscious intelligence. Thus, an unconscious computer, on its own, can no more make a measurement than a yardstick can.

5. Harrison, *Cosmology*, 2.

6. The anthropic principle is discussed in greater detail in George Greenstein, *The Symbiotic Universe: Life and Mind in the Cosmos* (New York: William Morrow, 1988).

7. Galileo, *Opere*, 1: 42; cited in Burtt, *Metaphysical Foundations*, 65.

8. Richard Feynman, *The Character of Physical Law* (Cambridge, MA: MIT Press,1983), 58.

9. Barfield, *Saving the Appearances*, 97.

10. Ibid., 85.

Chapter 15. Cosmology and a Participatory Universe

1. See Arthur Koestler, *The Ghost in the Machine* (New York: Macmillan, 1967).

2. Erwin Schrödinger, *Mind and Matter* (Cambridge: Cambridge University Press, 1958), 38.

3. Ibid., 1.

4. Winger, *Symmetries and Reflections*, 181.

5. Harrison, *Cosmology*, 287.

6. J. R. Gott III, J. E. Gunn, D. N. Schramm, and B. M. Tinsley, "Will the Universe Expand Forever?" in *Cosmology + 1* (San Francisco, W. H. Freeman, 1977), 83-84.

7. Dennis Sciama, *Modern Cosmology* (London: Cambridge University Press, 1973), 100.

8. Einstein, "Science and Religion," *Out of My Later Years*, 27.

9. Einstein, "On Scientific Truth," *Ideas and Opinions*, 262.

10. See Barfield, *Saving the Appearances*, 37.

11. Eric Chaisson, *Cosmic Dawn* (Boston: Little, Brown, 1981), 292.

12. Ibid., 187.

13. See Harrison, *Cosmology*, 390.

14. Chaisson, *Cosmic Dawn*, 199.

15. Ibid., 199.

16. Ibid., 299.

17. Cited in Davies, *Superforce*, 222.

18. Cited in Harrison, *Cosmology*, 118.

Chapter 16. Concept and Experience

1. Whorf, *Language, Thought and Reality*, 249.

2. Einstein, "The Fundaments of Theoretical Physics," *Out of My Later Years*, 98.

3. See Jean Piaget, *Six Psychological Studies*, ed. David Elkind (New York: Vintage, 1968).

4. Davis and Hersh, *Descartes' Dream*, 209, 212, 231-33.

5. Whorf, *Language, Thought and Reality*, 253.

6. This same point can be made with reference to ethical laws. Buddhist contemplatives identify as unethical various types of mental, verbal, and physical actions. These actions are motivated by such mental distortions as ignorance, hostility, and craving, and they result in suffering for oneself and others. There are natural laws governing the manner in which wholesome and unwholesome actions lead to well-being and suffering, respectively. They are objective in the sense that they are not subject to human whim; but they are conventional in that they exist as dependently related events, rather than as absolute things in their own right.

7. Louis de Broglie, *Matter and Light: The New Physics*, trans. W. H. Johnston (New York: Norton, 1939), 280.

Chapter 17. A Centrist View of Physical Science

1. Alternate views of the body, the mind, and the universe are introduced in chapters 21-24.

2. See John Boslough, *Stephen Hawking's Universe: An Introduction to the Most Remarkable Scientist of Our Time* (New York: William Morrow, 1985), 127.

Chapter 18. A Centrist View of Contemplative Science

1. For an extremely informative and authoritative account of many of the most fundamental practices in such mental training see Paravahera Vajirañāṇa Mahāthera, *Buddhist Meditation in Theory and Practice* (Kuala Lumpur, Malaysia: Buddhist Missionary Society, 1975).

2. We should also note that not all Indian philosophies have a contemplative basis. The most outstanding example of a noncontemplative view is that of the Cārvāka school, which arose around 600 BC. This philosophy is a fairly thoroughgoing positivism which admits the existence of no universal laws of nature, causal or otherwise. Every event is chance, and only matter is real. It refutes the existence of God and any objective ethical laws and declares that any action done for the sake of pleasure is justified. Consciousness is regarded as nothing more than an emergent quality of certain configurations of parts of the body, and it vanishes at death. For obvious reasons, the Cārvāka philosophy

was widely regarded by both Hindu and Buddhist contemplative schools as theoretically unintelligent and ethically perverse.

3. Renée Weber, *Dialogues with Scientists and Sages* (New York: Routledge & Kegan Paul, 1986), 210.

4. For an account of the twenty-four-year training of a monk in one of the major monastic universities of Tibet, see *The Life and Teachings of Geshé Rabten*, trans. and ed. B. Alan Wallace (London: George Allen & Unwin, 1980). It should be emphasized that this intellectually tremendously demanding course of training places heavy emphasis on logic and clarity of thought.

5. One of the great tragedies of recent history has been the genocide perpetrated in Tibet by the Chinese Communists. As a result of the Communists' brutal invasion of Tibet in 1950, and their subsequent concerted efforts to destroy Tibetan Buddhism, Tibetan contemplatives were forced to flee their country in order to continue their practice. Although the oppression of Tibetan Buddhism has relaxed somewhat, Buddhist institutions are strictly controlled by the Chinese Communist regime, and true religious freedom has yet to be regained by the Tibetans in their own homeland.

6. Not long ago I heard Jeremy Hayward speak of a conversation with a fellow physicist in which he suggested discussing the implications for physics if precognition were to exist. Hayward presented this simply as a hypothetical event, but his colleague refused to discuss it on the grounds that precognition is an utter impossibility. Scientific discussion foundered under the burden of dogma.

7. Bhadantacariya Buddhaghosa, *The Path of Purification*, trans. Bhikkhu Ñanamoli (Kandy, Sri Lanka: Buddhist Publication Society, 1979), chap. 13.

8. Ibid., chap. 12.

9. See Swāmi Hariharānanda Āraṇya, *Yoga Philosophy of Patañjali*, trans. P. N. Mukerji (Albany: State University of New York Press, 1983), book 3.

10. Weber, *Dialogues*, 208.

Chapter 19. Experiencing a Centrist View

1. Barfield, *Saving the Appearances*, 49.

2. The Buddhist philosophies known as *Vaibhāṣika* and *Sautrāntika* are included in this category. A type of contemplative practice that forms an excellent complement to the theoretical study of these two schools is the Four Applications of Mindfulness. In such training one experientially investigates the phenomenological nature of the body, feelings, mind, and other mental and physical events. On that basis one proceeds to examine one's fundamental mode of existence as well as the nature of the self. This practice is discussed in Soma Thera, *The Way of Mindfulness* (Kandy, Sri Lanka: Buddhist Publication Society, 1975).

3. This philosophy is known as *Vijñānavāda*.

4. For a detailed description of the intellectual training involved in exploring the centrist view of Madhyamaka in the monastic universities of Tibet see Wallace, *Geshé Rabten*.

Chapter 20. Realizing Personal Identitylessness

1. Herbert, *Quantum Reality*, 248.

2. See Shantideva, *Transcendent Wisdom*, commentary by His Holiness the XIV Dalai Lama, trans. and ed. B. Alan Wallace (Ithaca, NY: Snow Lion, 1988), verses 145-50.

3. C. A. F. Rhys Davids, *Buddhist Psychology* (1924), 32. Cited in Mahāthera, *Buddhist Meditation*, 364.

Chapter 21. A Contemplative View of the Body

1. For an introduction to this area of research see Elmer Green and Alyce Green, *Beyond Biofeedback* (New York: Delacorte, 1977). See also Patricia Norris, "Biofeedback, Voluntary Control, and Human Potential," *Biofeedback and Self-Regulation* 11.1 (1986): 1-20; and Richard J. Davidson, Gary E. Schwartz, and David Shapiro, eds., *Consciousness and Self-Regulation: Advances in Research and Theory*, vol. 3 (New York: Plenum, 1983).

2. The network of channels is discussed in much greater detail in B. Alan Wallace (Jhampa Kelsang), trans., *The Ambrosia Heart Tantra*, annotated by Yeshi Dönden (Dharamsala, India: Library of Tibetan Works and Archives, 1977), 58-61.

3. The winds, channels, and wheels are discussed in greater detail in Daniel Cozort, *Highest Yoga Tantra* (Ithaca, NY: Snow Lion, 1986), 42-45.

Chapter 22. Subjective Experience and Objective Science

1. Cited in Koestler, *The Ghost in the Machine*, 5.

2. Ibid.

3. Cited in Huston Smith, *Beyond the Post-Modern Mind* (New York: Crossroad, 1982), 136.

4. Koestler, *The Ghost in the Machine*, 7.

5. Francis H. C. Crick, "Thinking about the Brain," *Scientific American* (September 1979), 183.

6. Crick, "Thinking about the Brain," 183.

7. Jerry A. Fodor, "The Mind-Body Problem," *Scientific American* (January 1981).

Chapter 23. A Contemplative View of the Mind

1. See Geshe Kelsang Gyatso, *Clear Light of Bliss* (London: Wisdom, 1982), 67-99, 130-46.

2. See Lati Rinbochay and Jeffrey Hopkins, *Death, Intermediate State and Rebirth in Tibetan Buddhism* (London: Rider, 1979).

3. These practices are explained in some detail in Cozort, *Highest Yoga Tantra*, part 3.

4. John F. Avedon, *In Exile from the Land of Snows* (New York, Knopf, 1984), 3-12.

5. See Ian Stevenson, *Twenty Cases Suggestive of Reincarnation*, 2nd ed. (Charlottesville: University of Virginia, 1974).

6. A billionfold cluster of worlds is called in Sanskrit *trisāhasraloka*, or "a thousand thousand thousand worlds."

Chapter 24. Refining Human Consciousness

1. For a more definitive presentation of the above method of meditative inquiry see Nyanaponika Thera, *The Heart of Buddhist Meditation* (York Beach, ME: Samuel Weiser, 1984).

2. Takpo Tashi Namgyal, *Mahāmudrā: The Quintessence of Mind and Meditation*, trans. Lobsang P. Lhalungpa (Boston: Shambhala, 1986), 27.

3. Buddhaghosa, *The Path of Purification*, 3: 104-05. This fifth-century classic is a treasure of knowledge concerning Buddhist methods for developing mental stabilization (Sanskrit: *dhyana*, Pali: *jhāna*) and insight. It has been used as a major source for this discussion.

4. See Mahāthera, *Buddhist Meditation*, chap. 18; and Buddhaghosa, *The Path of Purification*, 8: 145-244.

5. See Gen Lamrimpa, *Shamatha Meditation*, trans. B. Alan Wallace (Ithaca, NY: Snow Lion, 1992). Reprinted as *Calming the Mind: Tibetan Buddhist Teachings on Cultivating Mental Quiescence* (Snow Lion, 1995).

6. This method is explained in Geshé Rabten, *Echoes of Voidness*, trans. Stephen Batchelor (London: Wisdom, 1983), 113-28.

7. Cozort, *Highest Yoga Tantra*, 48-56.

8. Pali: *uggaha-nimitta*.

9. Buddhaghosa, *The Path of Purification*, 8: 214-15.

10. Pali: *paṭibhāga-nimitta*.

11. Pali: *samatha*. In this account the term *quiescence* refers to what is technically

known as access concentration (Pali: *upacāra-samādhi*) to the first absorption (Pali: *jhāna*). It is upon the attainment of such concentration that one first gains experiential access to the form realm.

12. Lati Rinbochay et al., *Meditative States in Tibetan Buddhism* (London: Wisdom, 1983), 74. Chapter 4 of part 1 of this excellent text presents a lucid exposition of meditative quiescence based on Sanskrit and Tibetan sources.

13. See Buddhaghosa, *The Path of Purification*, chap. 13.

14. Ibid., chap. 12.

15. Sanskrit: *kāmacchanda, vyāpāda, styānamiddha, auddhatyakaukṛtya, vicikitsā.*

16. There is also an elaborate contemplative discipline in Tibetan Buddhism known as Tantra. Since the actual concentration of the first stabilization deeply suppresses attachment and desire, a tantric contemplative will not develop that concentration or any of the more subtle stabilizations. In tantric practice one engages in practices that yield meditative quiescence, and that level of concentration suffices.

17. Sanskrit: *bhāvanāmayī-prajñā.*

18. *Tattvasaṃgraha*, ed. D. Shastri (Banaras: Bauddhabharati, 1968), 3587; trans. Robert A. F. Thurman, *Tsongkhapa's Speech of Gold in the "Essence of True Eloquence"* (Princeton, NJ: Princeton University Press, 1984), 190.

Chapter 25. Worlds in Harmony

1. These are discussed in detail in the chapter on behavior between meditative sessions in Jé Tsong Khapa's treatise *The Great Exposition of the Stages of the Path* (the *Thun mtsams su ji ltar bya ba* chapter of *Lam rim chen mo*). To the best of my knowledge, this fourteenth-century Tibetan classic has yet to be translated into any Western language.

2. Pali: *brahma-vihāra*. Excellent discussions of this important subject are found in Mahāthera, *Buddhist Meditation*, chapters 20, 21; and Buddhaghosa, *The Path of Purification*, chap. 9.

3. *Upali Sutta, Majjhima-Nikaya* 1: 378.

4. Sanskrit: *bodhicitta*. See His Holiness Tenzin Gyatso, The Fourteenth Dalai Lama, *Kindness, Clarity, and Insight*, trans. and ed. Jeffrey Hopkins (Ithaca, NY: Snow Lion, 1985). See also Geshé Rabten and Geshe Dhargyey, *Advice from a Spiritual Friend*, trans. and ed. Brian Beresford (London: Wisdom, 1986).

Bibliography

Aitchison, I. J. R. "Nothing's Plenty: The Vacuum in Modern Quantum Field Theory." *Contemporary Physics* 26.4 (1985).

Āraṇya, Swāmi Harihārananda. *Yoga Philosophy of Patañjali*. Trans. P. N. Mukerji. Albany: State University of New York Press, 1983.

Aspect, A., P. Grangier, and G. Roger. "Experimental Tests of Realistic Local Theories via Bell's Theorem." *Physical Review Letters* 47 (1981): 460.

Avedon, John F. *In Exile from the Land of Snows*. New York: Knopf, 1984.

Barfield, Owen. *Saving the Appearances: A Study in Idolatry*. London: Faber & Faber, 1957.

Bell, John. "On the Einstein Podolsky Rosen Paradox." *Physics* 1 (1964): 195.

Bohr, Niels. *Atomic Theory and Description of Nature*. London: Cambridge University Press, 1961.

—. "Quantum Mechanics and Physical Reality." *Nature* 136 (1935): 65.

Boslough, John. *Stephen Hawking's Universe: An Introduction to the Most Remarkable Scientist of Our Time*. New York: William Morrow, 1985.

Boyer, Timothy H. "Classical Statistical Thermodynamics and Electromagnetic Zero-Point Radiation." *Physical Review* 186.5 (1969).

—. "The Classical Vacuum." *Scientific American* (August 1985).

Bruner, Jerome S. *Actual Minds, Possible Worlds*. Cambridge, MA: Harvard University Press, 1986.

Büchner, Ludwig. *Force and Matter, or Principles of the Natural Order of the Universe*. London: Asher, 1884.

Buddhaghosa, Bhadantacariya. *The Path of Purification*. Trans. Bhikku Ñanamoli. Kandy, Sri Lanka: Buddhist Publication Society, 1979.

Burtt, Edwin A. *The Metaphysical Foundations of Modern Physical Science*. New York: Harcourt, Brace, 1927.

Cajori, F., ed. *Sir Isaac Newton's Mathematical Principles of Natural Philosophy and His System of the World. A Revision of Mott's Translation*. Berkeley: University of California Press, 1934.

Callahan, J. J. "The Curvature of Space in a Finite Universe." *Cosmology + 1*. San Francisco: W. H. Freeman, 1977.

Capra, Fritjof. *The Tao of Physics*. Berkeley: Shambhala, 1975.

Casimir, H. B. G. "On the Attraction between Two Perfectly Conducting Plates." *Proceedings of the Koninklijke Nederlandse Akademie van Wetenschappen* 51 (1948): 793.

Casimir, H. B. G., and D. Polder. "The Influence of Retardation on the London-van der Waals Forces." *Physical Review* 73 (1948): 360.

Chaisson, Eric. *Cosmic Dawn*. Boston: Little, Brown, 1981.

Copleston, Frederick Charles. *A History of Philosophy*. London: Search Press, 1946.

Corwin, T. Mike, and Dale Wachowiak. "Experiment and the Nature of Quantum Reality." *Physics Teacher* (October 1984).

Cozort, Daniel. *Highest Yoga Tantra*. Ithaca, NY: Snow Lion, 1986.

Crease, R. P., and C. C Mann. *The Second Creation: Makers of the Revolution in Twentieth-Century Physics*. New York: Macmillan, 1986.

Crick, Francis H. C. "Thinking about the Brain." *Scientific American* (September 1979).

Dalai Lama, Tenzin Gyatso. *Kindness, Clarity, and Insight*. Trans. and ed. Jeffrey Hopkins. Ithaca, NY: Snow Lion, 1985.

Davidson, Richard J., Gary E. Schwartz, and David Shapiro, eds. *Consciousness and Self-Regulation: Advances in Research and Theory*. Vol. 3. New York: Plenum, 1983.

Davies, Paul. *Superforce*. New York: Simon & Schuster, 1985.

Davis, Philip, and Reuben Hersh. *Descartes' Dream: The World According to Mathematics*. New York: Harcourt Brace Jovanovich, 1986.

de Broglie, Louis. *Matter and Light: The New Physics*. Trans. W. H. Johnston. New York: Norton, 1939.

d'Espagnat, Bernard. *In Search of Reality*. New York: Springer-Verlag, 1981.

—. "The Quantum Theory and Reality." *Scientific American* 241.5 (November 1979).

Dirac, Paul A. M. "Is There an Ether?" *Nature* 168 (1951): 906.

Duch, W., and D. Aerts. "Microphysical Reality." *Physics Today* (June 1986).

Duhem, Pierre. *To Save the Phenomena: An Essay on the Idea of Physical Theory from Plato to Galileo.* Trans. E. Doland and C. Maschler. Chicago: University of Chicago Press, 1969.

Eddington, Arthur. "The Domain of Physical Science." *Science, Religion, and Reality.* Ed. Joseph Needham. Reprint. New York: Braziller, 1955.

Einstein, Albert. *Ideas and Opinions.* Trans. and rev. Sonya Bangmann. New York: Crown, 1954.

—. *Out of My Later Years.* New York: Philosophical Library, 1950.

—. *Sidelights on Relativity.* Trans. G. B. Jeffrey and W. Perrett. New York: Dover, 1983.

Einstein, Albert, and L. Infeld. *The Evolution of Physics.* Reprint. New York: Simon & Schuster, 1966.

Einstein, Albert, B. Podolsky, and N. Rosen. "Can Quantum-Mechanical Description of Reality Be Considered Complete?" *Physical Review* 47 (1935): 777.

Feynman, Richard. *The Character of Physical Law.* Cambridge, MA: MIT Press, 1983.

Feynman, Richard P., R. B. Leighton, and M. Sands. *The Feynman Lectures on Physics.* Reading, MA: Addison-Wesley, 1963.

Fodor, Jerry A. "The Mind-Body Problem." *Scientific American* (January 1981).

Gott, J. R., III, J. E. Gunn, D. N. Schramm, and B. M. Tinsley. "Will the Universe Expand Forever?" *Cosmology +1.* San Francisco: W.H. Freeman, 1977.

Green, Elmer, and Alyce Green. *Beyond Biofeedback.* New York: Delacorte, 1977.

Greenstein, George. *The Symbiotic Universe: Life and Mind in the Cosmos.* New York: William Morrow, 1988.

Gribbin, John. *In Search of Schrödinger's Cat: Quantum Physics and Reality.* New York: Bantam, 1984.

Gyatso, Geshe Kelsang. *Clear Light of Bliss.* London: Wisdom, 1982.

Hanson, Norwood Russell. *The Concept of the Positron: A Philosophical Analysis.* London: Cambridge University Press, 1963.

—. *Patterns of Discovery: An Inquiry into the Conceptual Foundations of Science.* Cambridge: Cambridge University Press, 1958.

Harman, P. M. *Energy, Force and Matter: The Conceptual Development of Nineteenth-Century Physics.* Cambridge: Cambridge University Press, 1982.

—. *Metaphysics and Natural Philosophy.* Totowa, NJ: Barnes & Noble, 1982.

Harrison, Edward R. *Cosmology: The Science of the Universe.* New York: Cambridge University Press, 1981.

Hayward, Jeremy W. *Shifting Worlds, Changing Minds: Where the Sciences and Buddhism Meet.* Boston: Shambhala, 1987.

Heisenberg, Werner. *Physics and Beyond: Encounters and Conversations.* New York: Harper & Row, 1971.

—. *Physics and Philosophy: The Revolution in Modern Science.* New York: Harper & Row, 1962.

Helmholtz, Hermann von. *Popular Lectures on Scientific Subjects.* Trans. E. Atkinson. 2nd series. New York: Appleton, 1881.

Herbert, Nick. *Quantum Reality: Beyond the New Physics.* Garden City, NY: Anchor Press/Doubleday, 1985.

Holton, Gerald. *Introduction to Concepts and Theories in Physical Science.* 2nd ed. Reading, MA: Addison-Wesley, 1973.

Hopkins, Jeffrey. *Meditation on Emptiness.* London: Wisdom, 1983.

Itzykson, Claude, and Jean-Bernard Zuber. *Quantum Field Theory.* New York: McGraw-Hill, 1980.

Kant, Immanuel. *The Critique of Pure Reason.* Trans. N. Kemp Smith. 2nd ed. London: Macmillan, 1933.

Kline, Morris. *Mathematics: The Loss of Certainty.* New York: Oxford University Press, 1980.

Koestler, Arthur. *The Ghost in the Machine.* New York: Macmillan, 1967.

—. *The Sleepwalkers: A History of Man's Changing Vision of the Universe.* New York: MacMillan, 1959.

Kuhn, Thomas. *The Essential Tension: Selected Studies in Scientific Tradition and Change.* Chicago: University of Chicago Press, 1977.

Lamrimpa, Gen. *Shamatha Meditation.* Trans. B. Alan Wallace. Ithaca, NY: Snow Lion, 1992. Reprinted as *Calming the Mind: Tibetan Buddhist Teachings on Cultivating Meditative Quiescence* (Snow Lion, 1995).

Lodge, Oliver. *Ether and Reality.* New York: Doran, 1925.

Mahāthera, Paravahera Vajirañāṇa. *Buddhist Meditation in Theory and Practice.* Kuala Lumpur, Malaysia: Buddhist Missionary Society, 1975.

Maturana, Humberto, and Francisco Varela. *The Tree of Knowledge.* Boston: Shambhala, 1987.

Medawar, Peter. *Pluto's Republic.* New York: Oxford University Press, 1984.

Mermin, N. David. "Is the Moon There When Nobody Looks? Reality and Quantum Theory." *Physics Today* (April 1985).

Nagel, Ernest. *The Structure of Science.* Indianapolis: Hacket, 1979.

Nagel, Ernest, and James R. Newman. *Gödel's Proof.* New York: New York University Press, 1964.

Namgyal, Takpo Tashi. *Mahāmudrā: The Quintessence of Mind and Meditation.* Trans. Lobsang P. Lhalungpa. Boston: Shambhala, 1986.

Nietzsche, Friedrich. *The Will to Power.* Trans. Walter Kaufmann and R. J. Hollingdale. New York: Random House, 1967.

Norris, Patricia. "Biofeedback, Voluntary Control, and Human Potential." *Biofeedback and Self-Regulation* 11.1 (1986): 1-20.

Pais, A. *Subtle is the Lord: The Science and the Life of Albert Einstein.* New York: Oxford University Press, 1982.

Petroni, N. C., and J. P. Vigier. "Dirac's Ether in Relativistic Quantum Mechanics." *Quantum, Space, and Time—The Quest Continues.* Ed. A. O. Barut, A. van der Merwe, and Jean-Pierre Vigier. New York: Cambridge University Press, 1984.

Piaget, Jean. *Six Psychological Studies.* Ed. David Elkind. New York: Vintage, 1968.

Poincaré, Jules-Henri. *The Value of Science.* New York: Science Press, 1907.

Popper, Karl. *The Logic of Scientific Discovery.* New York: Harper & Row, 1959.

Power, E. A. *Introductory Quantum Electrodynamics.* New York: American Elsevier, 1964.

Rabten, Geshe. *Echoes of Voidness.* Trans. Stephen Batchelor. London: Wisdom, 1983.

Rabten, Geshe, and Geshe Dhargyey. *Advice from a Spiritual Friend.* Trans. and ed. B. Beresford. London: Wisdom, 1986.

Rinbochay, Lati, and Jeffrey Hopkins. *Death, Intermediate State, and Rebirth in Tibetan Buddhism.* London: Rider, 1979.

Rinbochay, Lati, Denma Lochö Rinbochay, Leah Zahler, and Jeffrey Hopkins. *Meditative States in Tibetan Buddhism.* London: Wisdom, 1983.

Schilpp, Paul A., ed. *Albert Einstein: Philosopher-Scientist.* La Salle, IL: Open Court, 1969.

Schrödinger, Erwin. *Mind and Matter.* Cambridge: Cambridge University Press, 1958.

Schwinger, Julian. "Casimir Effect in Source Theory." *Letters in Mathematical Physics* 1 (1975): 43.

—. *Particles, Sources, and Fields.* Reading, MA: Addison-Wesley, 1973.

Sciama, Dennis. *Modern Cosmology.* London: Cambridge University Press, 1973.

Shantideva. *Transcendent Wisdom.* Comm. His Holiness the XIV Dalai Lama. Trans. and ed. B. Alan Wallace. Ithaca, NY: Snow Lion, 1988.

Smith, Huston. *Beyond the Post-Modern Mind.* New York: Crossroad, 1982.

Sparnaay, M. J. "Measurements of Attractive Forces between Flat Plates." *Physica* 24 (1958): 751-64.

Stevenson, Ian. *Twenty Cases Suggestive of Reincarnation.* 2nd ed. Charlottesville: University of Virginia, 1974.

Swenson, L. S., Jr. *The Ethereal Aether.* Austin: University of Texas Press, 1972.

Taylor, J. G. *The New Physics.* New York: Basic Books, 1972.

Thera, Nyanaponika. *The Heart of Buddhist Meditation.* York Beach, ME: Samuel Weiser, 1984.

Thera, Soma. *The Way of Mindfulness.* Kandy, Sri Lanka: Buddhist Publication Society, 1975.

Thurman, Robert A. F., trans. *Tsong Khapa's Speech of Gold in the "Essence of True Eloquence".* Princeton, NJ: Princeton University Press, 1984.

Wallace, B. Alan (Jhampa Kelsang), trans. *The Ambrosia Heart Tantra.* Annotated by Yeshi Dönden. Dharamsala, India: Library of Tibetan Works and Archives, 1977.

—, trans. and ed. *The Life and Teachings of Geshé Rabten.* London: George Allen & Unwin, 1980.

Weber, Renée. *Dialogues with Scientists and Sages.* New York: Routledge & Kegan Paul, 1986.

Westfall, Richard S. *The Construction of Modern Science: Mechanisms and Mechanics.* Cambridge: Cambridge University Press, 1977.

—. *Never at Rest: A Biography of Isaac Newton.* New York: Cambridge University Press, 1980.

Wheeler, J. A., and W. H. Zurek, eds. *Quantum Theory and Measurement.* Princeton, NJ: Princeton University Press, 1983.

Whitehead, Alfred North. *Dialogues of Alfred North Whitehead: As Recorded by Lucien Price.* New York: New American Library, 1956.

—. *Process and Reality.* New York: Free Press, 1978.

Whittaker, E. T. *A History of the Theories of the Aether and Electricity: Modern Theories, 1900-1926.* New York: Philosophical Library, 1954.

Whorf, Benjamin Lee. *Language, Thought, and Reality: Selected Writings of Benjamin Lee Whorf.* Ed. J. B. Carroll. Cambridge, MA: MIT Press, 1966.

Wigner, Eugene P. *Symmetries and Reflections: Scientific Essays of Eugene P. Wigner.* Bloomington: Indiana University Press, 1967.

—. "The Unreasonable Effectiveness of Mathematics in the Natural Sciences." *Communications of Pure and Applied Mathematics* 13 (1960).

Wilber, Ken, ed. *The Holographic Paradigm and Other Paradoxes: Exploring the Leading Edge of Science*. Boston: Shambhala, 1982.

Wilding, J. M. *Perception: From Sense to Object*. London: Hutchinson, 1982.

Wilson, D. *Rutherford: Simple Genius*. Cambridge, MA: MIT Press, 1983.

Index